HOBBY FARM™

LIVING YOUR RURAL DREAM FOR PLEASURE AND PROFIT

HOBBY FARM™

LIVING YOUR RURAL DREAM FOR PLEASURE AND PROFIT

BY CAROL EKARIUS

AN IMPRINT OF BOWTIE PRESS®

A DIVISION OF BOWTIE, INC.
3 BURROUGHS
IRVINE, CALIFORNIA 92618

Karla Austin, *Dir. of Op. and Prod. Dev.*
Nick Clemente, *Special Consultant*
Jarelle S. Stein, *Editor*
Jennifer Perumean, *Assistant Editor*
Jill Dupont, *Production*
Bocu & Bocu, *Book Design*

Library of Congress has cataloged an earlier printing as follows:

Library of Congress Cataloging-in-Publication Data

Ekarius, Carol.
Hobby farm : living your rural dream for pleasure and profit / Carol Ekarius.
p. cm.
ISBN-10: 1-931993-59-9
ISBN-13: 9781-931993-59-3
1. Agriculture—United States. 2. Farms, Small—United States. 3. Farm management—United States. I. Title.

S501.2.E3 2005
630'.973—dc22

2004017009

BowTie Press®
A Division of BowTie, Inc.
23172 Plaza Pointe Dr., Ste. 230
Laguna Hills, California 92653

Printed and bound in Singapore
10 09 08 3 4 5 6 7 8 9 10

Acknowledgments

Go confidently in the direction of your dreams. Live the life you have imagined.

– HENRY DAVID THOREAU

NO BOOK IS THE WORK OF ONE PERSON. THANKS FIRST AND foremost to Ken Woodard. He is my husband, my friend, and the one who makes everything else possible.

I want to thank the editors and staff at BowTie Press for helping make this book a reality, particularly Nick Clemente, Jennifer Perumean, Jarelle Stein, and Jen Dorsey. Annie Huang of Bocu & Bocu deserves special thanks for the wonderful job she did with the design and layout of the book. Karen Keb Acevedo, of *Hobby Farms* magazine is a wonderful editor—and friend—whose vision laid the groundwork for this book.

A number of people generously allowed me to interview them for the book and shared their personal triumphs and challenges. For their willingness to contribute their stories, I want to thank Dr. John Ikerd, David Muehleisen, Jill & Ken Giese, Jan & Tim Vala, Carol Ann Sayle & Larry Butler, Michele & Gustavo Huerta, Stephanie Caughlin, Judy & Sam Cavagnetto, Carol & Melvin Moon, Angel Henrie and Joseph Griffith, Susan & Stephen Robins, and Gary Dunn of the *Caretaker Gazette*.

Contents

CHAPTER 1

Back to the Farm

WHEN THE UNITED STATES FORMED "A MORE PERFECT UNION, to establish justice, insure domestic tranquility, provide for the common defense, promote the general welfare, and secure the blessings of liberty to ourselves and our posterity,"* over 90 percent of our population were farmers. They were the people who produced their own food and fiber, bartered for food, or bought food directly from someone else who produced it. Today, only about 1 percent of our population are considered farmers, making them the largest minority in this country.

At about the time Thomas Jefferson was penning the words of our Constitution, he wrote to President George Washington, "Agriculture ... is our wisest pursuit, because it will in the end contribute most to real wealth, good morals and happiness." Furthermore, "the moderate and sure income of husbandry begets permanent improvement, quiet life and orderly conduct, both public and private."

* *From the a Preamble to the Constitution of the United States*

In the heart of Virginia, on the estate of Monticello (above), crops and other plants still thrive on the plots originally designed by Thomas Jefferson (below). Jefferson believed farming to be one of the highest and best callings, and his farm was a showplace of progressive agrarian ideals and principals.

Jefferson's agrarian ideal was not new: it was a philosophy the earliest philosophers passed down. Yet we've seen the agrarian ideal give way over the last half-century or so, with an economic and social paradigm shift, resulting in a loss of *culture* in agriculture and fewer, bigger *agribusinesses* supplying our food and fiber. Corporately controlled operations, or factory farms, have steadily displaced the midsize, independent, family farm. At the same time, these corporately controlled operations have forced ex-farmers to move to the city. Iowa—the epitome of a farm state in many peoples' minds—provides a good example: It went through a landmark change sometime in the late 1950s, with more residents living in cities than on farms and in rural communities.

As the remaining farmers grow their operations to try to stay in business, agriculturally induced environmental problems have exploded. Iowa is also noted for having some of the most polluted lakes and streams in the world, and runoff from agricultural production in Iowa and other midwestern states has contributed to a dead zone in the Gulf of Mexico that has grown to more than 7,000 square miles (an area about the size of New Jersey). The dead zone has drastically hurt some of America's most productive fisheries. And, in spite of increased use of pesticides and herbicides for controlling invasive and noxious species of insects and weeds, the U.S. economy annually takes an estimated $137 billion economic hit from these pests.

Middle farms—those smaller, family farming operations that have tried to remain in the commodities game, but that have less than $250,000 a year in revenue—continue to be squeezed out. The squeeze comes because, according to John Ikerd, professor emeritus of agricultural economics at the University of Missouri and a strong supporter of sustainable agriculture, a farmer's net income on commodity operations (even on well run operations) generally runs about 15 to 20 percent of his or her gross sales. It doesn't take a wizard with a calculator to figure out that at that rate, a quarter-million dollars yields less than a living

wage for a family of four. In fact, over 90 percent of all family farms, including the really big ones, depend on nonfarm income, either from off-farm jobs or from government payments, for family support.

Industrialization in agriculture over the last century may be undeniable—but it is not unstoppable. People can, and are, reconnecting with the land, with the seasons, with life around them. Sometime in the mid-1990s for the first time since the United States Department of Agriculture began collecting data for the Census of Agriculture, farm size actually dropped. This change reflects more small-farm operations in the 10- to 179-acre size range. But many of the new small farm owners (the USDA defines a small farm as one with sales of less than $250,000 per year) are showing that there may be another approach to maintaining a diverse and vibrant agricultural community, while protecting rural values, responding to consumer wants, and ensuring a healthy environment for generations to come.

In a Minnesota orchard, two sisters gather a bounty of apples (above). People moving to the farm today often do so because they want their families to be able to work and play together outdoors.

THE NEW FARMERS

A number of the new small farms are simply lifestyle operations that provide the family with a nice place to live, good food on the table, and meaningful work for the kids but that generate very little revenue. Other farms are fully commercial operations, taking advantage of direct marketing, organic production, and other strategies to be self-supporting on a small acreage.

Lifestyle Farmers

Judy and Sam Cavagnetto are prime examples of lifestyle farmers. Sam's job as a full-time over-the-road trucker for a large moving van line allowed the couple to live anywhere they chose. They chose thirty-five acres in the mountains of Colorado. Judy and Sam wanted a great place to raise their kids, with a small-town atmosphere. They keep horses and the kids raise animals for 4-H.

DEFINING THE FARM

The USDA categorizes farms based on ownership, income streams, and farm sales.

Small family farms

- **Limited-resource farms** Any small farm with gross sales of less than $100,000, total farm assets less than $150,000, and total operator household income of less than $20,000 per year. Limited-resource farmers may report farming, a nonfarm occupation, or retirement as their major occupation.
- **Retirement farms** Small farms whose operators report that they are retired, but excluding those who fall into the limited-resource category.
- **Residential/lifestyle farms** Small farms whose operators report a major occupation other than farming, excluding those who fall into the limited-resource category.
- **Farming occupation/low sales farms** Small farms with less than $100,000 whose operators report farming as their main occupation, excluding those who fall into the limited-resource category. Household income may exceed $20,000 per year and may be based on one or more family members working off the farm.
- **Farming occupation/high sales farms** Similar to farming occupation/low sales, but with farm-generated sales of between $100,000 and $250,000 per year.

Other family farms

- **Large family farms** Farms with sales of between $250,000 and $500,000 per year.
- **Very large family farms** Farms with sales of over $500,000 per year.

Non-family farms

- Farms organized as a corporation (except family corporations) or a cooperative, as well as farms operated by hired managers.

Gustavo and Michelle Huerta also chose the country for a lifestyle. They were raised in Miami, but violence became too much a part of life there, so they decided to relocate to Tennessee. Here, Gustavo, a medical doctor, could establish his surgical practice, and the family could operate a small farm. With 200 acres, they raise a garden and horses, cattle, goats, and chickens. Although these lifestyle farms don't have to make money for their owners, they pay with quality of life values that, if purchased, would cost tens of thousands of dollars.

As John Ikerd says, "What would you have to earn to buy the quality of life that a farm offers, from scenic areas and recreational opportunities, to personal safety and a school for your children where the teachers know them and care about them? What is it worth if you are really living a life that has meaning in terms of a place to live? What would it cost for the view, the private schools, the clubs? In real economic terms, these are costs that shouldn't be marginalized."

For both the Cavagnetto and the Huerta families, it is that lifestyle value they seek. They believe that their children have experiences on the farms that they wouldn't get in the city or the suburbs.

A farmer holding a box of fruit on the porch of her Oregon produce stand (above) and another tapping away at a laptop on his gathered hay (far left) illustrate that the decision to farm can be a commercial one. Many people also like the life-long learning opportunities, as when children learn to care for animals (below).

Commercial Farmers

Other individuals want to turn their small farms into successful commercial enterprises. Some of them have done incredibly well, generating net incomes as high as 50 percent of their gross. How are small farmers able to make higher profits? Mainly by being more sophisticated and by wisely using capital earned elsewhere. David Muehleisen, program coordinator for the Small Farm Program at Washington State University, works with many of these new farmers. He sees the gamut, from people with five horses out in the meadow to "agripreneurs" (agricultural entrepreneurs) who are building successful operations on farms and ranches ranging from postage-stamp size to hundreds of acres. He says, "Most of

Specialty crops—such as the berries being picked above and resting in small containers below and the lavender stirring in the breeze at opposite—can provide good revenues from a relatively small piece of land. To maximize profits, though, you need to market directly to the public.

the people we are working with are serious; they want to make a profit. So what we do is teach them alternative production and business planning. We encourage everyone to make sure they have a market, that they are growing things that they will be able sell, so that they can make a profit. We tell everybody—'Do not put anything on the ground until you know you have a market.' That's the biggest mistake traditional farmers make; they grow a big crop (usually monoculture crops) and they don't have any place to sell it."

To underscore his point about markets, Muehleisen tells of the conventional raspberry grower Melvin Moon. "He was going broke marketing to wholesalers," Instead, Moon "cut his production in half, bought a big pot, and began making jams. He is doing better than anyone would have thought and has customers lined up."

Muehleisen also relates the success story of Susan and Stephen Robins, who grow lavender on San Juan Island, north of Seattle, and market over eighty handcrafted lavender products. Unlike Moon, the Robinses had no agricultural experience; he was a physician and she a journalist. They had run their own international communications business for fifteen years before retiring to the island. Once on the island, they quickly began seeking something more. As Susan says, "We had twenty-five acres on the island that we loved, and we had to think of something to do with it. We wanted to preserve it for open space so our first concept was that we would start an organic farm where we would have a crop that didn't use water, didn't use fertilizer and where we could make added-value products on a year-round basis so we could spread the enterprise over the entire year instead of being seasonal."

Today the Robinses have six of the twenty-five acres planted with 10,000 lavender plants, and they plan to continue increasing the size of their crop. They employ ten people year-round, and several dozen more during the summer season. Together with their crew, they grow and harvest the lavender—all by hand. Next they distill the oil and create the

A magnificent turkey standing in a yard (above), a man farming his land with draft horses instead of a tractor (below), and two boys gathering crops in a basket (opposite) show that every farm is unique. Location, personal interests, and goals help determine the type of farm you will have.

products (including lavender sugar, pepper, and vinegar; lavender soaps, shampoos, and body lotions; and lavender lip balm and massage oil). Finally, the Robinses market the products at an on-farm store and at the area farmer's market. Although they have a few retailers that sell their products, Susan says, "We have discovered that our products sell best when they're in a closed environment—that is a dedicated store—rather than sold among a lot of machine-made products. Our products are handcrafted and they are beautiful, but they get lost among the other ones that are slick." The direct marketing also enables them to capture a bigger portion of the consumer's dollar.

Not everyone in the small farm realm is ready for the kind of business that Moon and the Robinses are developing. Ken and Jill Giese raise a large garden on sixteen acres in New York, mainly to feed the family of six. They also raise turkeys and chickens, which the Gieses market directly or in cooperation with other small poultry producers. They didn't have much capital to get started, so while they grow their business to a sustaining size, Ken works part time on dairy farms and for construction companies in the area. The Gieses do much of their work with a draft horse, but when they need to use a tractor, they barter work for equipment use with some of the farmers Ken works for occasionally.

THE DRAWS

The draw of the farm is easy to understand. In our fast-paced, coffee-and-Tums driven society, the farm harkens to something simpler, quieter, and more meaningful. It provides the chance to experience nature, in both her glory and her fury. It is a place where family is more than a group of cohabitants who pass on the way to the next meeting, class, or soccer game. It allows the artist and the innovator in each person to emerge.

Farming allows parents and children to work together. As Jill Giese says, "The benefit to us is, as a family, we can work together and play together. Our kids have learned the

rhythms of helping; they know that animals need to be fed and watered, just like they need to eat and drink. They're seeing how you spend the money to feed the animals, and you get the money back when you sell them. They each have some work in the afternoon: Somebody feeds the turkeys, somebody does the watering. So they see responsibility and that we are depending on them and trusting them. They make their own games and run all over things, using a pile of hay bales to play king-of-the-hill. And they know about life, about how the male goat breeds the female goat, and that that's a natural part of life. They have seen baby goats being born, and this year we did a hatchery and had chicks coming out of their shells; they learned about the formation of the chicks and how different reproduction is from mammals to birds. It was exciting after three weeks, when the chicks came out, so Ken had them draw pictures and write things about the experience."

Many baby boomers are retiring early—often in their early to mid-fifties—and the farm offers them the chance to stay vibrant, learning new skills while they capitalize on their old skills. Susan Robins sums it up, "We weren't insecure about the business side of it, but we just were not experienced in the horticulture and product sides of it. It took over a year of *intense* research to get ready." However now, with the business up and running, the couple takes great satisfaction in the outcome: "We've been gratified to have created an industry on the island, in a place where that is very hard to do, and we have created wonderful jobs for artisans and others who want to be involved in it. We think we have created a landmark on the island that is open, free of charge, to anybody who wants to come and we get a huge amount of pleasure out of those people that come and picnic on the farm, bringing their kids and sitting in the fields when they're in bloom. Our harvest festival alone saw over 3,000 people visiting last year."

Farming also offers the chance to "experience the unusual or unexpected little adventure that lightens and even makes gladsome the work," as Gene Logsdon, a small-farmer

A chicken peers about in the late afternoon light (above). A woman and her granddaughter sit shucking corn on the porch (below). A little girl offers up a rainbow of gathered flowers (opposite). For some people, their farms generate no income, but they do offer beauty, good food, and the company of animals for their families.

Writer Gene Logsdon speaks of the "little adventures" farmers enjoy, such as seeing the fluttering of a pale green luna moth (above), or the chance to drive a tractor as the sun sets (below). Your adventures may include the melt-in-your-mouth taste of food freshly harvested from the garden (opposite)

from Upper Sandusky, Ohio, points out. He shares some of his own adventures—such as "a pale green luna moth fluttering in the porch light; a fungus that looks like a little pile of sand; an ant milking its own herd of aphids; a killdeer nest right in the middle of our gravel driveway. And three years after we planted paw paw trees, the gorgeous zebra swallowtail butterfly, which feeds only on paw paw, landed daintily on the tractor."

These "little adventures" may seem inconsequential to some, but for those of us drawn to the farm, they are grand payment for our labors. I have always been grounded by nature, and I love my own little adventures. As I broke the ice off the stock tank this morning, I smiled at a donkey nuzzling my work-coat pocket to find a treat, watched the mountain chickadees skipping in and out of the dried back leaves of the currant bushes, smelled the fine scent of pine smoke in the air from our woodstove, and listened to the wind singing through the trees. In the summer I can sit in an aspen grove and watch adult great horned owls teach their young to hunt, or enjoy the raucous fighting of a small flock of pygmy nuthatches as they bathe in the puddle where we empty the stock tank.

THE CHALLENGES

As gratifying as farm life can be, it is not always easy. It involves a level of physical work that many escapees from urban and suburban America have never engaged in, and it often involves new working patterns—like no weekends or holidays off—that can cramp previous lifestyles. If you have livestock, think again about all those vacations and extended weekend trips. If you are growing crops, get used to dawn-to-dark days during planting and harvesting. Dreaming of running a farmstead B&B? Get used to *no* privacy. Do you like to walk into a clean house, with shiny, polished floors and light colored furniture? Be prepared for mud and mess. Love to take in cultural events, like the opera or great museums? Instead, get ready for high school plays and cow-plop bingo at the town street-dance.

Gathering vegetables on a nice day may seem a pleasant task (above), but farmers must be prepared to work outdoors in all conditions, including the heat of summer (below) and the chill of winter, and cope with many other challenges, such as pests.

Be prepared, also, for the social challenges of moving into rural or rurban areas. These communities often seem backward and closed to newcomers. Although rarely hostile, people who were born and raised in the tight-knit, small-town atmosphere of rural and rurban America may be hard to approach. They are friendly and warm once you penetrate the surface, but penetration can take awhile. In the meantime you may feel isolated in your new community.

Expect that you may never become a local in your neighbors' minds, even if you stay the course and live there for twenty years. When we first moved to our farm in Minnesota, we were having coffee one day with our neighbors Bev and Willy. We had been able to break the ice quicker with them than any of the other neighbors, because Willy had been renting the fields when we bought the place, so we had an immediate business relationship. In their sixties at the time, the couple lived on the farm that Willy's grandfather had homesteaded almost a hundred years earlier. We asked if the neighbors on the other side of them, Kathy and Jim, were originally from around the area. "Oh no," Willie said, with a shake of his head, in a way that clearly indicated that Kathy and Jim were like us—real foreigners, "They are from over near Deer Creek." Deer Creek was only about twenty miles away, but despite the fact that they had lived on their farm for well over a decade, Kathy and Jim were still not locals.

At the same time, I can say most of the rural people we've befriended over the years retain a kind of neighborly charm and support often missing in urban and suburban America as well as a generosity that often exceeds their means. I never understood the term "salt of the earth" until I had rural neighbors. Your rural neighbor might own only three shirts, well worn and patched, but if he thought you needed a shirt he would give the one off his back without a second thought.

HOT SPOTS FOR HOBBY FARMING

Most new small farms are in the rurban zone. These areas boast good roads and proximity to large groups of consumers for direct marketing. They benefited from the burst of technological innovations in communications and computing during the 1980s and early 1990s that enabled more people to work from home. These features make these communities most attractive for those seeking small farm life. Areas along both coasts—and in a belt ranging from Dallas to Washington, D.C., with a 200-mile-wide strip on either side—are the current hot spots for the rurban, small farm explosion. And because of the increase of small farms in these areas, there are support services, ranging from Cooperative Extension programs for small farmers, to tractor and implement dealers catering to small farmers with tools like compact tractors, springing up to meet their needs.

Although the majority of viable small farms are in these areas, other rural areas too are beginning to see the transition. This is in part the result of ex-urbanites taking advantage of lower-priced farmland that's found in truly rural communities, but it's also being helped by increasing numbers of farmer's markets outside of urban centers together with programs sponsored by the USDA that allow low-income people to use food stamps and federal coupons at farmers markets. According to USDA research, the number of farmers markets in the United States has grown dramatically, increasing 79 percent from 1994 to 2002. The 2002 National Farmers Market Directory listed more than 3,100 farmers markets operating in the United States. These markets are providing a crucial source of revenue for small farmers, with more than 19,000 farmers reportedly selling their produce only at farmers' markets.

Last, many farms are located right in urban core areas and near suburban homes. Today, up to 30 percent of agricultural production in the United States originates from

Residents work together on a community vegetable garden located in the heart of Chicago (above), but such urban gardening may not satisfy those who really want to get "back to the land." Scenic areas (below) found within a couple of hours' drive of a city or resort community are among the hot spots for members of the modern back-to-the-land movement.

RURBAN

Rurban communities are those that offer a rural lifestyle and still have traditional rural populations, but that are strongly influenced by urban areas. They are usually located within a couple of hours' drive from a major metropolitan area or a major resort community. They may have a fair population of telecommuters that occasionally go to the city for work, but rurban areas are just a little too far out for many day-to-day commuters.

within metropolitan areas. Most city farms are currently community collaboratives, sprouting up in some of the poorest and most violent neighborhoods in America through the efforts of nonprofit organizations trying to improve the quality of food and provide positive opportunities for inner-city dwellers, but small-scale agripreneurs run other city farms. These agripreneurs seek a viable business in the place they live. Typically operated on less than five acres and using the CSA (community supported agriculture) model, these farmers are taking advantage of their ability to build close relationships with families who purchase from them.

Since 1991, Larry Butler and Carol Anne Sayle have built Boggy Creek Farm in East Austin, Texas, into a very successful urban farm. With five acres, and a 160-year-old farmhouse, located just blocks from the Texas state capitol, they market a wide variety of produce and flowers, grown on site, value-added products created from their surplus, like smoke-dried tomatoes and salsa, and products like goat cheese and free-range eggs, which other farmers in the region raise.

"I was getting burned out remodeling houses and selling real estate," Larry recalls. "We started growing vegetables on some land we owned that's about an hour and a half outside of town. Once we grew all this stuff, it was like, 'Well now, what are we going to do with it?' A friend of mine had a liquor store here in Austin and let me sell from a card table in front of the store on Saturday mornings. The first Saturday, I made about forty dollars on carrots and onions and greens. The rest of the story is, it got nuttier every week, and now we are running four cash registers."

In 1992, they saw the Austin property with nut trees, irrigation water, and the historic house listed in a real estate book. As Larry says, "Ninety days later, we were signing the papers on an old junk car out under the trees, and we were farming full time." They haven't looked back and have no regrets.

Picked, packed, and ready to be sold at market, the tomatoes, peppers, squash, carrots, and other fresh produce shown on this page and the next represent only a portion of the bounty realized by those who have chosen farming as a way of life.

CHAPTER 2

Are You Ready for the Country?

I LOVE THIS LIFE. I WOULDN'T TRADE IT FOR A FASHION MODEL'S body, a vault full of money, or a best-selling book. How could you want to trade something that fits so well, like a treasured old coat that warms you to the soul? I love our compact house, nestled in a saddle between two pine dotted ridges, overlooking Pikes Peak to the east and the Continental Divide to the west. I love that our house is charged (electrically) by rays of the sun bouncing off sparkly blue solar panels, and is heated by wood from nearby beetle-killed trees, which my husband, Ken, brings home with the donkeys, or with an old three-wheeler and a trailer. I love the fact that I can look out my window and see animals—both our own animals, and wild animals—gamboling about, healthy and happy, as animals should be. I love the new potatoes that come from the garden, and the greens grown in pots in the living room that freshen our winter plates. I love to sit in the evening and listen to Ken serenade me with his guitar, both with wonderful songs he has written and covers of some of my favorites.

Though the winter field above has an austere beauty, heavy snowfalls cause extra work on the farm and can damage buildings, particularly older ones such as the farmhouse below. Thankfully, spring comes, the world turns green again, and flowers, such as those of the nasturtiums interplanted with zucchini and beans on the next page, benefit from the moisture winter snows brought.

I can go to the city if I need a city-type fix, but I hardly ever do. Mostly Ken and I stay home, both working from right here, though occasionally we go to one of several nearby small towns for shopping or an out-in-public spree.

But as much as I love my life, I have to be truthful: It can be really challenging, and I know it isn't for everyone. For example, as I write this chapter, we are coping with a frozen water service line (our first at this house after six winters, though sadly, not our first ever—and not likely to be our last). Yesterday, we spent our Saturday fighting the water line, thawing snow on the woodstove to keep the critters watered, and unloading our mid-winter delivery of hay, all while Ken was combating a cold. Since we were unable to get the line thawed, we went to bed dirty. Luckily it was a sunny and pleasant day, but it was the tail end of a three-week spell with night temperatures dropping to the –30s degrees Fahrenheit.

We have had other bad times, as have most people who relocate to a farm from a suburban/urban life, and those bad times should give you pause. Moving to a farm is a family lifestyle change, and the whole family needs to want to face the challenges that don't exist for most Americans today. If your wife's idea of a challenge is picking out a shade of nail polish that will match her silk blouse, and her idea of fun is spending a whole day cruising through Saks Fifth Avenue, she probably won't like it on the farm. If your husband's idea of hard physical work is mowing the 100-square-foot lawn on a Saturday morning, and he is quite proud of the fact that he has never had a blister, he may not be ready for a farm. If your kids haven't been outside in a year, except to go from building to vehicle and back, they might not appreciate the fresh air and sunshine of farm life.

If in doubt about the family's sincere commitment to the lifestyle change, consider practicing farming in your own backyard before you make a big move. The potential to grow a food-supplementing garden exists in most places. Many cities even have community gardens, where residents who lack an adequate yard for a garden can acquire a small bed to

GREEN BEANS
ZUCCHINI

The best way to wet your toes may be to start "farming" where you live now, growing a few vegetables, such as the freshly picked carrots being rinsed above. Many small farms that run a "community-supported agriculture" operation or an on-farm store (looking something like the general store shown below) happily take on volunteer interns.

work. A few backyard chickens, if there isn't a rooster to wake up the neighborhood, are a great addition to most yards.

There are also some other approaches to wetting your toes, without drowning: Agritourism, or vacationing on a working farm or ranch, provides a taste of the lifestyle, but after a weekend or a couple of weeks, you get to go home. Find agritourism opportunities in areas where you think you might like to relocate by contacting that state's department of tourism, or go online and check out www.farmstop.com.

Many working farms also offer an opportunity to work as an intern, and if there is a CSA near you, then by becoming a member of the CSA, you can usually opt to participate in farm activities. Check out Web sites such as the ATTRA (Alternative Technology Transfer for Rural America) at attra.ncat.org/attra-pub/intern.html or the Organic Volunteers at www.organicvolunteers.com for intern opportunities. Another approach to testing the farming life without making a final commitment is to work as a caretaker for a farmer, rancher, or rural landowner. Gary Dunn, editor of the *Caretaker Gazette*, says there are thousands of opportunities for caretakers. Some caretaking prospects are relatively short-term commitments, like farm-sitting for a month, but others are long-term arrangements that can go on for years.

Since 1983, the *Caretaker Gazette* has listed opportunities for caretaking around the world. About 150 ads, such as "Couple, or a single person able to handle isolation, is needed on a remote southern Arizona ranch," run in each issue—or you can opt to run a situation-wanted ad. Visit the *Caretaker Gazette* Web site for more information at www.caretaker.org.

WHEN IN ROME

One of the first things to think about with your move to the country is that you are changing cultures. The further you move from the urban fringe, the starker the cultural differ-

ences will seem. These differences are not insurmountable, but they are easiest to overcome if you think that, in a way, you have moved to a foreign country with different mores and traditions than the one you've just left. Remember the adage: When in Rome, do as the Romans do.

Rural people have long lived with different economic and social realities than their urban and suburban brethren. When they invite you for coffee, expect freeze-dried instant, not freshly ground beans or latte, and drink the former as though it were the latter. Expect less emphasis on clothing, cars, and home furnishings, and more on tractors, homemade crafts, and the high school football team.

Those differences can quickly result in bad feelings and problems, though the problems you'll encounter depend on how you approach your new neighbors. Our experience in Kremmling provides a perfect example. We found ourselves neighbors to a codgerish old fellow (probably not much older than we are now) who ran a junkyard and who seemed distinctly unfriendly at first. Turns out the people who had built the house we were living in tried to get his junkyard (which was there long before they bought the land and built the house) closed down by the county. Erwin suspected we were more of that ilk—city slickers tryin' to change the countryside.

The rancher who owned a large expanse of land up behind ours began dropping cows and calves (hundreds of them by the semi-load) down at the bottom of the valley, and he, along with his kids and hired hands, drove them up through our place to get to his land. Like Erwin, George too had had a run-in with the previous residents, who hassled him about moving the cows through and left gates open when they were supposed to be closed, or closed when they were supposed to be open. He eyed us with suspicion that first spring morning.

It turned out to be fairly easy to break the ice with these rural neighbors. We smiled at them when we saw them and followed the rural tradition of waving when we passed them on

Most of your new neighbors, like the woman harvesting from her garden above and the farmer with his horse below, will gladly share their knowledge with you. Break the ice with rural neighbors by offering a big smile and waving when you drive by.

The man tending his vineyard above and another baling hay at opposite depend on heavy-duty equipment to get their work done. These tools of the trade can easily cause sticker shock when you start shopping for your own line of farm equipment.

the road. We tried really hard not to judge them by our citified criteria, and before long, we were on good terms. They began visiting us and would offer advice and help. By late summer, George had given us permission to ride our horses on his ranch, which ran for tens of thousands of acres up behind our house.

Michelle Huerta (Tennessee) had similar experiences. "It is a quantum leap [moving from the city] and in a way I felt like we'd landed on Mars. At first when we were shopping for farms, we'd see a really nice farm next to a terrible-looking old trailer or a rundown old farm, but finally we decided, we couldn't let that stop us from getting the piece we wanted. Once we got here, we realized that those are pretty nice folks in the trailer. I am so much happier living in the country than I was in town or in the city. The farmers are so nice, they are helpful, and they're so real; they laugh at your mistakes, but it is good-natured laughing."

Hard work and hard economies shape your new neighbors. They are dedicated to their land and their family, which is often an extended network within the community. They value tradition in work and in worship. Older neighbors in particular may be uncomfortable hammering out the details of a business deal in a contract (they tend to stick to the handshake approach of doing things) or in talking about business with a woman.

Accept your neighbors for who they are, and they will be more likely to try to accept you for who you are.

ECONOMICS OF FARM LIFE

People coming from towns or cities soon discover that although real estate in the country is somewhat cheaper than comparable real estate in developed areas, farm living isn't automatically cheaper than life in the city or suburbs. Rock stars and corporate executives looking to get away from the craziness of their day-to-day lives don't have to think much about the money, but if you don't fall into the multi-millionaire category, you will need to think about it. You may need to consciously make a change in spending habits.

The job market in rural and rurban areas is often limited, and the pay scales are often lower than those found in cities. You may take advantage of good roads to get in and out of the city into work (especially if you have the ability to arrange flexible scheduling with your employer), but you should still think about what commuting long distances will mean to your life, and the life of your family. Our hi-tech boom has made telecommuting possible for large numbers of people, but some rural areas still have limited access to the Internet—and don't expect high-speed service.

Sustainability and Self-Sufficiency

Farm living can be comfortable, but sustainability and self-sufficiency must be the pillars of this life. You can raise at least some of your own food, and reduce your dependence on energy and outside resources that eat up your money; your entertainment can be right in your own backyard, with little need to spend money on fancy trips and expensive restaurants.

Michelle Huerta from Tennessee says that when her family moved to the farm, they had both pleasant surprises and sticker shock about the economic differences between the city and the farm. "The first thing that struck us was that we could go out to eat a lot more often, because the restaurants are so much cheaper here. I know it sounds so silly, but the little things, like free refills on drinks, came as a surprise to us. The six of us could go out for a

To take care of their fields (above) attendees of the Four State Farm Show in Pittsburg, Kansas, inspect a line of tractors (below). At farm shows held throughout the country, the Cooperative Extension Service and farm equipment suppliers are always on hand to answer questions about equipment.

meal for twenty to thirty dollars. At the same time, it is very expensive having a farm; there is no doubt about it. It's shocking to look at the price of a tractor or farm equipment, and a lot of services, like having a plumber or an appliance repairman out, are much more expensive here than in the city."

Michelle also addressed some of the other changes as we talked: "When we were in Miami I wouldn't have shopped at a Dollar Store or a Wal-Mart. You had to have eighty-dollar Nikes from the mall instead of ten-dollar sneakers from the discount store. What I've figured out is that you can live on a lot less money when you get out of that environment that tells you that you have to go the upscale stores, and you have to wear this brand."

Maybe your plan is to create a moneymaking enterprise out of your farm—to be a real farmer. You can make money off a small farm, but it is hard work, and if you aren't going in with some cushion of money in the bank, things can careen into a financial wreck before you know what happened. For planning purposes, assume you won't make money on your enterprise for at least the first couple of years. Can you get by with outlay and more outlay when there is no significant farm-generated income? (Chapter 10 dives into agripreneurship, or the marketing end of farming, which is critical if you plan to make money off the farm.)

Farms and the IRS

Our accountant once told us that the surest way to find yourself at the uncomfortable end of an IRS audit is to show a farming loss, while showing significant off-farm income. The IRS considers that if farming is a business, it must be setup and run with the intention of earning a real profit. When a farm is set up and run as a profit-making endeavor, you can deduct the expenses of running the business, even if your expenses exceed your income, and you have a loss—and the loss may be applied to other nonfarm income under the federal tax code. But the IRS is also wise to the fact that many people set up a farm with no *serious* intention of

making a profit, yet they deduct those "farming losses" from their income. If the IRS determines that your farm is an "Activity Not Engaged in for Profit," then you fall under section 183 of the tax code, which governs "hobby losses."

Losses incurred in connection with a hobby are generally deductible only to the *extent of the income produced by the hobby*. In other words, you can't use a hobby to generate a tax loss that shelters your other income. And, all of your hobby income is supposed to be reported as "other income" on Line 21 of your Form 1040, *Individual Income Tax Return*, though the expenses incurred earning that income are only deductible if you itemize your deductions, because they are considered "miscellaneous itemized deductions." You can only deduct the portion of expenses associated with hobby income that exceeds 2 percent of your adjusted gross income.

When determining whether you are operating a business, as opposed to engaging in a hobby, the IRS considers the following points.

The manner in which the taxpayer conducts the activity. Do you operate in a business-like manner? Do you keep complete books and a separate business checking account? Do you advertise your products? Do you study what is going on in your industry and adopt new techniques to increase profits?

The expertise of the taxpayer or his or her advisers. What is your background in the activity (including number of years of practical experience and formal training)? Do you consult with professionals, such as an attorney and a CPA? Do you seek advice from experts, such as county extension personnel? Can you demonstrate that you have responded to the advice offered by your advisers? For example, have you fertilized a pasture based on the extension agent's advice?

The time and effort the taxpayer spends on the activity. Do you spend a significant amount of time on the business and its related activities? Do you actively spend time marketing your products? Do you keep any kind of time log that documents your work and efforts to make a profitable operation?

When April 15 rolls around, use caution in deducting farm expenses on your tax forms (above) unless you are confident that you can pass the IRS tests for running a business. Thinking of farming as a retirement nest egg (below)? Farms can eat up savings the way pigs chow down on corn—with great abandon.

A small herd of cows, such as the Angus grazing above, may look beautiful in your field, but think twice about using their expense or any other farming expense to offset nonfarm income. The IRS frequently audits taxpayers who file farm returns with a loss. Dairy farms such as the one below are rarely selected for auditing, however, because the IRS assumes their owners work too hard for this type of operation to be a hobby.

An expectation that assets used in the activity may appreciate in value. Do you anticipate that certain activities, like breeding purebred stock, will show a profit down the line through appreciation? Are you in an area where actively farmed land is going up in value faster than other land? Can you demonstrate that your efforts—say a program you have undertaken to reclaim your land from a noxious weed, like leafy spurge—will increase the value of your land?

The taxpayer's success in similar activities. Have you started other similar enterprises where you did show a profit? For example, if you started a successful kennel, you demonstrated the ability to create success for profit. The IRS doesn't consider success in your primary field as proof. In other words, it doesn't count for you to have been a successful banker. But if you have been a successful banker who started a profitable restaurant as a secondary business, the IRS is more likely to concede that you are in this for a positive business result and not a hobby.

The taxpayer's history of income or losses with respect to the activity. Did you have a farm at some other point in your life that was profitable? Or has your bottom line been steadily improving over several years and your losses getting smaller?

The amount of profit from the activity. Have you had some profitable years already on the farm (even if the profit was slight)? Make sure the profit is legitimate farm-generated income and not from an unrelated activity.

The taxpayer's financial status. Where does your income come from? How much money do you have from other sources? Is the farm your only source of income?

Elements of personal pleasure or recreation. This is probably the most interesting factor, because even the IRS acknowledges that you can derive personal pleasure from an activity that is intended to make a profit, beyond the profit itself. Yet the IRS expects that the pleasure is secondary to the profit motive.

SEARCHING FOR THE IDEAL FARM

Farm shopping is fun, but it is best to take your time. First make a list of what you want in a farm and your general preferences for things like climate, terrain (mountains, seashores, plains, forests), cultural resources, churches, medical needs, educational needs, proximity to your family, the job market, and markets for farm products you are thinking about raising. This list will initially help you to target areas that meet your needs and will later help you narrow the field of farms in the area in which you're interested.

Once you identify areas or regions of the country that interest you, try to find out as much about them as you can. The Internet makes a lot of this kind of research easy. But even if you don't have access to the Internet, you can research by calling state economic development and tourism offices, town and county clerks, county extension agents, school districts, or the chambers of commerce for places that tickle your fancy. Assess how the area is doing economically—growing, stagnant, or losing business and population. If you have school-aged children, ask questions about graduation rates and standardized test scores. How are healthcare facilities in the community? (Find out about the quality of healthcare organizations by contacting the Joint Commission on Accreditation of Healthcare Organizations (JCAHO). The JCAHO provides quality reports on most hospitals and surgery centers, nursing homes, home care services, and other types of healthcare operations. Their Web site, www.jcaho.org, offers a searchable database of reports, or call 630-792-5000 to purchase a report. Are there recreational or cultural resources available? What is the climate like? What crops grow well in the area?

If you are not in a big hurry to move, consider subscribing to local newspapers for the communities that interest you. Contact numerous real estate agents in the areas that seem to meet your general preferences. They'll all be happy to send you information on the farms they have listed. By dealing with multiple real estate agents in the same vicinity, you get a

Coming across your dream farm, whether it includes a white picket fence (above), lovely old farmhouse (below), a pond (opposite), or all three, can be exciting, but take your time before signing any papers. A farm is a big investment, so evaluate properties carefully.

Above, a river winds through one farm, while opposite, water gushes from a private well in the yard of another. A river offers stock watering, fire protection, and recreation, but it means a significantly higher price tag. A buyer looking at a farm with a private well (most have them) should have it tested to make sure the water meets safe-drinking standards.

better range of properties and prices. United Farm Country Real Estate has the largest network of rural real estate agents in the country. They publish a catalog that you can request by calling 1-800-999-1020. You can search their online database at www.unitedcountry.com.

As the field narrows further, plan some trips to visit the top two or three areas you have identified. While visiting, look at farms that are for sale, but try to resist the temptation to make an offer until you have really gotten to know the area. If possible, revisit the area during a different season, even if the subsequent visit is shorter than your initial trip.

Serious farm shopping comes after you have settled on an area. Again, your earlier questions will help you compare different farms, but for this phase you should do some pre-planning that will help you do an even more thorough analysis of the individual properties that interest you. We use a technique known as matrix analysis when we shop for real estate (or any other major investment). Put simply, with this approach you set up a worksheet that allows you to "compare apples to apples." The criteria on which properties will be judged are written down before you head to the field, with scoring established for each criterion. Points to consider on your matrix may include the broad things, like quality of schools, healthcare, and recreation. But, more importantly, remember to look at detailed specifics: What type of soil does the farm have? Is the land in pasture or field crops? Does the size and condition of the house and outbuildings meet your needs? If not, what will it cost to make repairs or upgrades? Are there land amenities, like a live stream or a nice old hardwood forest? Is the well good? Does the septic tank appear to work? Are the utilities suitable to meet your needs? How far are the buildings from roads and neighbors?

Four of the most important issues to consider are water, drainage, septic systems, and utilities.

Water

I think water is the most important single issue when shopping for a farm. People living in towns and cities generally have municipal water—turn on the tap and out comes good, safe water; but farms are almost always on private wells. The first concern therefore is, "Is the well good"? A good well produces adequate quantities of safe water for your family and animals to drink and for necessary irrigation.

Quantity may not be a problem if you are looking in a high precipitation area of the country, but if you are looking in the arid West, it could be a major consideration. Judy

PONDS

According to the USDA, there are more than two million constructed ponds on private lands. Landowners construct them not only for livestock watering and wildlife habitat, but also for irrigation water, fire protection, fish production, recreation, erosion control, and landscaping.

Large ponds, or those needing a concrete dam, will probably require the services of a civil engineer, but under most circumstances, you should be able to design and construct a small pond without the use of an engineer. If you decide to go it alone, there are many variables you'll have to take into account when selecting a site and sizing your pond, ranging from estimating runoff to assessing soils. In most western states, you should also check with the state's water resources department to find out if there are water-law concerns. (For example, where I live, in Colorado, it is legal to build a pond that has less than one third of an acre of surface area on an intermittent stream without a water right, but it is illegal to build any pond along a live stream without owning a water right.)

The Natural Resources Conservation Service, or NRCS (a branch of USDA), has an excellent publication on ponds, *Ponds: Planning, Design, Construction* (1997). It is an eighty-five-page handbook that describes the requirements for building a pond. It can be downloaded from the NRCS Web site (go to *www.nrcs.usda.gov* and search under the "publications" heading) or ordered from your local NRCS office.

Cavagnetto says that she and Sam learned this the hard way. "We had our house built and then moved from Wisconsin. We ended up having to have a cistern put in the basement, because the well wasn't producing enough water. That's something we found out the day we moved here, when I went to water the twelve horses; there wasn't enough water, we could only get about fifty gallons. The drillers drilled to 250 feet and they got water, but it was the minimum gallons per minute for a well. Now I wish they would have drilled deeper so we would have been closer to the maximum than the minimum."

Check with neighbors, the county, or the state agency responsible for water resources to find out if there have been any dry wells, or wells with poor production, in the area. You can hire a well driller to test a well if there is any reason for possible concern. When purchasing bare land (especially in the West), add a condition to the contract that says you have a certain period of time to drill a well that gets sufficient water by a certain depth (well drillers, or the state water resources department, should be able to give you guidance on how deep that is). If the well driller can't hit water you are out the drilling cost, but you aren't stuck with a piece of dry land.

Make it a condition of the contract for purchasing your farm that the well meets "Safe Drinking Water Act Standards" for all constituents. If the well doesn't meet the standards, you don't want the place. Test for herbicides, pesticides, and nutrients, as well as bacterial contamination. (Contact the county or state health department for recommended labs.)

A farm that has a river or creek running through it offers aesthetic and recreation values, but it may be subject to flooding, and just because it hasn't flooded yet, doesn't mean it won't. Look around you. Buildings should be located away from the banks of the river or creek and on high ground. The Federal Emergency Management Agency, or FEMA, is the national lead agency on flooding, and it often has flood maps available. If you are in a FEMA designated flood zone, you'll want to check into what flood insurance will cost.

Finally, is there the right amount of water for the kind of farming you plan to do? In some areas, crops need irrigation. In other areas, swampy pastures grow poor quality forage. County extension personnel are the best folks to provide information on water needs and availability for crops in the area you are looking at.

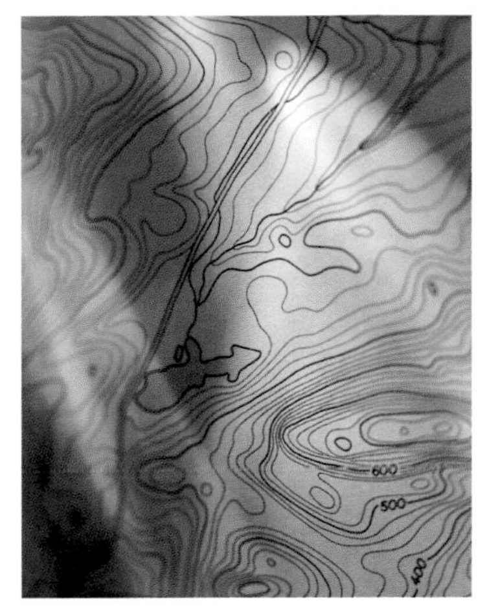

When searching for your farm, study maps (above) and the lay of the land (opposite) to get a better understanding of drainage. Swampy areas are a concern for animal health and safety, damp ground yields poor crops, and eroding hillsides pollute rivers and ponds.

Drainage

Life in a swamp can be miserable, for both you and your critters. Over the years, we've known a number of neophyte farmers who bought farms during a dry spell, only to have their dream drown in knee-deep mud when the rains returned. Their crops weren't good, and their animals suffered from myriad health problems like hoof rot and mastitis (an infection of the mammary gland, primarily in lactating animals). Their equipment spent more time stuck in a field than operating, and their buildings had water-related problems, including wet basements. Though you can usually correct minor drainage problems through the use of French drains and grading, it is best to avoid low-lying areas.

Even if you are shopping for a farm during a drought, you can assess the potential of drainage problems in several ways. The first option, and what might be easiest, is to talk to people in the area about the land. Locals will know.

Another option is to get a topographic map and study the area on the map. The United States Geological Survey (USGS) prepares these maps, which display a wealth of information about elevations, waterways, and vegetation. A topographic map will display marshy areas by showing blue

A cleaner pumps out the waste from a septic tank (above). Many people moving to the country for the first time must learn to maintain septic systems—or they may have to resort to even more primitive sewage disposal (opposite).

dashes and blue vegetation. Also look for intermittent lake beds, which are displayed by a dashed blue line with light blue lines within its boundary.

Get topographic maps and aerial photos from terraservice.net. This Web site is one of the world's largest online databases, providing free public access to a vast data store of maps and aerial photographs of the United States. The Microsoft Corporation operates it as a research project for developing advanced database technology, in partnership with Hewlett-Packard Corporation, the USGS, and other partners. Topographic maps can be purchased at stores that cater to hunters, fisherman, hikers, or other outdoor sports enthusiasts, or by calling the USGS Map Store at (800) ASK-USGS.

The third approach is to study vegetation. Plants that grow in wet ground have adapted to having their "feet" wet; they tend to have thick, waxy-surfaced leaves.

Septic Systems

A civil engineer or health department employee designs standard, modern septic systems according to uniform design specifications. Each system consists of a tank and a drain field (also called a leach field or absorption field). These systems efficiently treat wastewater, thereby protecting groundwater, rivers and lakes, and drinking water wells. However, in some areas of the country or for certain types of uses (like business uses), systems may have additional components, such as effluent filters, surge tanks, or grease traps. These additional requirements are sometimes needed where geology limits the effectiveness of drain fields, or where water quality needs to be protected at a higher level— for example, near small streams with cold-water fish populations or where the density of development is expected to affect nearby lakes.

The designer sizes the components of a system according to estimated usage. A two-bedroom house will have a smaller system than a five-bedroom house, and a shop will have a smaller system than a restaurant.

Most modern tanks are concrete, though in some areas local authorities may permit the use of fiberglass or polymer tanks. Older tanks were often steel, which rust through after

MAXIMIZING YOUR SEPTIC SYSTEM

Here are four steps to help maximize the life and efficiency of your septic system, and to protect the environment:

- **Inspect regularly** Have the system inspected on a regular basis (every two to three years). This extends the life of a septic system and helps avoid unnecessary and expensive repair and replacement costs.
- **Conserve water** Hydraulic overload is a major cause of septic system failure. Low-flow plumbing fixtures, faucets, and showerheads will minimize the amount of water entering a septic system. Stagger water use throughout the day to minimize the strain on your septic system.
- **Protect the drain field** Do not plant trees and shrubs with deep, penetrating roots near the drain field—the roots can plug the perforated pipe structure. Do not drive or park vehicles and equipment over the drain field because their weight can compact the soil and damage drain field components.
- **Manage household waste** Limit the types and amounts of waste poured down the drain. Garbage disposals can double the amount of solids added to the system, so use them sparingly, if at all. Cooking oils and fats harden after disposal and block the septic tank inlet, or outlet, and they can even clog the soil pores surrounding the drain field, reducing its effectiveness for filtrating wastewater. Never dump chemicals like paints, solvents, drugs, and pesticides down the drain, as these items may kill the microorganisms that help purify wastewater and they can potentially enter into groundwater and contaminate drinking water supplies. Low-phosphate detergents can reduce phosphorous loads to surrounding lakes and streams by as much as 40 percent.

OUTHOUSES

twenty to forty years of use. (If you purchase a really old farm, the "tank" may actually be a buried car body.) In the tank, solids settle to the bottom and partially decompose through a biological process known as digestion, and scum from soaps and oils floats to the top.

The liquid in the middle exits the tank and flows through a series of perforated pipes and out the drain field. The soil is the final and most important component of a septic system. This is where the majority of wastewater treatment actually occurs. Through physical and biological processes, the soil consumes most bacteria and viruses in wastewater, as well as some nutrients, as the wastewater effluent travels down through the soil layers.

To maintain efficient operations, you need to pump the tank from time to time. Pumping removes the solids from the bottom and the scum from the top. If not removed occasionally, the solids and scum begin to take up the entire volume of the tank. Once this occurs they move into the drain field, quickly clogging the soil-matrix that is critical to treatment. Usually, when this happens, you need to dig up and rebuild the drain field, which is far more expensive than keeping up with pumping.

Windmills are a common sight in some farm communities (above); most older ones operate wells for livestock watering. If you are looking for land far from electric lines, solar panels (such as ours below) can convert the sun's rays into electricity. These systems are best used in high-sunlight areas (opposite).

Utilities

Most towns and cities have readily available utility services for electricity, natural gas, phone, and even cable television; wires and pipes run into the house, and essentially all you have to do is pay the bill. Farmers may or may not have these services that townies take for granted. Few rural areas have cable television; natural gas rarely runs to farms; and in some areas, even electricity and phone services aren't readily available.

We live "off-the-grid," in a house powered by photovoltaic solar panels, with a gasoline generator for operating our water pump. Off-the-grid living is great, but to develop an alternative-powered home requires a little more planning and initial expense, though

Though land such as this gorgeous pasture may seem the fulfillment of a dream when you see it, protect yourself from later headaches and heartbreaks by investigating the property thoroughly before making a purchase.

you will never see an electric bill again, and can laugh when your town friends complain about power outages. (And you will be helping to protect the environment by reducing nitrous oxides, sulfur dioxide, and carbon dioxide emissions.) You also need to be more diligent in turning off unused lights and appliances, but it seems a small sacrifice for the benefits you reap.

We have six solar panels, four batteries, and an inverter, which run the lights, television, stereo, computer, and other small electronic devices. We have all propane major appliances, including the refrigerator. (Electric refrigerators and freezers draw a lot of power, so if you want to go with them, you will need to significantly increase the size of your system.) Our water pump is fairly deep, so we opted to go with the gasoline generator to run it. That cut down the capital expense, though down the line, we may redesign our water system to eliminate the generator. We run the generator once or twice a day.

For those considering off-the-grid living, I'd recommend solar as the first choice in areas of the country that are blessed with plenty of sunshine. Wind generators will often do the job in areas that lack enough sunshine to make solar a viable power supply, but they have moving parts, which means wear and tear, and maintenance and repairs, and they can be kind of noisy. Solar panels, on the other hand, are pretty much maintenance free and absolutely quiet.

Small hydro systems are an option if you have live water in the form of a stream or river running through your property. Hydro systems use one of man's oldest inventions—the waterwheel—to turn a generator turbine. Hydro applications work best where there is a good drop along the river's course, which creates head that turns the wheel. Three feet is about the minimum head needed to produce electricity.

Whichever off-the-grid system you choose, you'll need to perform routine maintenance on your batteries. Ken checks our batteries twice a year, cleaning terminals, replacing corroded battery cables, and checking water levels in the batteries.

REAL ESTATE LEGALITIES

It is best to have someone who is highly knowledgeable (in the state where the transaction is taking place) to represent you. This could be a real estate agent or an attorney, but keep in mind that if you are looking at real estate with a real estate agent who has a listing on the property, he or she is legally representing the interests of the seller—not your interests. No matter how knowledgeable your representative, however, it is important to educate yourself on real estate legalities. Be aware, for instance, that there are different types of deeds—with very different warranties and securities—and that land interests and codes that could affect your future plans may exist.

Types of Deeds

The owner of real property is said to hold the title to the property, and a deed is a legal instrument that transfers title from one party (typically the seller) to another (the buyer). There are several types of deeds to transfer title, but there are two common ones: the quitclaim deed and the warranty deed.

The quitclaim deed is a simple document that essentially says one party ceases to have any claim or interest in a title. People often use quitclaim deeds when settling a divorce, an estate, or a gift transfer; but you should *never* accept a quitclaim deed on real property, because it provides you with no warranty. For example, some person of low character could sell you something that he or she didn't even own, say the Statue of Liberty. Since this person didn't own anything in the first place, you have nothing when you file your quitclaim deed at the courthouse. You might find a prosecutor who'd be willing to charge this person with fraud, but you would have no assurance that you'd ever see a dime of your money again.

When a seller signs property over to you using a warranty deed, on the other hand, he or she is making certain written guarantees that will provide you with some protection against future claims on the property. The guarantees normally include:

- The seller has full title and the right to sell the property.
- There are no unspecified encumbrances (for example, liens, mortgages, or easements).
- The buyer is assured the right to "quiet enjoyment" of the land—meaning that no spouse, child, partner, or other party will come out of the woodwork and force you off the land.
- If a problem should arise with the title after transfer, the seller will do whatever is necessary to clear up the problem.
- If another party brings a "rightful claim" against the title, then the seller will reimburse your losses and damages.

If a title has some problems, the seller can go to court to clear the title through a *Quiet Title* suit. This should be the seller's responsibility. How do you find out about problems prior to purchase? Depending on which state you live in, you'd get either a "title search," or an update of the abstract. These are prepared by searching through courthouse records. If you purchase property with a loan from a commercial lender (mortgage or promissory note), the lender normally requires "title insurance." In this case, a professional "abstractor," or title company, will provide a title search as part of the process of supplying the title insurance. If you are purchasing with an owner-carry loan, you can do a title search yourself, or hire a title company to perform one for you.

The local Cooperative Extension agent or Natural Resources Conservation Service (NRCS) officer can help you evaluate the land's suitability for various crops (above). Area bankers, the county assessor, or competing realtors can offer opinions on the fairness of the asking price.

A deed of trust is a financing system used in some states. In states that use the deed of trust system, a third party acts as a "trustee" for the financing of property. The trustee may be a bank, a title company, or a government agent (for example, a county clerk). The trustee holds the actual deed until you pay the loan in full. If there is a dispute between the lender and the borrower, the trustee has rules to follow to resolve the conflict. In some states, the borrower pays the trustee, and the trustee pays the financer; in others, the borrower pays the financer directly. But if the borrower fails to make payments, it is up to the trustee to dispose of the property and pay off the loan.

Issues perspective farmers need to consider aren't limited to the condition and size of the property, the kind of crops that can be grown, and what type of irrigation is available. Other land interests and legal codes must be investigated as well.

Land Interests and Codes

Before signing on the bottom line for your dream farm or ranch, there are a few other things you should investigate: access to the land, access through the land, reservations, and zoning and building codes.

Access to the land. Let's say you are looking at a piece of land that isn't adjacent to a public road. There is an old dirt track leading to it through a meadow. The seller or the real estate agent says, "No problem, you can access the land on the dirt track." But after you buy, the owner of the meadow puts a lock on the gate and tells you that you can't drive through his meadow. Can he do that? The answer is maybe. When a piece of land *isn't* adjacent to a publicly maintained road, you should require proof in writing that a legal right-of-way exists to access the land. This proof comes in the form of a deeded access easement.

Access through the land. The flip side of this coin is when you look at a piece of land along a public road, with other private, road-less land behind it. You don't give it any thought and buy the farm, but one day several years later you look out to see a bulldozer driving through the middle of your hay field. Wait just a gosh-darn minute you say, but the owner of the land behind you points out the deeded easement to the parcel he bought

Neighboring farmers or utilities may have access through your land (above). A long gravel road such as the one below may seem an amenity in good weather but be impassible during bad. Zoning laws may preclude you from building anything in farm fields (opposite).

behind you. You won't be able to stop this person from tearing up your hay field for his big, gated driveway to his new dream house, if he has an easement.

Other easements. Our farm in Minnesota had a utility easement running through the middle of our pasture. There were no utility lines in the ground because the gas company that had acquired the easement decades earlier ended up taking a different route with the line when they installed it. But they still had an easement and could theoretically show up one day to run a gas line—or they could transfer their right to that easement to some other utility company. Easements aren't necessarily bad, and most utility companies that access their system where it goes through your property will work hard to minimize damage to fields and infrastructure (like fences) when they do installations or maintenance. Still, you should know what the easements are before you buy.

Reservations. Deeds can include reservations for certain "rights," like mineral, oil, gas, or timber rights. For example, all lands that the federal government offered for homestead after 1901 included a reservation by the government of all mineral rights (including oil and gas). What this translates to is that at some time the federal government could authorize a private company to come onto your land to extract valuable minerals. This may never happen, but then again, new technology may make extraction of heretofore unusable minerals possible—coal-bed methane wells, which have popped up over large areas of Wyoming, Utah, and Colorado in just the last decade or so, are a prime example. Although there may be little you can do about reservations, you should be aware of them.

Zoning and building codes. Before buying, you should check with the local government to find out how the land is zoned, which affects its possible uses (and the possible uses of neighboring parcels). You should also find out what kinds of building codes are in effect if you plan to build a new house or outbuildings. Like reservations, there may not be much you can do about local requirements, but if you know what they are ahead of time, you can evaluate their impact on your plans.

CHAPTER 3

Jumping In

WHEN KEN AND I MOVED TO KREMMLING, WE WERE FULL OF enthusiasm. *Everything* was new to us. But our enthusiasm could not make up for our inexperience and our lack of practical skills. The house sat back from the highway a rough three quarters of a mile; our vehicles consisted of an Audi and a Le Car (not exactly vehicles intended for rough roads). We had a woodstove for heat, but we didn't have a chainsaw. The woodstove had a chimney that needed cleaning, but we didn't have a chimney brush. Our tools consisted of a mishmash of screwdrivers, hammers, and wrenches, stuffed in a well-worn fishing tackle box.

We had read about gardening and raising livestock, but had never done either. We stumbled through many mistakes and problems, yet managed to do many things right, all the while learning skills that our grandparents knew through to their bones. (If they have been looking down on us over the last two decades, I'm sure all four of our grandparents have had some good belly-bustin' laughs at our expense; but my guess

Winter is a relatively easy time for crop farmers (above), but if you keep livestock your work will be harder (below).

is they've also been impressed by our perseverance and our old-fashioned common sense.) I know that you, too, can live on a farm and enjoy a great life. Just jump in and paddle like hell.

THE RHYTHM OF THE FARM

A farm has its own rhythm, which changes somewhat by seasons, but which is ultimately dictated by chores. Animals need to be fed and watered; fences need to be repaired; buildings and equipment need to be maintained and repaired; crops and gardens need to be planted, weeded, irrigated, and harvested. The harvest needs to be put-up, stored, and possibly marketed. Let me run down our current chores by season.

Winter

Winter is the time to plan and study, the time to do as much indoor work as possible. We burn wood as our primary heat source, so firewood chores dominate this time of year. Ken cuts trees that have succumbed to old age, insects, or disease. He cuts and splits these into pieces that fit in our stove. I actually love to split wood, and help regularly with this chore. The chimney requires regular cleaning to reduce the likelihood of an accidental chimney fire (which can easily lead to a house fire) and to keep the fire burning well. We have found that about four times a year is a good number of cleanings.

This time of year also makes for more onerous animal chores. The animals are not getting much feed (or if the snow is deep, no feed at all) from grazing, so hay is fed morning and night. We also provide fresh water daily. Our watering system requires us to run about a hundred feet of hose, which has to be well drained each day in order to protect it from freezing. Sometimes the hose freezes despite our best efforts, and we must drag it into the house to let it thaw.

Doing outdoor chores when temperatures are falling well below freezing (here we have had temperatures as cold as −37 degrees Fahrenheit; in Minnesota we had −52 degrees) can sap your energy. Trudging around with twenty pounds of extra clothing—winter overalls, heavy coats, big boots, hats, gloves, over-mittens, and face protection—adds to the work, as does having to break trail when there is new snow on the ground.

I maintain indoor planters full of greens during the winter. I reseed on a regular basis to maintain a continuous supply. I have found that EarthBox planters work well for this application in the winter; then I use them outdoors in the summer.

Beautiful pink and yellow bouquet of freshly picked flowers (above) and a new calf standing in a field (below) signal that spring has arrived. This is a time of promise.

Spring

Spring is glorious and busy, though it is also known in these parts as mud season. Early spring—which is really just the unexpected nice days when winter begins to relinquish its hold on the earth—is a time for cleaning up around the place, digging garden beds, checking on the fences, and performing minor repairs that had been on hold waiting for a fine day. I try to turn the winter accumulation of compost as early as possible in the spring. I start only a small number of plants inside these days, because our house is tiny, but when we lived in a bigger house, I lined every window with soil blocks and plants to transplant later in spring or early summer.

These are also the days when the animals begin to shed, so we often spend time currying them to get out the excess winter hair. They love it, and so do we. This is a fun time for simply watching the critters. They play wildly and with abandonment on these early spring days. Our donkeys, Jessie and Duke, will have mock stallion battles that rage for hours. Wild things begin moving around more if they are year-round residents, and the "snowbirds" begin returning, first in ones and twos, then in droves. We are thrilled to see the first mountain bluebirds return, flashing a streak of intense blue past a window in early March.

The harvest begins in summer, when crops such as these delicious berries are picked, and runs through fall, when long-season crops such as the squash below are gathered. Crops for feeding livestock, such as the dried feed corn opposite, are also harvested during late summer and fall.

Late spring is the time of green. I begin planting outside in the garden, and Ken starts getting construction projects going (there seems to be at least one every year). It is also the time when colts, calves, and lambs are hitting the ground running, and chicks arrive (via the U.S. mail). Life is exploding everywhere.

Summer

Summer is a time for lots of work, but also a time for enjoying the fruits of your labor. The garden begins providing some fresh greens and other short-season crops and will continue to produce through late fall. Even a small garden provides an unbelievable bounty. As time allows, I try to can some of the harvest (and some produce purchased at farmers' markets) for later use.

Construction, repairs, and maintenance are now in full swing. The work always takes longer than we had hoped, but we have come to understand that this is the way of do-it-yourself projects.

During the summer we try to allocate some time for fun things, too, such as riding horses, hiking, and fishing. Ken brings home fresh trout often, and we fry it the same evening with a touch of olive oil in cast-iron frying pans. Our only chance of traveling is now, because the must-do-daily workload is at its lowest of the year. Ken's dad comes up and stays so we can get away for a few days.

Fall

Fall is a splendid season. The pesky flies and mosquitoes disappear as the nights get colder. The aspens blaze against the blue sky in yellow and gold. Birds are drunk on the fermenting currants. The roads around here are almost empty, as summer tourists have left and skiers have yet to show up. We enjoy the crisp days, and we try to spend as much time outdoors as possible.

Potatoes (above) are one of my favorite crops because they have such a long season of harvest, with early potatoes coming in late spring and storage potatoes ready for harvest in the fall. Beginning farmers often find pumpkins (below) to be a good market crop.

We harvest the remaining garden produce (the root crops are ready for storage) and cleanup the garden. Fall is also hunting season, and Ken regularly participates in this food gathering tradition—something his grandfather, father, and uncles taught him as a boy. He hunts with a muzzleloader, a time-honored weapon, loaded with powder and ball. It's a weapon that had its heyday in the early nineteenth century. A muzzleloader holds only one shot, which you must shoot at close range. Ken doesn't succeed in shooting an animal every year, but when he does, we eat elk, deer, or antelope through much of the winter.

Because we no longer have hay fields, we buy all our hay; we try to get a large portion of our year's supply purchased and stored now. It is the time to start collecting firewood again. We try to have at least half of our winter's wood supply before fall gives way to the deep freeze. The chimney gets its first cleaning of the season, as night temperatures cool off enough to send us to the stove for a small fire.

ACCESSING EXPERTS

Old Abe Lincoln may be best known for his role in ending slavery in this country, but he also performed an important service that still benefits farmers and ranchers each and every day. In 1862, Abe signed the Morrill Act into law. Morrill provided states with at least 90,000 acres of land (the actual amount was tied to the number of representatives the state had in Congress) that the states were to sell, the proceeds earmarked for the endowment of "land-grant" colleges. These land-grant colleges were to "teach such branches of learning as are related to agriculture and mechanic arts."

In 1914, President Woodrow Wilson signed another act into law. The Smith-Lever Cooperative Extension Act authorized federal support at the state level for extension services associated with each U. S. land-grant university. Today, land-grant colleges not only provide agricultural education for students but also play a key role in research. Most U.S.

counties have a cooperative extension office, with extension agents to help disseminate information and act as a bridge between the university researchers and farmers.

Your local extension agent is one of the first people you should meet. He or she is there to help. Although no one person can know the answer to every question or have a solution to every problem that might crop up, extension personnel have a web-like support structure that allows your agent to find an expert who can answer your question or help solve your problem. Extension agents have a wealth of free or low-cost literature on subjects ranging from apples to zucchini, air conditioners to wells. They can also help interpret information and clarify concepts that may be new to you, such as deciphering a soil report from a lab and determining an approach to improving soil health.

The extension service also runs 4-H programs and provides a backbone for county fairs throughout the country. Through 4-H, kids develop confidence at the same time as they learn new skills. Programs are still largely centered on agriculture and home economics, but there are also opportunities for kids to learn about construction, photography, music, rocket science, and just about anything else that might interest them and that has a practical side to it. I participated in 4-H from the time I was nine until I was eighteen, and I believe it was the one of the very best things I ever did. It obviously hasn't become a thing of the past, as both Michelle Huerta and Judy Cavagnetto say their kids have enjoyed and benefited from participation in 4-H.

Most counties in the country also have offices (or have access to offices in a neighboring county) of the Natural Resources Conservation Service (NRCS) and the Farm Service Agency (FSA). These are both agencies of the USDA, started during the later years of the dust bowl and the Depression. Today, NRCS is the lead federal agency in the effort to help people conserve, maintain, and improve our natural resources and environment on private lands, working with farmers and other landowners. District conservationists are available at these offices to advise you on conservation programs (many of which have cost-share funding available for project implementation) and projects. The FSA acts as the financial arm of the federal government with

In Texas, an NRCS officer talks with a farmer about the protective grass she has seeded her land with to prevent erosion (above). New farmers face a multitude of unexpected problems; fortunately, the NRCS and the Cooperative Extension Service have agents in most rural counties. Those agents also coordinate 4-H programs for youth and county fairs (below).

A local NRCS officer discusses range management with a Hawaiian rancher (above). To keep your animals from wandering, you can choose more traditional fencing material (below) or something "new fangled," such as electro-plastic wire fencing (opposite).

respect to agriculture. It works to stabilize farm income, help farmers conserve land and water resources through administration of certain funding programs, provide credit to new or disadvantaged farmers and ranchers, and help farm operations recover from the effects of disaster.

Large animal veterinarians, who come right to the farm with their mobile clinic, are generally available in areas where there is a tradition of livestock farming or hobby-horse operations. Shop around for a vet, and develop a professional relationship with this person before you actually need to have him or her out for an emergency. Good vets don't only doctor the critters; they also act as advisers, answering your questions and making suggestions to improve both your animal's health and your bottom line.

Don't forget the experts in your own backyard—your neighbors. They willingly answer question upon question about farming. You should listen to their wisdom, which exceeds all the book knowledge in the world. After a time, you yourself may become an "expert" in their eyes. While your new neighbors know much about farming, they are often locked in handed-down systems that can be improved upon, or adjusted, to address modern needs and markets.

Our electric fence provides a great illustration: When we first moved to the farm, no one in our immediate vicinity was doing managed grazing, and no one had seen an electro-plastic wire (a thin and lightweight fencing wire made of plastic twine with tiny strands of aluminum woven in to carry the current from an electric fence charger). When we showed Willy our two-strand fence around a previously unfenced cornfield that we had converted to pasture, he looked at us as though we were completely crazy. He fingered the plastic wire strung on plastic fence posts that are simply "stepped in" to the ground on short metal spikes, and said, "Well that's different." (That is ruralese for "Not only is this the craziest idea I've ever heard in my life, but I know I'm gonna find all their cows in my corn tomorrow morning.") Tomorrow came, our cows didn't get into his corn, and soon he, and all the other old-timers, were driving by our place very slowly to study the new fence.

With a topper, the sheep above could be carried in the pick up below, which can easily transport it's present load of watermelons to market without extra equipment. While trucks are a must-have for farmers, sometimes ATVs, such as our 3-wheeler on the opposite page, can be used for jobs otherwise done with more expensive tractors.

Don't be surprised if some of your neighbors look at you as though you have three ears and a beak when you mention new-fangled ideas such as organic production, niche marketing, specialty crops, or agritourism. Understand that when they say, "Well a fella could do that if a fella wanted to," they think you are pursuing a folly.

But also, don't be surprised when they begin asking you how you did something. We became involved in the Sustainable Farming Association of Minnesota at its inception and hosted one of its earliest field days in the central part of the state. A surprising number of traditional farmers from right around us came and asked questions. By the time we moved back to Colorado, many had adopted ideas we had pioneered in the area, including easy-to-install electro-plastic fencing for subdividing paddocks in a rotational grazing system.

ESSENTIAL TOOLS OF THE TRADE

Running a farm requires a variety of tools and equipment; some are highly specialized, others rather general. Over years, you will accumulate things, but to me, this is the list of first things to begin acquiring as soon as possible.

Vehicles

Pickups: Before we bought a pickup, we bought an old Chevy Blazer. We quickly realized that an SUV is not, and never will be, a pickup. Pickups are probably the most versatile and useful long-term investment you'll make for your farm. They are indispensable for hauling everything from building supplies to feed, and firewood to sod. When you team a pickup with a trailer, you can move livestock and much more. Although a pickup is a big investment, when well cared for (remember to change that oil every 3,500 miles), it is an investment that can last for decades, and good, used pickups can often be bought at a reasonable price.

Toppers: Add a basic topper to your pickup, and you can keep items dry while hauling, use the truck for camping, or haul small animals. We've gotten some entertaining looks at gas stations and other stops over the years when the topper held a menagerie. Some of my favorites were the time we were driving thirty rather large turkeys to the poultry processing plant, and the time we had half a dozen ducks and geese and several big rabbits hanging out in the back. You can also easily move goats, sheep, and small pigs under a topper.

Tractors and ATVs: Even if you dream of working your land with animals, a tractor or a farm utility vehicle (an ATV, or a cargo-ATV, often called a "ute") is a practical thing to have. Although we like to use our donkeys for packing firewood when time permits, winter often finds us out with the ATV, equipped with its own trailer, bringing in wood. Compact tractors are versatile pieces of equipment that are perfect for small farms. Depending on the attachments you have, they can do just about anything. Mowing acres of lawn, digging a foundation, baling hay, pushing snow, setting fence posts: It's all possible with a compact tractor.

For those in the under-sixty-acre category, a ute will often do all the work you need done. Manufacturers now make attachments ranging from front-end loaders to manure spreaders that are specially designed to work with these rigs. The fat tires, light weight, and low center of gravity make these units easy on the land. If money is not a big issue, and you have a larger piece of land (say 160 acres or more), having both a tractor and a farm utility vehicle is the way to go. The tractor can do heavy work, such as baling hay, but the utility vehicle can haul supplies or get you across the farm quickly to move a paddock fence or check on the stock and crops.

Two-wheel drive trucks, tractors, and utility vehicles are OK for flat ground that's not too muddy, but if you're in hilly terrain, a snowy climate, or tend to have frequent muddy conditions, invest the extra money up front in four-wheel drive.

BEGINNING FARMER LOANS

One FSA program worth knowing about is the Beginning Farm and Ranch Loan Program for new farmers and ranchers. The loan program will help beginning farmers and ranchers with low-interest loans. For purposes of the program, a beginner is an individual who has not operated an agricultural enterprise for more than ten years; who materially and substantially participates in the farm or ranch; who provides substantial day to day labor and management on the farm or ranch; who demonstrates a need for assistance; and, for the purpose of farm real estate loans, who does not own land which in aggregate exceeds 30 percent of county average farm size. This definition applies to all credit programs and to conservation cost-share programs. Look in the phone book under United States Government for the FSA office nearest you, or check the Web site at www.fsa.usda.gov, for more information on the program.

Our mustang and donkeys investigate the contents of our two-wheeled wheelbarrow (above), which we find handy for all kinds of chores. The owners of a handcart overflowing with grapes (below) obviously find it an equally useful piece of smaller equipment.

If you plan to have large livestock (horses, cows, llamas, yaks), plan on getting a stock trailer. We don't actually use our trailer all that frequently for hauling livestock, but I still consider it one of the best investments we've made in twenty-some years of buying. When we do need to haul our animals, we don't have to borrow or rent a trailer. In between animal trips, we have used the stock trailer to haul firewood, feed, hay, and lumber. During the several household moves we've made since we purchased our trailer, it has done duty as a moving van, hauling furniture and household items. In addition, it often serves as a temporary storage shed. Although two-horse trailers are readily available, opt for a bigger trailer that can accommodate four or more animals.

Smaller Equipment

Handcarts: A handcart is the first tool I would invest in. Priced between $100 and $400, depending on capacity, handcarts are bargains that are hard to beat. They are lightweight, yet they carry big loads easily. Unlike their single-wheeled cousins, they are sturdy and steady over uneven ground or through mud or snow. And they are just plain hard to tip. Best of all, they are balanced in such a way as to be easy on the back. Some carts come with an accessory that converts them to a trailer for pulling behind a ute or small tractor.

We have used our two-wheeled wheelbarrow and carts for everything around the farm. In the garden or yard, they're great for moving topsoil, plants, seed, fertilizer, or tools. In the barn, they are handy for cleaning up small piles of manure, or dragging tack from point A to point B. They are a perfect size for moving a bale of hay, or a few fifty-pound bags of feed. We have also brought newborn calves from the field to the barn in bad weather, with mama tagging along right next to the cart.

Manure spreaders: If you are going to have any livestock, sooner or later you need a manure spreader. Even if your animals will spend most of their time on pasture, piles of

manure accumulate, and spreading this manure thinly over the land improves fertility, reduces contaminated runoff, and helps keep fly numbers down. Several manufacturers have come up with compact manure spreaders that are ideal for small farms. The tractor-driven units carry more manure in one trip and are probably the best way to go if you have a significant number of animals. The ATV units are good for operations with only a few animals stabled regularly, or with a larger herd that is out on pasture most of the time.

Composters: Compost is an almost-magical substance. Break down organic waste, such as food scraps, leaves, grass clippings, and manure in a compost pile, and you have the best soil amendment in the world—an absolute must-have item for a gardener. You can purchase composters, or you can construct them out of wood or old tires. (See Chapter 5 for more on composting and composters.)

Hand and Electric Tools

Hand tools: Every farm needs to keep a variety of hand tools. Companies such as Sears (with its line of Craftsman tools) and Snap-On (available at many auto parts stores) make hand tools that will last for generations and that come with a lifetime warranty to prove it. At the top of my list of items to purchase are: 25-foot and 100-foot tape measures; a good claw hammer with a comfortable grip; an electrician's pliers; a socket and driver set; adjustable wrenches in several sizes; and a screwdriver set with both flat head and Phillips head drivers.

Electric tools: There are dozens of electric power tools available at hardware and home stores, but there are two must-have electric hand tools for any type of around-the-farm construction project: 1) a 7-inch circular saw; and 2) a drill/driver (preferably the rechargeable battery-operated type). Need to build your own compost bin? Out comes the saw and drill. Hanging a new barn door? Get the saw and the drill.

The circular saw slicing through the piece of lumber above is an essential tool for farmers. If you are thinking of farming hundreds of acres for crops such as corn or soybeans, you'll need a fairly large tractor, such as the one below, pictured with a springtooth harrow.

With the versatility of projects you'll find to use these two tools on, invest in the best and the heaviest-duty models you can afford. If you plan to do lots of heavy construction and remodeling (thinking about that sunroom addition on the house or that new barn?), consider adding a heavy-duty reciprocating saw to the electric tool collection. Other electric tools don't tend to be of much use, unless you have somebody who gets seriously involved in woodworking as an avocation. So save your money on all those table saws, routers, and other cool-looking tools on display at the store.

Fencing tools: Farms and fences go hand-in-hand, so plan to purchase a fence-post driver. Drivers are heavy iron tubes with handles on the side that go over the top of a T-post. You use it to pound the post into the ground. A pair of fence pliers is a great, and fairly inexpensive, specialty tool to have. We are fans of electric fences—they are economical, efficient, and safe—but when you have an electric fence, you also need a fence tester.

Miscellaneous tools: We always have pocketknives when out working. A "Leatherman" type of all-in-one tool is also handy to carry. A round-pointed shovel and a good spade are always in use. Garden hoses are a must, but when buying them, purchase the longest and strongest available (fall is a great time to find really good buys on garden hoses). The good ones come with long-term guarantees (often twenty-five years or lifetime). We save the guarantee card with the receipt stapled to it, because under farm conditions, a "lifetime" can turn out to be only a few years. The last miscellaneous tool you should buy is a digging bar. We use ours for breaking ice in winter; for digging large rocks out of the garden, construction sites, or fence holes; and for prying apart incorrigible packages.

Older tractors, such as the Farmall above, work well for many applications but require lots of care. Implements such as the harrow attached to the tractor below are necessary additions to your tool lineup for farming on any scale.

ALL ABOUT TRACTORS

For most people who are new, or aspiring, to farm life, tractors are central to their dreams. They see themselves puttering across a field, baling hay, spreading manure, or planting and

The monster tractor moving across the field of a large-scale commercial farmer uses a lot more horsepower than is needed for the work on most small farms.

caring for a crop. Yet for the neophyte farmer, tractors are also intimidating, requiring familiarization with a unique language and skill set that few Americans have today. The following pages will help you learn the language and set out shopping for the perfect tractor.

Horsepower

Since horses provided power for pulling loaded wagons and plows long before people invented engines, early tractor manufacturers rated their product on its ability to do work that was comparable to a horse's work. For example, 1 horsepower (HP) was approximately equivalent to the power exerted by one horse pulling something and is mathematically equal to 33,000 foot-pounds per minute. Another way to think of it is that one horse could typically pulls a 3,300-pound wagon a distance of 10 feet in one minute; a 10 HP-tractor can apply 330,000 foot-pounds of power per minute.

When it comes to modern tractors, there are three different parts of the tractor that manufacturers and dealers talk about when they discuss horsepower. The first is engine, or gross, horsepower. It represents the amount of power the engine produces, but the engine loses some horsepower simply through its own operation. The second part of the tractor that manufactures rate is residual horsepower after engine loss. This is known as the PTO—or power takeoff—horsepower. The PTO is the device that powers the moving parts on farm implements such as mowers, combines, manure spreaders, and balers, and it is critical to doing work with a tractor. The third place manufacturers rate horsepower is at the drawbar. A tractor's ability to do tillage-type work, such as plowing and disking, is affected by its drawbar horsepower, which steps down from the PTO horsepower. PTO horsepower is usually about 90 percent of gross horsepower, and drawbar horsepower is 75 to 85 percent of the PTO horsepower.

A tractor's actual performance may be lower in some circumstances than its rated capability. All tractors lose some power at higher elevations; the rule of thumb says that for every 1,000 feet above sea level, there is a 3 percent reduction in horsepower. Tractors also lose power when operating on wet ground and on hilly terrain and when tilling in heavy soils. Over time, the tractor also loses power as wear and tear takes its toll on the engine. This will be even worse if you ignore routine maintenance.

TRACTOR TALK DEFINITIONS

- **Three-point hitch** A standardized mechanism for attaching implements to tractors. The three-point hitch can raise and lower implements. Thanks to a hydraulic pump that delivers oil under pressure to a control valve, it can also hold implements in a desired position.
- **Power take-off** A standardized shaft that spins, providing power to implements from the tractor's engine. In the United States, PTOs are standardized at 540 or 1,000 revolutions per minute (RPM). Older tractors often have a PTO that is driven by the tractor's transmission; new tractors use an independent hydraulic system to operate the PTO. Even with these independent systems, which are significantly safer than the old units, the PTO is dangerous when spinning. So keep the safety shield on the tractor, wear tight-fitting clothing when using the tractor, and make sure the shaft has completely stopped turning before you get near the unit.
- **Torque** This is the measure of twist that an engine can apply to the driving wheels or the PTO. Let's say, for example, that you have two tractors advertised with the same horsepower, but one has higher torque. The higher-torque model has an engine that runs slower to create the same amount of turning action, thereby using less energy than the lower-torque model to do the same amount of work. In practical terms, this means you won't have to rev the engine as much, the engine is less likely to stall when working under a load, it is quieter, it will use fuel more efficiently, and it will typically last longer.

Tractors that are appropriate for small and hobby farms come in three general classifications. Read below for which types are best suited for your needs.

Categories of Tractors

There are three general categories of farming tractors: lawn and garden tractors, subcompact and compact tractors, and utility tractors. Lawn and garden tractors are light-duty tractors that range from about 10 to 25 HP. Lawn and garden tractors are relatively slow; most use gasoline, though a few offer diesel engines. They are suitable for mowing grass on an acre or two but not good for mowing acres and acres. They can tow light loads and some are suitable for operating small, ground-driven implements; but few have a three-point hitch or PTO, so they can't operate a wide variety of implements.

Subcompact and compact tractors are built for heavier duty than their lawn and garden counterparts, with engine horsepower ratings ranging from 15 to 50. They were introduced by Kubota in the late 1990s and are now offered by several other companies. Kubota and others intended them for the consumer market—designed with comfort, ease of operation, and low maintenance in mind. Subcompact tractors also act as a bridge between the lawn and garden tractors and compact tractors. They can accommodate a range of implements and have a two-speed transmission. Compacts, also called estate tractors, are versatile, and at the top-end, may be appropriate for baling hay on a small acreage with a small-square baler.

Most models of subcompacts and compact tractors come with diesel engines and offer four-wheel drive (making them good buys when they will have to operate on hills or for plowing snow). They're faster than their lawn and garden counterparts, and they can do more work: All models come with a three-point hitch and PTO, so they can operate a wide range of implements.

Utility tractors are heavy-duty units, generally designed for commercial-scale farms. They have PTO horsepower in the 45 to 110 range. As with compact tractors, manufacturers

The farmer above drives a utility-size tractor on his land, the right choice for most small farms. However, upkeep is a real considera tion with all farm equipment so when time for repairs comes around, you may wish your tractor was the size of the one pictured below!

A loader such as this one is one of the most versatile and important additions you can buy for your tractor. You also can have buckets, hay forks, or forklift type attachments added.

offer most new models with diesel engines, and four-wheel drive is a readily available option. All utility tractors have a three-point hitch and a PTO. For farms up to about 160 acres, these are the workhorse tractors, doing most of the jobs the farmer needs done. On larger commercial farms, they do many of the jobs that don't require big power, such as raking hay or hauling round bales to feeders. The smaller units readily operate a small-square bale baler, and the top end can easily operate a round baler or "big-square" baler.

The Implements

A tractor by itself is like a foot without a shoe: It can go places, but there's a limit to the kind of *hard work* it can do. Implements are the shoes—or maybe the "magic work boots" would be a better term. They take your tractor from being just an engine and wheels, to being the do-anything rig you dreamed of someday owning. Among the implements for the tractors are mowers, tillage tools, loaders, blades, backhoes, fencing tools, and snowblowers.

Mowers: There are many kinds of mowers available, depending on your circumstances. They can be either "belly mounts" (a mid-mounted mower that sets under the center of the tractor), rear-mounted units, or front-mounted units. Finish mowers yield a manicured look for lawns. Rotary cutters are heavy-duty—designed to cut thick grass and brush. Sickle mowers cut hay and clip weeds and grass off at a desired height.

Tillage tools: Farmers use cultivators, tillers, discs, plows, and harrows to prepare seed beds in gardens or fields and to reduce weed pressure during the growing season. For small gardens, a tiller is generally sufficient, but for larger operations of a half-acre or more—say a sweet corn or pumpkin patch—cultivators, disks, plows, and harrows may become necessary pieces of your tool inventory. The plow does the first rough turning of the soil, the disk smoothes it over, and then the harrow does the fine smoothing. Farmers use the cultivator while the crop is growing to reduce weed pressure between the rows.

Loaders: A loader is the tool of tools. It allows you to dig and scrape; to move materials such as hay, manure, compost, or snow; to grapple equipment or machinery by lifting heavy items with a chain; and to do light grading of roads and driveways. The loader fits on the

MAINTAINING YOUR TRACTOR

Here are some tips to keep your tractor running in top shape and to protect your investment.

- **Check and change fluids and filters.** Check the fluid levels regularly (while the engine is cool), and keep all fluids at their recommended levels, including engine oil, water, and hydraulic, transmission, and brake fluids. Change fluids and filters according to the manufacturer's recommendations (which are generally based on hours of use), but for engine oil, do so at least each spring and fall.
- **Grease zerks.** Learn the locations of all the grease "zerks" (grease nipples) on your machine, and give them a squirt or two from a grease gun once a month for heavily used equipment, quarterly for lightly used machines. This goes for implements as well.
- **Oil nuts, bolts, and screws.** Get a can of machine oil, and place a drop or two on all the nuts, bolts, and screws. Repeat monthly if machines are stored outside or used hard and often; apply quarterly for machines stored inside with lighter use. When you oil nuts, bolts, and screws, check to ensure that they are snug.
- **Store out of weather.** If at all possible, store out of the weather, which ages equipment prematurely. North Dakota State University found that resale values for five-year-old tractors stored indoors were 16 percent higher than comparable units stored outdoors, and that they had half the downtime for major repairs.
- **Keep fuel tank full.** Fill the fuel tank after each use to avoid air and moisture problems. When air is present in the tank overnight, it cools and permits moisture from the air to run down into the fuel. During extended periods of storage, consider adding a fuel stabilizer, and run the engine at least once a month for fifteen or twenty minutes.

front of the tractor and comes with a bucket. Other attachments are readily available, including a fork for spearing and moving big round bales of hay and a forklift for raising pallets and other flat items. Modern loaders not only lift, but also have powered control for downward movement and tilting capability.

Blades: Blades are available as rear-mounted or front-mounted implements. They are good for heavier scraping jobs, including grading roads and shaping ditches, and they can drag soil or gravel for short distances. Some blades are straight, but angle blades, though a little more expensive, are far more versatile and worth the upfront cost.

Backhoes: Backhoes are rear-mounted and make digging a snap. Depending on the size, you can excavate fairly large holes in rough ground, quickly; for example, digging for a building's foundation or a septic system is a reasonably easy chore with a backhoe.

Fencing tools: Post drivers and posthole diggers are available for tractors. They make large fencing projects go quickly. Post-hole diggers also come in handy for constructing pole-buildings and for planting trees and shrubs.

Snowblowers: In most areas of the country, a loader bucket and/or blade will take care of snow; but if you happen to live in a place known for heavy snowfalls, a blower will cut through the drifts with the greatest of ease. It will also take much less time than it would take to move the snow with buckets and blades.

Other PTO-driven tools: Many other tools are available, depending on your workload. There are seeders and planters; manure spreaders; feed augers, grinders, and mixers; cement mixers; and wood splitters and saws. Name a task, and there's probably a tool to make that chore easier.

If you are planning on keeping livestock, a manure spreader such as this one is another crucial tool. These come in a variety of sizes, from small enough to be pulled with an ATV, to giant units that can keep up with the manure from hundreds of animals.

ALTERNATIVES TO A NEW TRACTOR

The idea of a new tractor may sound great, but cost could place a damper on the idea. There are alternatives to purchasing a new tractor if money is an issue. For occasional projects, you can lease tractors and implements from rental supply companies. Or you might consider paying a neighboring farmer to do the work for you. These options also work well if your tractor and implements are too small to undertake a one-time big job. We've used this option ourselves frequently over the years. Once we hired a neighbor to plow a cornfield that we were putting into permanent hay and pasture; the neighbor's big rig did in a day what would have taken Ken a few weeks with our equipment.

On small hobby farms, an ATV, or utility vehicle (for example, John Deere's "Gator"), may be a better, less-costly choice than a tractor. You'll find a variety of implements available—from manure spreaders to snowplows and hydraulic front-end loader attachments—that work with these versatile machines.

Another option is to shop around for used tractors. We've had good experiences with tractors that are older than we are, but when purchasing used models (even newer used ones), expect to incur more repair and maintenance expenses. If you aren't mechanically inclined or don't have the time to do a lot of maintenance and repairs, used equipment can make your life miserable. When shopping for older units (and there are many tractors still hard at work that are fifty years old or more), stick to brands that are common in your area of the country. And find out if parts and service are still available from a reputable local dealer. Tractor tires are expensive, so look at the condition of the tires. Check fluids for condition and quantity.

Gray-market (imported brands of) tractors are a special class of used tractors. Gray-market dealers import units for resale into the United States without the consent of their trademark owner. For example, Kubota produces a line of tractors for the United States. Kubota designed the tractors to work correctly with U.S. implements and to meet United States environmental and safety standards. Kubota produces a separate line of tractors intended for use in Japan. That line of tractors run implements found in that country (which often run at higher PTO speeds than U.S. implements) and that meet different standards required in Japan. Kubota doesn't import the Japanese models into the United States, but gray-market dealers purchase used tractors in Japan, bring them to the United States, and sell the tractors to farmers. These tractors sell for less initially than comparable used U.S.-market tractors, but the original manufacturers don't provide parts, service, or support of any kind. Purchasing a gray-market tractor may seem like a money-saving step up front, but it could cost you far more over time.

CHAPTER 4

Nature's Troublemakers and Farm Safety

YESTERDAY AFTERNOON, KEN AND I WATCHED ABOUT ONE hundred antelope having a grand time playing on the hill behind our house. Then last night, we stood on the deck under the stars, listening to an owl hoot in the trees on the ridge next to the house. He asked us, "Who...? Who...? Who...? Who...?" We couldn't answer him.

Counting wildlife encounters as part of our daily lives is what makes this life so appealing to us, but there are some encounters we're less fond of. Weeds, predators, and a host of other troublemakers think of our place as a fine home, or a good place to visit; they likely will think of your home much the same way.

WEEDS

To quote Emerson, "A weed is a plant whose virtues have not been discovered." Undoubtedly when it comes to most noxious weeds, such as thistles, knapweed, and leafy spurge, it's hard to imagine them having

any virtues. But even they do, as butterflies would tell us if they could talk. Nevertheless, when weeds are on your land, it's hard to share the butterfly's view of the world. So what can you do?

Completely eliminating weeds is an impossible task, even with herbicides (as is evidenced by the fact that we have more acres of weed-infested land today than we had before the introduction of chemical herbicides). But control of weeds is possible, so make that the goal of any weed project.

When you opt to work on a control strategy for weeds, it has to be a long-term commitment. It can take three to seven years of consistent application of controls (mechanical or biological) to have a significant impact. If you make the commitment, you will succeed. There are many different weed-control methods you can use.

To control weeds in small plots, dig them up (above)—it's the best strategy because it removes the roots—then transport them for proper disposal elsewhere (below). Weeds (opposite) rob nutrients and water from crops and reduce habitat for wildlife. If the weeds have begun going to seed or have flowers about to open, they may reseed the area.

Mechanical Techniques

Many weeds are susceptible to mechanical techniques, including pulling, mowing, hoeing, cultivating, and burning. Pulling weeds is still the most effective method of control for small areas or limited infestations. You will accomplish this most easily when the soil is slightly moist. During our first summer on the Hartsel farm, the loco weed (which can be toxic to livestock and wildlife when eaten in sufficient quantities) had a bumper crop throughout the mountains of Colorado, thanks to a moist spring. Most people sprayed to get rid of it. But the moist spring made for easy pulling. I spent an hour or so each afternoon for a couple of weeks pulling out the biggest patches, keeping the loco weed down to a minimum. Then, because we hadn't sprayed, a shiny green beetle showed up in August. Those beetles ate all the remaining plants. The next summer, the beetles arrived again and cleaned up any loco that tried to sprout on our place. People who had sprayed before had to keep spraying, because they had not eliminated the roots (which pulling did), and they didn't have the helpful beetles cleaning up for them.

The sheep above are eager to chow down on many invasive plants that other types of livestock won't touch. Using a very different approach, the farmer below destroys intruders by flame weeding, an option for large fields and pastures.

A good sharp hoe makes easy work of weeds in garden beds. The key to hoeing is to hoe frequently; don't let weeds get too thick or too large before you nip them—just below the soil surface—with the hoe.

Mowing and Controlled Burning

Mowing and controlled burning are both good approaches for pastures, fence lines and roadways, orchards, and any other area where the land is in a permanent cover crop. Mowing works best when the flowers are just beginning to set but before more than the first few are opening. This timing is absolutely critical: If you cut before the flower heads form, the plant has plenty of spare energy left in the roots; it simply sends up a bunch of new shoots. If you cut after the flowers start opening in earnest, the seeds will continue to form and spread, even though the plant is lying dead on the ground. But if you mow just as the flowers first open, the plant has put most of its reserved energy into making flowers and will have a tough time regrowing. Controlled burning is done in the spring. It is a field-scale fire kept burning at low temperatures. It takes all vegetation back to the growth point, giving grasses and legumes a chance to compete with the weeds. If a weed infestation is too serious, a hotter burn, followed by reseeding of grasses and legumes, might be required.

You can use grazing animals for "mowing," but to be most effective, you must use managed grazing. Sheep and goats are often the top choice for weed control, but other critters will work in some circumstances. For example, ordinarily cattle won't touch thistles, but Gregg Simonds, a clever rancher in Utah, decided to try spraying Canadian thistle patches with molasses and water before letting his cattle into an infested paddock. The result: The cattle "ate the thistles right into the ground."

In early spring, when weeds are just emerging, cultivating and spot burning with weed flamers are the best mechanical approaches in field crops. You can use either technique several times before the crop is well established. You'll find a number of cultivator styles designed to dislodge, cut, or bury plants, or all three. The type of crops you'll be growing and the types of weeds you are trying to control will determine which style you choose.

Biological Techniques and Herbicides

Biological control techniques use beneficial insects ("beneficials") or plant-specific disease organisms for controlling weeds, but each insect or disease tends to be specific as to which weeds it will control. Using beneficials for weed control is less expensive than herbicidal sprays, and once a population of organisms is established, minimal effort is required to conserve it. It's also less disruptive ecologically, so you maintain the natural biodiversity. Many states are now running beneficial insectaries, where you can purchase insects for some of the most troublesome weeds in your area. The key to using beneficials is to provide them with good living conditions, and that means avoiding the use of chemicals that kill the good bugs as well as bad.

Herbicides should be the last choice in weed control or limited to new infestations of fast-spreading nonnative weeds. Native plants evolved over millions of years to fill unique ecological niches. Nonnative weeds developed in other countries. Insects, disease, and competition with other species keep these weeds in check in their native environment, just as they do our native plants. Without their natural enemies, many of these non-native weeds become highly invasive when they get to the United States. They spread like wildfire, reducing the diversity and quantity of native plants. Federal and state agencies list fast-spreading nonnatives as noxious weeds, those that are "competitive, persistent, and pernicious." Learn about noxious weeds in your area and take steps to control them.

For best results, combine herbicides with other techniques. For example, cutting followed by herbicide applications or controlled fires followed by spot-applications of herbicides work better than just spraying. The problem with relying on herbicides is that they will reduce natural biodiversity, which results in more problems over time.

CONTROLLING WEEDS

For more information on controlling weeds, check out the Wildland Invasive Species Web page at tncweeds.ucdavis.edu. The Nature Conservancy and the University of California at Davis co-sponsor this site. The site has excellent photos and management strategies for weeds ranging from acacia and alligator weed to wormwood and bitter yam. You can also download an excellent weed control handbook in Adobe Acrobat.

TYPES OF WEEDS

- **Summer annual weeds** grow every spring or summer from seed. These weeds produce seeds, mature, and die in one growing season. Their seeds germinate mainly during a two-month period in late spring and early summer. The seeds are dormant until the next spring. Thanks to their self-seeding nature, they may seem like perennials.
- **Winter annual weeds** grow in late summer or fall from seed, then mature and produce seeds the following summer. Some, including chickweed, can germinate under snow.
- **Biennial weeds** grow from seed anytime during a growing season. They normally produce a rosette of leaves close to the soil surface the first year; then they flower, mature, and die the following growing season.
- **Perennial weeds** establish themselves in new areas by seed. Once established, they can proliferate from the roots. They live for more than two years. Because they can grow from pieces of roots, perennial weeds may take off after soil preparation and cultivation. Most perennial weeds that spread from extension of their roots grow in circular patches if left undisturbed. In cropped fields, the patches are often oblong, following the pattern of cultivation. Well-established perennials are the most difficult weeds to control.

A coyote sniffs at its latest victim. Predators such as this one cause serious losses for livestock producers; the chart on pages 84 and 85 provides information on the various kinds of predators and their hunting tactics.

PREDATORS

The USDA estimates that predators (wild and domestic) account for an almost-$100-million bill to farmers and ranchers annually. So if you have livestock and pets, you may have good reason to fear for your animals' safety. However, according to Dr. John Shivik, a wildlife biologist at the USDA's Predation Ecology Field Station in Utah, there are things you can do to reduce the impact of predators. (Dr. Shivik reminds us, though, that predators are important components of ecosystems.) In nature, predators feed not only on large herbivores, but also on lots of small rodents and rabbits (in fact, several studies show that rodents make up about 90 percent of the diet of coyotes). They'll also eat insects and carrion.

When they do kill livestock or pets, predators aren't trying to ruin your day, cut into your profit, or break your heart; they're simply struggling to survive. As Dr. Shivik says, "Predators kill things for a living; that is their job."

Those who live in remote areas primarily have problems with wild predators. In small farm towns and rurban areas, the domestic dog does most of the damage, though coyotes are moving into the 'burbs, finding it an easy place to make a living (they've even been seen dodging traffic in the Bronx). Fido and Spot don't have to be wild, vicious, or even brave to chase sheep or kill chickens: They're simply following their natural impulses. They are capable of carrying out the hunting sequence of their forebear, the wolf—from orienting and tracking, to stalking, chasing, herding, attacking, and killing—though they usually do so for sport rather than survival.

Not all predators kill livestock. When they do, they tend to be opportunistic killers, seeking whatever is easiest to meet their needs. In other words, they usually go for young, old, weak, or sick animals first. As they become desperately hungry though (like during a drought), they become much more aggressive and will attempt to take healthy, mature animals. Since healthy animals suffer less predation, good feed and adequate healthcare pay in more ways than one.

There is no magic answer to all predator situations; each predation event includes unique circumstances, so it will require unique responses. Overall, the best approach to protect your livestock (and pets) is to make predators think that eating at your house will be harder than chasing mice and rabbits. You can do this by gaining knowledge, developing an understanding of predators, and learning to apply nonlethal techniques that reduce predation.

Although Wile E. Coyote may have looked the fool in his encounters with the Road Runner, he's not a good example of the species, or predators in general. Since it is the "job" of predators to kill, predators are intelligent, curious, and most of all, adaptable. Consequently, changing their behavior—although it may be possible—is harder than changing your own.

Becky Weed is a producer who has learned how to successfully adjust her behavior. Becky and David didn't grow up on a farm, but in the 1980s they started raising sheep in Montana and have been farming full time since 1993. Early on, Becky and David lost 20 percent of their flock to coyotes. They called an Animal Damage Control agent, who shot and trapped a few coyotes, but as Becky says, "We knew we couldn't kill all the coyotes that came through, and we didn't want to, even if we could." She has since built a very successful marketing strategy around her wishes. As founding members of "predator-friendly" wool, a co-op that brands and markets an environmentally friendly product, they have seen their business grow steadily.

Identifying Predation and Predators

The first step is to identify the predator, but keep in mind that sometimes predators get a bum rap. A farmer comes upon the corpse of a dead animal, and because there are obvious bite marks, he or she assumes a predator killed it. But animals die from a number of causes, and unless you see the predator in the act of attacking a live animal, the death may have been from natural causes, with predators simply scavenging afterward. Nature's cleaning system at work.

When you suspect predator damage, assess the scene. Signs of a struggle, like drag marks, torn hair, wool or feathers left on brush or fences or blood spread around a large area all point to predation. If there are no signs of a struggle, examination of the carcass may help. When a predator feeds on a dead animal, that animal will *not* bleed under the skin at the bite marks. This type of bleeding, known as subcutaneous hemorrhage, is only present when the heart was beating while a predator inflicted bites.

When signs of struggle or subcutaneous hemorrhage are present, the next step is to try to confirm the kind of predator. Each species leaves its own telltale signs at a kill. For example, canid species (coyotes, dogs, wolves, foxes) tend to attack from the sides and the hindquarters, grabbing their prey under the neck. whereas cats tend to jump up on the back, biting the top of the head or back of the neck. Close examination of paw-print size and shape, tooth spacing and size, feeding habits, and pattern of killing help correctly identify the predator responsible for the kill.

Though sometimes predators themselves, domestic dogs (above) often serve as guardian animals, protecting livestock. Other guardians include donkeys (below), horses, ponies, and llamas.

Guardian Animals

For thousands of years, farmers in Europe and Asia used guardian dogs to protect their sheep and goats. However, during the early 1900s, farmers switched from using guardian animals to protect their flocks and herds, to using guns, poison, and traps. Today, farmers like Becky and David are showing that this old approach is still practical.

OUTSMARTING COMMON PREDATORS

Predator	Where	Domestic Prey	Characteristic
Coyotes	Traditionally in rural areas west of the Mississippi, but they are extending their range to towns and cities, and east of the Mississippi, with a significant increase in the Southeast.	Take sheep, goats, calves, and poultry, and small domestic dogs or cats	Hunt alone, in pairs, or occassionally as a family pack
Wolves	Found in pockets of the West and around the Great Lakes	Capable of taking mature cattle, llamas, horses, as well as all small stock	Hunt in a pack
Foxes	Throughout the country; often live in towns	Mainly lambs/kids or poultry	Hunt alone or in pairs
Domestic Dogs	Found anywhere that people are	Capable of taking mature livestock, as well as all small stock	Hunt alone or in packs
Bears	Remote areas and wildland/urban interfaces over much of the country	Capable of taking all classes of livestock	Hunt alone or with cubs
Bobcats	Remote areas over a fairly large portion of the country, but in largest numbers in Western states	Small stock, poultry, domestic dogs and cats	Hunt alone
Cougars/Panthers	Mountainous regions of the West; the South has remnant populations of native panthers	Capable of taking all classes of livestock	Hunt alone
Birds of Prey	Found throughout the country	Small stock, poultry, domestic dogs and cats	Hunt alone
Raccoon	Almost everywhere	Poultry	Hunt alone or in family group
Mink/Weasel	Large areas of the country	Poultry	Hunt alone
Opossum	Large areas of the country, with greatest numbers in Southeast	Poultry	Hunt alone

Attack Pattern	Feeding	Fencing
Attack from sides or hindquarters. Bite marks and subcutaneous bruising under neck and throat, bloody foam in the trachea. Usually attack right before dawn, or right after dusk.	Usually begin on flank just behind the ribs, consuming organs and entrails	Six feet high, with 3 feet buried underground or 5 feet high electric fence
Similar to coyotes, but large tooth patterns, and often multiple kills in one night	Similar to coyotes	Woven wire 6 feet high with electric wires along top and bottom
Similar to coyotes but small tooth patterns	Similar to coyotes	Net wire 4 feet high with openings less than 3" square buried to 3 feet with a 1 foot apron
Indiscriminate mutilation of prey, bite on multiple areas of body, often attack during day	Often kill large numbers of animals at one time, but do very little feeding	Same as coyote fencing
Kill with crushing bites to spine, skull, and dorsal side of neck. Claw marks often found on the neck, back, and shoulders of larger prey. Often kill more than one animal.	Consume the udder and flank, and remove the paunch and intestines intact; carcass may be almost entirely consumed. Prey often dragged to cover, sometimes covered with grass and dirt.	Electric fence at least 3 feet high
Usually kill small animals by biting on the head or back of neck. Often leap on the back and bite the neck and throat of larger prey. Hemorrhaging from claw punctures often can be found below the skin on the neck, back, sides, and shoulders. Paired upper and lower canines usually are 3/4-1 in. apart.	Often begin feeding on the viscera after entering behind the ribs. May drag and cover kill.	Woven wire 5 feet high
Usually bite to the back of the neck and skull causing massive hemorrhaging. Large canine tooth punctures, upper canines 1 3/4-2 in. apart, lower canines 1-1 3/4 in. apart. Large claw marks on head, neck, shoulder, flank.	Usually eviscerate the carcass, remove entrails and move aside. Consume lungs, heart, liver, and larger leg muscles first. May drag and cover the carcass.	Heavy woven wire 9 feet high or electric fence 9 feet high
Often kill poultry or small mammals (new lambs and kids are fairly vulnerable). Talon punctures in head and body with internal hemorrhage from talons. Tufts of feathers, wool or hair scattered and carcass often "skinned out." Presence of white-streak feces.	Consume entrails, organs, sometimes opens skull and eats brains. Ribs removed near the spine on young animals.	Wire topped cages. Also, respond to scare balloons or aluminum pie pans strung on poles.
Usually come on a schedule, once every 5 to 7 days. Often kill more than one bird. May clean out eggs from nest boxes. Mainly night hunter.	May eat just the head and crop	Two electric wires at 6 in. and 12 in. off ground
Several birds (or fish in aquaculture operations) are killed, and neatly piled together or lined up. Strictly night hunter.	Usually only eat the back of the head and the neck	Close animals in buildings at night. Cover all openings with 1/2 hardware cloth.
Usually only attack one bird per visit. May eat eggs. Mainly night hunter.	Usually just the abdomen is eaten	Wire mesh fence with electric 3 in. outside mesh at ground level and top

Head thrust between a fence's wooden boards, an Ayrshire calf examines the world outside his corral. You can reduce losses of young animals—who are particularly vulnerable to predators—by placing birthing areas near your farmstead where you can keep an eye on activities.

Killings usually occur at night or in very early morning, when you're normally asleep. A guardian animal is on duty twenty-four hours a day. They are alert and protective during these hours of greatest danger. Dogs are probably the most common guardian animals, but farmers also use donkeys, ponies, mules, and llamas to protect sheep and goats.

You'll need to raise guardian dogs very differently than pets. Bond guardian dogs to the animals they are going to protect as puppies, not to the family members. At the same time, be sure to handle them often enough that you can safely feed them, take them to the vet, chain them when you will be working with the flock, and perform other necessary tasks with them. Although certain breeds are characteristically used, not all individuals within those breeds are suitable.

When coyotes and domestic dogs are the problem, one or two guardian dogs are sufficient to protect a farm flock, but if wolves or other large predators are of major concern, dogs may or may not work: Although some producers report success with three to five dogs warding off large predators, Dr. Shivik says, "In the western U.S., guardian dogs are often killed by large predators, particularly wolves."

Donkeys and llamas, which live longer than dogs and don't require special feed, really dislike coyotes and dogs but tend to be scared of, or even vulnerable to, larger predators. In the United States, you can purchase these likable critters for between $50 and $500—a bargain compared with the cost of good guardian dogs, which usually start at $500. As with dogs, it is best to purchase these guardians early and raise them with the flock or herd they will protect.

A single female or gelded male is less likely to harass the animals it is meant to protect than multiple animals or ungelded males, and it will stay with the flock for companionship. If you use a herding dog for working your animals, the guardian may interfere with its ability to work.

Whichever type of guardian you're considering, remember the following.

- The guardian needs to bond with the animals it's protecting, and bonding can take time.
- Introduce guardians slowly, across a fence. It's usually easiest to make the introduction in a small area rather than in a large pasture.
- Each animal is an individual and will react differently in different situations. Some individuals don't make good guardians.

Physical Barriers

Fencing and enclosures are designed to place a physical barrier between the predators and their prey. As Dr. Shivik says, "Exclusionary devices can be as simple as an easily strung electric-energized temporary corral, or as complex and expensive as a dingo-proof fence stretching from one side of Australia to the other."

People build most fences to keep livestock in. Fences designed to keep predators out are more expensive than those, so they are rarely cost effective for large areas. Night penning is a cost-effective fencing approach that works well, especially for small- and medium-size operations. It involves bringing animals back into a small, predator-fenced area in the evening. Adding lights to night pens increases the effectiveness of the pens.

Since young animals are most vulnerable, having babies near the farmstead house reduces predation, particularly if you can move mother animals into a shed or barn near parturition. Buildings are also crucial for keeping small animals, like poultry and rabbits, safe from predators. Small animals are vulnerable to a wide variety of predators, ranging from raccoons and opossums to large predators. Timing when your babies will hit the ground can also influence predation. Lambs, calves, and other babies that are born in late spring and early summer are less subject to predation than those born in winter or early spring because small prey, like rabbits or voles, are abundant.

FARM SAFETY

It is a dangerous world, but farms are more dangerous than most other places, so farm safety is one of the most important things to think about. Consider some statistics:

- In 2002, the U.S. agriculture industry had the second highest rate of deaths due to accidents.
- In an average year, tractor rollovers crush 110 American farmworkers to death.
- Every day, about 500 U.S. agricultural workers suffer lost-work-time injuries, and about 5 percent of these result in permanent impairment.
- Farming is particularly dangerous for children. On U.S. farms and ranches an estimated 104 children younger than 20 years of age die annually of agricultural injuries. Over 30,000 serious injuries occur annually to children under the age of 20 who live on, work on, or visit a farm.

Heavy equipment, such as tractors and combines, can be involved in rollovers, run-overs, or in the pinning of someone against a stationary item. Visit older farmers, and you'll notice that a very large percentage of them are missing appendages (especially fingers) from working with high-speed spinning and chopping devices, such as PTO-driven equipment, which can easily catch hair, clothing, and hands. This equipment is very noisy and can reduce hearing capacity over time, so you should wear hearing protection.

It can be particularly dangerous to work in enclosed spaces, such as silos and manure pits, which lack sufficient oxygen or contain toxic gases, such as methane. These conditions often result in multiple deaths as untrained rescuers succumb to the same problem that caused a worker to collapse. Test enclosed spaces with gas and oxygen testers before you enter. If the air isn't suitable, set up an air pump to provide a suitable atmosphere. When

Above, a person encased in protective clothing sprays a field with pesticides. Below, farm children attend a lecture on farm accidents, such as the tractor rollover before them, and safety. Everyone in the family needs to learn about farm dangers and how to be safe.

The billy goat munching on grass above may appear cute, furry, and fun to people new to livestock, but he and other farm animals can be dangerous. Below, smoke still chokes the air around firefighters after their fierce battle with a barn fire. Such fires are all too common so take proper precautions.

working in an enclosed space, have someone outside the enclosed space and wear a safety harness. The harness allows rescuers to get you out without having to enter the enclosed space themselves.

Farmers often handle and store hazardous chemicals. Herbicides, pesticides, and fertilizers are dangerous chemicals (many are known carcinogens) so use the utmost care if you to opt to use them: Read the directions carefully, wear personal protective equipment as specified by the manufacturer, and dispose of according to the manufacturer's instructions.

Livestock hazards are abundant, and the animals don't have to necessarily be *mean* to hurt you. Any animal may kick, bite, buck, butt, or stomp out of fear or stress. Breeding males are especially dangerous during the breeding season because fighting is one of the steps to winning females in nature, so a normally mellow bull, stallion, buck, ram, or boar can suddenly become an aggressive terror.

Purposefully make yourself aware of the hazards around your farm and then make sure your family, visitors, and workers are aware of them as well. (Your local fire department or extension agent may be happy to come out and walk through the farm with you for a voluntary safety audit.) Do not tolerate unsafe behavior from anyone on your farm. Wear appropriate personal protective equipment (PPEs) at all times. Basic PPEs include hearing protection, goggles, steel-toed work boots, and good leather gloves, but many jobs require specialized PPEs.

Barn Fires

Although it is big disasters that garner the majority of the attention, the most common disaster for farmers is a barn fire. There are a number of steps that you can take to reduce the chances of a barn fire and to improve the likelihood that your animals will survive in the event of a fire.

Barns are usually full of highly flammable materials, such as hay chaff. A stray ash, an electrical short, or a hot engine can set off a conflagration in no time at all. Absolutely forbid smoking in and around the barn—and enforce this with guests as well as family members or employees. Be extremely conscious when using electrical appliances or heavy equipment around the barn, and don't leave them on unattended. Inspect electrical wiring annually. And, probably most importantly—don't store damp hay in a barn or haymow. Hay that is put up damp can spontaneously combust.

Keep fire extinguishers near every entry point, and make sure they are up to date and large enough to be effective. If you regularly keep animals stalled in the barn, consider the possibility of installing sprinklers. And invest in a good heat-and-smoke sensor with an alarm mounted outside the barn and in the house. The new sensors will pick up any sudden increase in building temperature, even if there isn't active smoke yet.

If a fire has started, use extreme caution when entering the barn. Ask yourself if your family can afford for you to be seriously injured or killed trying to rescue the animals. If you think you can enter safely, evacuate the easiest-to-reach animals first. This is another case when some pre-designed facilities will help: Construct a fenced area far enough away to safely keep the animals, but close enough so that you can quickly get animals to it if you are evacuating them from a barn.

Muddy water spraying up around his vehicle, a driver attempts to get through a flooded country road. Listen to local emergency managers and evacuate when they tell you to—before rising waters endanger your family and animals.

Disaster Preparedness

For most Americans, disaster is something we see on the evening news. Yet each year, hundreds of thousands of us personally suffer through some type of disaster, like floods, hurricanes, power outages, and wildfires. Disasters can be even more of a problem in rural areas because volunteers often operate rural emergency service providers, which cover large areas.

Lara Shane, spokesperson for the Federal Emergency Management Agency (FEMA, the lead federal agency for emergency response) says, "You don't want to be thinking about what you're going to do in an emergency situation for the first time, as that crisis is occurring."

She adds, "There are three key things we urge people to do:

- Have a plan. We think it's the most important thing people can do.
- Have a disaster supply kit.
- During a disaster, listen to your local emergency managers. These officials will guide you safely through a crisis."

If you have pets or livestock, make sure your plan addresses their needs. As Shane says, "Animals are generally not allowed in emergency shelters, so if you have to evacuate, you need to know where you can take your animals."

Creating a Disaster Plan

To create a disaster plan, take the following steps:

Learn and evaluate. Learn and evaluate what types of disasters could occur. Consider the following types of natural and manmade events when doing your evaluation: floods, hurricanes, thunderstorms (including tornadoes), extreme winter events, earthquakes, mudslides, wildfires, hazardous materials incidents, and terrorist attacks. Your local fire department or county emergency services personnel can help you consider possibilities you might overlook. (For example, the fire department may know about hazardous chemicals being transported through your community.)

Above, a child plays contentedly beside a pond. Most of us go through our daily lives enjoying the good things, not thinking about the bad, but catastrophes, such as the ominous storm approaching over Iowan fields below, do occur. Prepare your disaster plan and kit.

Determine means of contact. Determine how you will make contact with other members of your household if separated by an emergency. Identify two meeting places: one near your home (perhaps a nearby tree or telephone pole)—in case of fire—and the other farther away, in case you cannot return home. In addition, identify an out-of-town contact to act as a family communicator.

Draw up a floor plan. Draw a floor plan of your home. Mark two escape routes from each room. Likewise, if you keep animals in a barn, plan escape routes from it.

Post emergency numbers. Post emergency telephone numbers by telephones, including numbers for veterinarians and livestock handlers. Teach children how, and when to call 911. If you live off main highways, post written directions to your home along with the emergency numbers, so you can clearly tell emergency dispatchers how to find your home. "Turn left after the first cattle guard, drive three miles, then turn right after the green barn" is not something you want to have to think about while the barn is burning.

Know shut off switches. Make sure everyone in your household knows how and when to shut off water, gas, and electricity at the main switches or valves. If you have to evacuate (and you have time without endangering yourself or your family), fill the bathtub, sinks, and other containers with water before you turn off the water. Then when you return, you will have water immediately available for cleaning and other uses, even if the electricity is off. Consult with your local utilities if you have questions.

Reduce economic impact. Reduce the economic impact of disaster on your property and your household's health and financial well-being. Review property insurance policies before disaster strikes—make sure policies are current and be certain they meet your needs (type of coverage, amount of coverage, and hazards covered). Floods aren't covered under normal homeowner's policies unless you have a flood policy. In addition, review life and

health insurance policies. Consider starting an emergency savings account to use in a crisis. It is advisable to keep a small amount of cash or traveler's checks at home in a safe place where you can quickly gain access to it in case of an evacuation.

Inform emergency personnel. Does someone in your household have special needs (mobility impairment, children home alone during the day, a person without a vehicle, or other special circumstance)? If so, let local fire and emergency response personnel know what the situation is at your home.

Consider others. Do you have neighbors that will likely need help? Can your community use assistance in developing the capacity to meet an emergency?

Consider your animals. Where will you evacuate them to if you need to leave? If you face an extended power outage, how much water will your animals need and how will you supply it? A gasoline-powered generator can provide electricity during an extended power outage, both for watering your animals and for supplying electricity to your home.

PREPARING A DISASTER KIT

- **Water.** Stocking water reserves should be a top priority. It is *not* okay to ration drinking water in emergency situations. Therefore, it's critical to store adequate amounts of water for your household. Because you will also need water for sanitary purposes and cooking, store at least one gallon of water per person per day, in thoroughly washed plastic, fiberglass or enamel-lined metal containers. Sound plastic containers, such as soft drink bottles, are best. You can also purchase food-grade plastic buckets or drums. Seal your water containers tightly, label them, and store them in a cool, dark place.
- **Food.** Unlike water, you may safely ration food, except for food to children and pregnant women. Use canned foods, dry mixes, and other staples that do not require cooking, water, or special preparation. Be sure to include a manual can opener in your survival kit. Replace food items every six months. Consider including ready-to-eat meats, fruits, and vegetables; canned or boxed juices, milk, and soup; high-energy foods such as peanut butter, jelly, low-sodium crackers, granola bars, and trail mix; vitamins; foods for infants or persons on special diets; cookies and hard candy; instant coffee; and cereals and powdered milk.
- **First aid kit.** Assemble a first aid kit for your home and for each vehicle. Each kit should include a first aid manual, adhesive bandages in assorted sizes, safety pins, cleansing agents (isopropyl alcohol, hydrogen peroxide), antibiotic ointment, two pairs of latex gloves, petroleum jelly, two-inch and four-inch sterile gauze pads (four to six of each size), three triangular bandages, three rolls each of two-inch and three-inch sterile roller bandages, cotton balls, scissors, tweezers, needles, moistened towelettes, thermometer, two tongue depressor blades, and sunscreen. Also include an extra pair of prescription glasses or contact lens. Have nonprescription drugs, such as pain relievers, antacids, laxatives, and cough/cold medicines, in your disaster kit. If you require routine prescription medications, ask your physician or pharmacist about storing them.
- **Tools and other items.** Include a portable, battery-powered radio and flashlight, extra batteries, signal flares, matches in a waterproof container, shut-off wrench, pliers, shovel, whistle, A-B-C-type fire extinguisher, tube tent, mess kits (or paper cups, plates, and plastic utensils), all-purpose knife, household liquid bleach to treat drinking water, sugar, salt, pepper, aluminum foil and plastic wrap, re-sealing plastic bags.
- **Sanitation and hygiene items.** Include a washcloth and towel, soap, hand sanitizer, liquid detergent, toothpaste, toothbrushes, shampoo, deodorants, comb and brush, razor, shaving cream, lip balm, insect repellent, contact lens solutions, mirror, feminine supplies, heavy-duty plastic garbage bags and ties, toilet paper, medium-sized plastic bucket with tight lid.
- **Household documents and contact numbers.** Have copies of household documents and contact numbers ready to go on short notice and stored in a watertight container. Include your personal identification; cash or traveler's checks and a credit card; copies of important documents (birth certificates, marriage certificate, driver's license, social security cards, passport, wills, deeds, inventory of household goods, insurance papers, immunization records, bank and credit card account numbers, and stocks and bonds); an emergency contact list and phone numbers; a map of the area and phone numbers of place you could go; and an extra set of car keys and house keys.
- **Clothes and bedding.** Keep one complete change of clothing and footwear for each household member and three sets of socks and underwear, sturdy work shoes or boots, rain gear, hat and gloves, sunglasses, blankets or a sleeping bag for each household member, and pillows.

CHAPTER 5

Gardening: The Land

WHETHER YOU PLAN TO GARDEN COMMERCIALLY, OR JUST want to reduce your reliance on grocery store food, no farm is complete without some kind of garden. The garden is a sacred place, loved by those who know it. It provides a respite from the hectic world, a chance to enjoy nature at her finest, and the opportunity to feast on a gift of the best food available anywhere. After all, who can resist the flavor of garden-fresh vegetables? Fruit so juicy that you have to wash your face, hands, and arms after eating it; berries you can't stop eating, with a sumptuousness never found in the grocery store; sweet corn so sugary you know how it got its name; carrots that are perfectly crunchy, and potatoes that are naturally creamy; greens so light and crispy that they don't taste like something your mother forced you to eat; and squash that melts in your mouth. Who can remain unawed by the miracle of new life pushing up from the soil after a warm spring rain where just days or weeks before you set out seed (often so small it looks like a speck of dust)? And who isn't cheered by spring-flowering bulbs poking up through the snow?

Over the years, my own garden has changed in size, shape, and style. It will continue to change, as a garden should do. At one time, we gardened on over two acres and sold a good deal of our produce to friends and acquaintances. We thought about operating a CSA garden (community supported agriculture), but by then we were milking cows—two labor-intensive enterprises. We couldn't do both well so we cut back on the size of the garden.

Now our garden is small, consisting of some outdoor beds and indoor containers that help to keep us in fresh, organic produce all year-round. We don't grow all of our fruits and vegetables by any means, but we put a good dent in our need to purchase. Our plans for the future include a year-round greenhouse just large enough to meet our needs. We want it attached to the house, but as that's an expensive step, it won't happen for a while. We treat it as part of the evolution of our current farm.

You can grow crops on the field scale size: acres instead of a row or a bed. Some—such as field corn, soybeans, and hay—are the main enterprise, year-in and year-out, for many midsize and large commercial farms. Small and hobby farms often incorporate some field cropping, too. For example, they may grow several acres of pumpkins or a sweet corn patch, or put up hay for use on the farm. Field cropping and gardening follow many of the same practices, just on really different scales, but the principals, and the underlying kernels that predispose for success, all count on the same things: soil, sun, water, seeds.

Crops, such as the peppers being gathered above and pumpkins and corn shown below, can be grown on a small scale for personal use or as a commercial enterprise. Gardening, from starting seedlings for transplant (opposite) to the harvest, is perhaps the essence of hobby farming.

CHOOSING THE SITE

Where you place a garden has a lot to do with its success. Traditionally, gardeners placed kitchen gardens close to the kitchen door. When possible, it is still a good idea to place your garden within proximity to the kitchen. A garden that is near the kitchen door is inviting, and you are more likely to keep it up than one placed farther away. Water for irrigation is readily available close to the house.

To succeed in growing a wide variety of crops, your garden must receive at least six hours of sunlight a day, though more is even better. In shady patches, you can grow cool-season crops like lettuce, broccoli, cauliflower, cabbage, carrots, and radishes; but warm-season plants like tomatoes, peppers, corn, melons and berries will not fare well at all. A level or gently sloping site, with southern exposure, is ideal. On steep slopes, you will need to incorporate terracing.

Wind can damage plants, especially young transplants, so selecting a site that is somewhat protected by a natural or manmade windbreak will increase the success of your garden. Although trees can provide a windbreak, they also create unwanted shade and rob the garden soil of water, so try to keep them at least 50 to 60 feet from the edge of your garden.

THE WATER CYCLE

The water cycle is the movement of water between the atmosphere and the earth. Some water runs off land to enter streams, rivers, lakes, and ultimately, the ocean; but in a healthy ecosystem with soil that is high in organic matter, much of the water that falls from the sky as precipitation is absorbed into the soil. Some of what is absorbed enters the groundwater, some evaporates directly from the soil to atmosphere, and plants use the rest for transpiration. Transpiration is essentially the process by which plants carry nutrients from the soil up through the aboveground portion by water sucked in through the roots. Eventually, the excess water evaporates from the leaves of the plants.

EVALUATING THE SOIL

Most people look at the ground and just see dirt, but to a farmer dirt is something greater. It is soil, and when combined with solar energy, air, and water, it forms the life force of the planet.

Types of Soil

Soil starts with minerals. Most of the mineral was formed into rock eons ago by geologic processes (like volcanoes and earthquakes), and then over more eons, the rock has been crushed and pulverized, and moved by erosion from wind and water, which carries it from mountains to plains and river bottoms. Forces like wind, sun, and rain break large rocks into smaller ones, and then those smaller still. Bacteria, lichens, algae, and insects get in the act, helping to further break down rock. Chemicals in the soil, like acids and enzymes, keep the process going. This broken rock combines with humus, or organic matter from decaying plants and animals, to yield soil minerals.

At right, a gentle slope and fencing protect a young vegetable garden from wind damage while a scarecrow stands guard against animal intruders. On the opposite page, freshly tilled soil awaits the planting.

Soil high in organic matter, such as that shown above, retains moisture, yet drains well and is high in nutrients. Check soil quality using methods such as the easily executed soil texture test detailed in the box below.

You can generally classify soil minerals into three different size categories. Sand is the largest particle, silt is intermediate, and clay is the smallest. The percentage of each category in a soil determines the soil's texture as well as its physical properties. An ideal soil texture consists of equal parts of each size category and is called loam. Most of the time, however, one size category dominates so you end up with breakdowns like sandy loam or clay loam. The sizes affect how quickly soil drains and dries out. (Soils high in sand drain and dry quickly; clay, slowly; and silt, in between.)

Some soils contain little or no organic matter; they grow poor vegetation, if any at all. But healthy soil is vibrant and alive, containing more living tissue, in the form of roots, worms, insects, bacteria, and other microorganisms, than lives above its surface. Soil scientists estimate that a single tablespoon of good soil contains tens of millions of living organisms. These healthy soils grow abundant crops and native plants.

Some folks are lucky enough to enjoy naturally fertile soils that are rich in humus and can grow bountiful crops with little effort—just throw some seeds in the ground and wait for harvest. But most of us are not so fortunate; either the soil was never rich in organic matter (like my current situation in the Rocky Mountains, where the breakdown of rock hasn't progressed too far, and the long winters and dry conditions don't favor the quick conversion of dead plants, animals, and manure to humus), or the soil is worn out from bad practices (like mono-cropping; applying too much or too many years worth of chemical fertilizers, pesticides, and herbicides; or applying too much surface irrigation water that was high in salt). We need to take measures to improve our soil through the addition of amendments that increase humus in the soil, adjust the pH, increase or balance the nutrients (or both), and improve the texture of the soil so that it is easier to work with and drains well while still retaining moisture. After choosing a site for a garden (or field crop), it's a good idea to have some tests run that will help you decide on what amendments to make and when to make them.

Soil Tests

Although you can purchase home test kits, I recommend checking with your extension agent to find out about labs that do the tests commercially in your state (many state land grant universities have their own testing labs that provide reasonably priced service to residents). Under most circumstances, you won't have to run tests more than once every three to five years, so the cost isn't too much of a burden. Lab test results are usually more

DETERMINING SOIL TEXTURE

A quick and dirty way to approximate the soil texture is to determine the percentages of sand, silt, and clay in your soil by running a simple jar test. First, fill a quart jar two-thirds full of water, and gradually add a soil sample until the water reaches the top of the jar. Cover and shake the contents well, then allow it to settle for twenty-four hours. The sand will settle to the bottom, followed by silt, and then the clay particles. Some very fine clay particles may remain in suspension, and organic matter may float to the top.

Using a ruler, measure the total depth of soil in the bottom of the container. Write down the number of inches of soil. Next, measure each soil type, then divide that soil type by the total, and multiply by 100 to determine the relative percentage of that soil type in the total sample. Let's say, for example, that you measure a total of 6 inches of soil. One inch is sand, so you divide 1 by 6 to get 0.16, then multiply by 100. Your sand percentage is approximately 16 percent.

accurate than those you get from a home test kit. (When pH results come back highly acidic or highly alkaline, purchasing a home test kit specifically for pH is a good idea so that you can monitor changes to pH as you adjust it with soil amendments.)

Commercial labs (including those run by land grant universities) will generally supply a container and paperwork to complete. Most ask you what crop you are growing, because they will make recommendations according to that crop's needs. A technician will interpret the test results and make recommendations for soil amendment based on the type of crop you will be growing.

Soil tests evaluate the pH of your soil, the major nutrients (nitrogen, phosphorous, and potassium), and micronutrients (such as calcium, magnesium, sodium, and sulfur). The results can help you decide on appropriate plants for your soil, on soil-preparation techniques, and on amounts and types of fertilizer to apply. They will also help you avoid overfertilization, which can stimulate excessive plant growth, increase the likelihood of some diseases, or cause pollution of your drinking water supply and your area's rivers and lakes.

Whether running a home sample or having a lab run one, the accuracy of your test results is highly dependent on the quality of the sample you take. Follow these steps:

Avoid contamination. The best tool to use is a soil probe, but if you don't have access to one (they are available through most garden supply catalogs—see resources in the appendix) use a stainless steel or chrome-plated trowel or spade. Avoid using brass, bronze, or galvanized tools, as these can contaminate the sample with copper, zinc, or both. Use a clean container (even small amounts of residual fertilizer, lime, or cleaning chemicals can give false results) to combine all samples

Take samples in different spots. To fully represent the garden or field, you need to take samples in different spots, anywhere from five to twenty samples. Sample throughout

In central Iowa, an NRCS agent helps a farmer take a soil sample using a soil probe (above); in eastern Arkansas, two other agents check soil moisture on a farm (below). USDA personnel and other knowledgeable advisers offer valuable information and help to farmers.

the rooting zone—the top six to eight inches for gardens and crops other than hay, and three to four inches for hay fields.

Create soil composites. Mix the samples from your garden or field together to create a soil composite. If you are looking at distinct growing areas (say a garden, a hayfield, and an orchard), take separate composites for each, and have them analyzed separately. Mix the soil thoroughly.

IMPROVING SOIL HEALTH

For most soils, the first step to improving soil health is to increase the organic matter, and adding compost, leaf litter (partially decomposed leaves), or well-aged manure is the best way to do that—particularly for garden-size plots. From here on out, any time I say anything about adding compost to the garden, you can substitute well-aged manure or leaf litter in the application.

Compost

Compost is like black gold, and I have a hard time imagining why anyone would forego making compost. By composting organic waste, you reduce trash going to landfills and incinerators, and you feed the plants around your home. Even for urban and suburban dwellers, a compost tumbler or bin is a great way to do something good for the planet and for yourself.

Composting is a natural biological process carried out by organisms such as bacteria, fungi, insects, and earthworms. The organisms responsible for composting consume organic materials and oxygen in order to grow and reproduce. They produce carbon dioxide, water vapor, and heat as byproducts of their activities. From start to finish, the composting materials change from a diverse mixture of individual ingredients, such as grass clippings and leaves, food waste and manure, to a uniform soil-like material. Six key elements affect the process.

Above, a county extension agent checks the contents of a metal compost bin in suburban Virginia. Below, a young man out in the country adds material to a small compost pile contained by wire fencing. You can greatly improve soil with the addition of organic matter from a compost pile, leaf litter (opposite) or green manure.

COMPOSTING NO-NOS

Never compost the following materials:

- chemicals such as cleaning products, drugs, pesticides, and gasoline
- meat scraps, unground bones, dairy products *
- grease, fat, oil
- human, dog, cat (including used kitty litter), or pig waste**
- diseased plants, toxic plants (for example walnut leaves contain a toxic substance), and weeds with mature seed heads
- glossy paper, colored paper, and paper with colored ink
- treated or painted wood

*The best management practice, or BMP, for disposal of dead animals on many large-scale commercial farms is to use composting techniques, but the process has specific design requirements not covered here.
** Composting these kinds of wastes may be appropriate if you do not intend to use the finished compost on crops grown for human consumption—for example, if the compost will be spread on ornamental plantings.

Carbon to nitrogen ratio: Carbon materials are the "browns" that go into the pile. They include dried, dead leaves; twigs; corn stalks; hay; straw; dried grass clippings; sawdust; wood chips; finished compost; and shredded newspaper. They provide bulk and air gaps, and they help keep the pile from going sour. Nitrogen materials are the "greens." They include fresh grass clippings, fruits and vegetables, coffee grounds, eggshells, garden waste, and manure. A well-balanced proportion of carbon and nitrogen ensures a good supply of all nutrients and allows composting to proceed rapidly.

Surface area: The smaller the materials are that go into the pile, the better they are for speedy composting. Smaller chunks give more surface area for organisms to work on, so break up those branches and shred that newspaper.

Aeration: Aerobic organisms carry on the process of composting. You need good airflow throughout the pile to supply these workers with the oxygen they need to breathe. Turning the pile from time to time can aid aeration. We turn ours in spring as soon as it thaws, and then once a month or so during the summer and fall. At each turning, we take some finished compost off the bottom of pile. For small operations that are primarily dealing with household waste and a small amount of yard or garden waste, commercial compost tumblers work well. For a mid-size operation, running several bins or piles works well. Large operations, like those with lots of manure, typically build free-form piles and turn them with a tractor. Medium and large piles also benefit from several perforated plastic pipes inserted vertically into the pile to increase airflow.

Moisture: Your pile needs to be damp most of the time, but not sopping wet. A dry pile leaves the organisms thirsty, but a too-wet pile looses critical air space that allows them to breathe.

Temperature: The organisms generate heat while they work, thus raising the temperature of the composting materials. The ideal temperature is in a range from about 135 to 160 degrees Fahrenheit, though temperatures in a pile can sometimes exceed 160 degrees.

Time: It can take anywhere from several weeks to over a year to produce compost, depending on the ingredients and conditions in a pile. Compost is typically ready for use in three to four months during warm weather, given regular turning, adequate moisture, and a good mixture of materials. Methods that involve little or no turning usually require more than a year to produce compost that is ready to use.

You can easily create compost piles by alternating layers of green and brown material. The ideal ratio is about three parts of carbon to one part of nitrogen by volume. In other words, if you place a layer of browns that is about three inches deep on the bottom of your pile, the next layer of greens can be about one inch deep. We pick up some night crawlers from a bait supply store each spring and dump them in our compost piles to help speed up activity.

Manure and Fibrous Plant Matter

If you have livestock, you have a readily available supply of fertility for your land. Never use fresh manure in the garden during the growing season, as it can burn plants, and may contain viable weed seeds or pathogens. However, you can work some fresh manure into the garden during the late fall, and by spring it will be broken down sufficiently to not cause problems. Applying some fresh manure to farm fields in the spring, prior to tillage and planting, is okay if you spread it thinly with a manure spreader. The spreader lays it out in well-broken pieces that sun and precipitation quickly breakdown.

Another approach to improving soil health is to grow a "green manure" crop. Green manures are plants grown for the sole purpose of being turned back into the soil. Crops like clovers, field peas, oats, annual rye, wheat (spring or winter), and buckwheat are common green manures. When you use legumes (plants that fix nitrogen from the atmosphere in their roots, such as clover, alfalfa, or field peas) as green manures, you get an extra boost of free nitrogen fertilizer. Whereas compost, leaf litter, and well-aged manure can go on immediately before planting, green manures need to breakdown somewhat after you have turned them under, but before you plant your crop. After you turn down the green manure, wait three to four weeks before planting your next crop. If you have a site where the soil is really worn out, planting several successive green manure crops is the best way to bring it back.

The final approach to improving soil organic matter is to turn fibrous plant matter, such as sawdust, chopped straw, or shredded newspaper into the soil. However, there is a problem with turning these materials directly into soil. Because of their high carbon concentration, these materials are slow to break down, and they can steal nutrients such as nitrogen from your crop while they are breaking down.

Some crops, such as the potato plant shown above, are heavy feeders, so you may need to provide supplemental nutrients even when the soil already boasts good organic content. When growing field crops, including cereal grains such as green wheat below, take soil samples from several areas of the field that seem fairly representative of the overall area to determine quality.

Fertilizers and pH Adjustment

Although compost, manure, green manure, and fibrous materials add some nutrients as well as organic matter, your soil may require additional amendments to feed the plants that you plan to grow. There are two approaches to feeding the plants you grow. The first is to feed the soil and let it take care of the plants, and the second is to feed the plants directly with soluble feeds that they can take up through their leaves. (The latter approach is known as foliar feeding.)

I believe in feeding the soil and letting it take care of plants through the natural system Mother Nature developed. However, if you are starting new with soil that is far out of balance,

foliar feeding sometimes can be an excellent short-term fix to help your crops along while you rebuild the soil. If foliar feeding is necessary, you may need to do it frequently (six to ten times) during the growing season, starting with seedling emergence and continuing until just before harvest. Apply foliar feeds in the early morning or early evening, rather than during the heat of the day, so that you lose fewer nutrients to plant transpiration. You can brew compost-tea and use it as a foliar feed, or purchase fertilizers that are appropriate for foliar feeding.

The letters *pH* stand for the percentage of free hydrogen ions, and they describe the acidity or alkalinity of a substance on a scale from 0 to 14. If a substance has a pH value below 7, it is acidic; above 7 it is alkaline, and 7 itself is neutral. The pH scale is interesting, because as you move up and down the scale, changes multiply by factors of 10. For example, a pH of 6 is 10 times more acidic than a pH of 7. A pH of 5 is 10 times more acidic than a pH of 6 or 100 times more acidic than a pH of 7. A pH of 10 is 1,000 times more alkaline than a pH of 7 (10 times for the change to 8; 100 times for the change to 9; 1,000 times for the change to 10).

Most of the plants we want to grow do best in soils with a pH between 6.0 and 6.8, which is slightly acidic—though certain plants (such as azaleas, blueberries, and cranberries) prefer more acidic soils, and others (such as peppers, yams, and legumes) appreciate slightly alkaline soils. In the United States, most soils have a pH between 4 and 9. You can bring up acidic soil by adding limestone. You can bring down alkaline soil by using sulfur or aluminum sulfate. It is best to adjust pH in several smaller applications of sulfur or limestone spread throughout the year, versus one big application.

PREPARING THE LAND

Whether growing crops in a field or planting a garden, there are some steps required to prepare the seedbed for your crop. Farmers use the term *tillage* for the process of preparing the seedbed. For smaller gardens, I prefer the deep-bed method to row plantings with traditional tillage. However, if you have the space, the tractor-driven equipment, and the urge to spend most of your time driving the tractor, row planting definitely works.

Deep Beds

Many people credit an Englishman named Alan Chadwick with pioneering the deep-bed method in the United States, as early as the 1930s, when he began experimenting with the practice at the University of California at Santa Cruz. The method is based on the traditional raised beds of French market gardeners. During the nineteenth century, Parisian gardeners were able to grow more than one hundred pounds of produce annually for every person in the city. They did this through the use of beds that were dug deeply and then built up (to heights of 18 inches) above the paths that bordered them, adding plenty of well-aged horse manure (something that was quite abundant at the time). By spacing plants closely, they could maximize the production in a given area, and by using glass cloches (bell-shaped mini-greenhouses that sat over individual plants or clumps of plants), they were able to produce throughout the winter.

The ideal design for a bed is wide enough that you can straddle it from the two paths that border it (say, about 3 feet). Though beds can be any length you want them to be, I prefer relatively short beds (10 to 20 feet long) with cross paths, which make moving around the garden convenient. I like most paths wide enough to accommodate a two-wheeled wheelbarrow or a garden wagon. Mulching paths with 3 inches or so of straw, wood chips, or shredded newspaper helps control weeds and maintain moisture in the beds, yet reduces

TOOL TIPS

For small gardens, you'll need a flat spade and a pointed spade for digging. A good digging fork is a multipurpose tool, used for breaking up and turning soil in the garden, harvesting potatoes, and for manure cleanup around the barn. My preference for hoes is the collinear hoe designed by gardening guru Eliot Coleman and available from Johnny's Selected Seeds (see Resources). This style of hoe takes the "back-breaking" out of controlling weeds, as it allows you to stand up straight while you work.

For medium-size gardens (say, more than a couple of beds, but less than an acre or two) a walking tractor can be a cost-effective alternative to a compact tractor or utility vehicle with implements. A walking tractor is like a big, heavy-duty rotary tiller, but the tiller isn't permanently mounted—instead it is one of several different attachments that you can add, such as seeders, hillers, and mowers.

Before you begin digging your garden (opposite), determine which tools will be best for the job at hand. As the tips box above explains, you shouldn't pick up just any old shovel if you want a healthy back at task's end.

A young boy works diligently on a dug bed (above), a great way to grow garden crops as it yields big harvests from small areas. Create the raised bed as a mound with no structure or in a frame (see below).

mud and mess. Try to never walk on the bed itself, as this compacts the soil. (The success of the beds is in part due to the airy soil structure you create.)

Arrange your crops in blocks instead of rows and use an equidistant spacing pattern to create a nearly solid leaf canopy or "living mulch." This reduces weed pressure and conserves moisture.

Vegetable and herb gardens have traditionally been oblong, because an oblong plot was easier to work with a tractor. But when using beds, you can design your beds in fanciful patterns. In recent years, I have been developing a series of beds in unusual shapes that follow the natural lay of the land. In the beds, I intermingle flowers, herbs, and vegetables. They add a landscaped feel to the area around the house, while producing food.

Double-digging beds

Some gardeners advocate a method called double digging. To double dig your beds, follow the steps below.

1. Dig out a layer (about the depth of the spade) in a trench that runs the width of the bed. Set this aside. (It's convenient to put it in your wheelbarrow or garden cart.)
2. Loosen the soil at the bottom of the trench by digging it with a fork and turning it over.
3. Add compost or manure to the bottom of the trench so that it reaches about half way to the top of the trench. Also add any other slow-release amendments.
4. Dig another trench adjacent to the first, placing the soil from it on top of your first trench.
5. Repeat from step 2 until you have dug and treated the entire bed.
6. Use the soil from the first trench to cover the last trench.
7. Shape the bed to mound it slightly in the middle.

Lazy person's bed

I find double digging to be too much work. My method of preparing a bed does require one over-wintering period, so it has a disadvantage if you are in a hurry, but if you plan ahead it is quite easy. First, in late summer or early fall, mark the area where you want to create your bed with rocks or stakes at the corners. Using your round-pointed shovel, turn over the top 4 to 8 inches of soil (depending on how easy it is to dig and turn) to put the existing vegetation down under the soil surface. As you're working, remove any large rocks from this layer. Next top-dress the bed generously with three to six inches of compost (this is one time you can substitute fresh manure if you don't have compost or aged manure). Last, sprinkle a layer of straw mulch lightly over the bed (one to two inches is good). Now sit back and wait for spring.

In very early spring, head out with your spade and dig around, mixing up the soil, compost, and straw as well as you can to about the depth of the spade. (If you live where soil freezes, do this step as soon as the soil thaws enough to work it; in less severe climates, a nice afternoon in early February would probably be the time to do it.) If you are adding any slow-release amendments such as wood ash, greensand, lime, or sulfur, put them on top before you do your mixing. Add another inch or so of compost to the top of the bed, and take another break until the weather warms up enough to start thinking about planting.

As planting time approaches in late spring, remix the bed lightly to incorporate the last top dressing. Slightly mound the bed in the middle with a rake. Each fall you can add compost and some mulch, and each spring you can turn it under. Over several years, your beds will improve and you will see the difference in your crops.

TILLAGE: A WORD TO THE WISE

Never perform any tillage operations in fields or gardens when the soil is wet and muddy. Doing so causes soil to become compacted, which blocks root penetration and results in more sheet runoff (water running along the surface of the ground rather than being absorbed by the soil) and erosion.

Field Tillage

Traditionally tillage involved plowing and harrowing. Plowing breaks up the soil surface, turns under vegetation and crop residue, and incorporates manure, lime, or fertilizer.

In Texas, a farmer tills, plants, and fertilizes his field with a single, unique piece of machinery.

CONTRACTING PAYS

Field preparation is a skill—as much art as science—that lifelong farmers learned as youngsters, and for any kind of sizeable project it is best done by somebody with really big equipment who has been doing it forever: We were converting a sixty-acre field from corn to hay ground one summer. With our smaller utility tractors this would have been an onerous job, so we contracted with one of our neighbors to prepare the field with his giant Versatile tractor and implements. (At 200-plus horsepower, this is a tractor that could pull a house down, if you were so inclined.) This worked out well for both of us; we got our field prepped in a couple of days, and Dan earned some ready cash to help pay for the big rig. Ken then seeded the field easily with our Farmall M (a 50-plus-year-old tractor) and a seed drill.

Several types of plows are available. The moldboard plow, which earned the name *prairie buster* as settlers opened the frontier in the nineteenth century, can turn over up to 2 feet of soil, with sod or dense vegetation on it. Chisel plows are narrower and don't dig as deeply, making them inadequate for plowing a field for the first time. Their advantage comes into play on fields that have previously been planted in annual crops. Chisel plows disturb less soil, causing less compaction of subsoil layers. Chiseled land is less erosive.

When plowing land that has been farmed for annual crops in the recent past, a compact tractor may do the job, but if you are plowing land that has been in sod for years, you will need at least a utility-size tractor. (See Chapter 3 for a discussion of tractors and implements.)

Harrowing follows plowing and is intended to create a smooth soil surface by breaking up the furrows and clods of dirt thrown up by the plow—it's comparable to giving a garden bed a final raking. It prepares a fine and even seedbed that creates the ideal environment.

Harrowing is often a multi-step process, depending on the type and depth of plowing and the crop for which the field is being prepared (very fine seeds require a more even and finely prepared seedbed than larger seeds). A disk harrow is often the first tool used following the plow, because it is capable of quickly breaking down the rough surface and clods of soil left by the plow. For a field that doesn't require a very smooth seedbed, you can often do the work in a single pass by using a disk harrow with a set of chains following it, but for a really smooth field, you should make a second pass with a spring-tooth harrow.

Try to minimize the amount of tillage you do, as every pass of a machine ultimately compacts soil and reduces tilth. Often you will find that area farmers won't plant into anything but a perfectly smooth seedbed, out of habit, but their crops (particularly those with large seeds) don't always need that level of perfection to perform well.

One last chore of seedbed preparation is rock picking. In areas with rocky soils, freezing and thawing actually lift rocks to the soil surface. Remove large rocks from the field, because they can damage equipment.

The neat rows of soil shown at right are the result of several days of hard work, like the one the farmer on the opposite page is putting in as he prepares his fields for planting.

CHAPTER 6

Gardening: The Planting

SEEDS ARE SIMPLY MIRACULOUS. THEY ARE BUNDLES OF LIFE—plants in embryonic form—just waiting for the right conditions to grow and reproduce.

GETTING TO KNOW PLANTS

You can group plants into three primary classes, depending on their life cycles. Some plants are annuals. They must go through their whole life cycle, including producing seeds, in the year that they sprout. Biennials are plants that take two years to complete a growth cycle and yield seeds. Perennial plants live from year to year; shrubs and trees are all perennials. Some annual plants are self-seeding, so from a gardener's point of view, they behave like perennials.

Annuals reproduce strictly from seeds, so gardeners consider their reproduction sexual. Biennials and perennials can reproduce sexually from seeds, but these plants may also reproduce asexually from existing roots.

Plant Families

Think of plants, like people, as part of a family. Like human families, plant families share significant traits. Some of the important families that farmers and gardeners deal with are:

Apiaceae (formerly Umbelliferae): Carrots are probably the most common member of this family in gardens, but you may also plant celeriac or celery. Apiaceae herbs include anise, coriander, cumin, dill, fennel, and parsley.

Chenopodiaceae: Beets and spinach are the two most common members of Chenopodiaceae, but quinoa (a grain from Central and South America that is finding its way into our diet), Swiss chard, and sea kale are other members you might consider planting. The "seeds" that you plant are actually tiny fruits containing the real seeds inside them, so when you plant one "seed," multiple plants come up. This means you have to thin your plantings. An advantage of planting Chenopodiaceae is that the members of this family have a dense root system that breaks up compacted soil. Grow beets for livestock feed as well as for humans.

Compositae: Lettuce is probably the most famous member of the Compositae family. Included as well are artichokes, cardoons, chicory, endive, salsify, and scorzonera. Unfortunately, this family also brings us some weedy members—such as dandelions and thistles—that find their way into gardens, lawns, and fields against our wishes.

Cucurbitaceae: Yum, yum, yum. This family brings us cucumbers, melons, pumpkins, and squash. All members of this family are warm-season crops, so do not place seeds or transplants in the ground until the danger of frost has passed. Though generally grown for their fruit, Cucurbitaceae blossoms are edible, and you can add them to salads.

Even a small garden can provide enough vegetables, such as the carrots above and pumpkins below, year round.With the warm sun on her back, a woman (opposite) enjoys the peacefulness of her garden, gathering her homegrown peas.

Like other of members of the Cruciferae family, broccoli (above) and cabbage (opposite) are some of the first treats to pop up in your garden. The legumes, such as green beans (below), are popular crops, too, because they enrich the soil.

Cruciferae: Also called the cabbage family, or the Brassicas, the Cruciferae family includes broccoli, Brussels sprouts, common and Chinese cabbage, cresses, kale, kohlrabi, radishes, rutabagas, and turnips. All the plants in this family are biennials. They have a two-year growth cycle to create seeds, though for garden produce, you pick the crop during its first year. The Brassicas are cool-season crops, so they can go in the garden early, producing some of the first goodies to come from the garden. Plant brussel sprouts in summer for harvest in the fall, as frost sweetens the result.

Lamiaceae: Known as the mint family, this group brings us a wide variety of herbs, ranging from basil and bee balm to sage, rosemary, and thyme. These are highly aromatic herbs that are widely used in cooking. You may also use them for their medicinal properties.

Lauraceae: This is a family that doesn't rest on its laurels. It brings us a number of perennials, including avocados, as well as the herbs bay leaf and cinnamon.

Leguminosae: Most living organisms use the ammonia form of nitrogen (NH_3) for building protein that is required for body functions. The atmosphere consists of about 80 percent nitrogen; however, this nitrogen is available in a non-useable form of gas (N_2). The legumes are unique in that they are able to "fix" that atmospheric form of nitrogen in their roots, changing it to the useable NH_3 form. By doing this, they provide part of their own fertilizer while increasing soil fertility that other plants can take advantage of. Legumes accomplish this feat thanks to a mutually beneficial, relationship that they have with a group of soil microorganisms, known as rhizobium. Rhizobium lives in nodules on the roots of the legumes. The plant contributes energy, in the form of sugars and other nutritional factors, for the bacteria, so the bacteria can provide the nitrogen that the plant needs in a form it can use. To enhance nitrogen fixing, inoculate seeds with appropriate rhizobium before planting.

The legumes are also special, because they provide more dietary protein for animals (including us two-legged creatures) than any other plant can provide. The legumes include

such garden favorites as peas and beans, lentils, and peanuts. Crops for livestock feed include field peas, alfalfa, clovers, vetches, and birdsfoot trefoil.

Liliacae: This is one of my favorite families. Its members include asparagus, chives, garlic, leeks, onions, and scallions. This family has flowering members as well, such as day lilies, camas, crocuses, daffodils, hostas, hyacinths, lilies-of-the-valley, and tulips. The aloe plant, known for its medicinal properties, is also a member of the clan. All members of this family are monocotyledons.

Poaceae (formerly Gramineae): Better known as the grass family, Poaceae is represented in the garden by only one family member—sweet corn. Outside the garden environment, poaceae includes many cereal grains, such as oats, rice, rye, and wheat, and forage crops for the pasture, such as bromegrass, orchard grass, and timothy.

Polygonceae: Rhubarb and sorrel are the two members of this family found in the garden, but the most famous member is buckwheat, a major green manure crop as well as a minor grain crop. Buckwheat hulls can be used as stuffing for pillows.

Rosaceae: As the name implies, roses are members of this family, but also included are many of our favorite fruits: almonds, apricots, apples, blackberries, cherries, nectarines, peaches, pears, plums, raspberries, and strawberries. All members of this family are dependent on insects (primarily bees) for pollination.

Rutacae: Those of you who live in southern-tier states and some parts of California are probably familiar with Rutaceae, which support a large amount of economic activity in your regions. These are the citrus family members: grapefruit, lemons, limes, oranges, and tangerines. For those relegated to northern climes, if you are dedicated, you may get fruit from trees grown indoors in pots.

Soanaceae: This group includes some all-time favorites—potatoes, tomatoes, peppers, and eggplants. Soanaceae also includes some dark horses, such as tobacco, belladonna, and deadly nightshade. Petunias, ground cherries, and jimson weed are members of the tribe as

These vibrantly colored oranges beg to be picked (above). Nothing tastes better than fresh fruits and veggies from your own yard (below and opposite).

To save grapes (above and below) and other fruits in orchards and vineyards, owners often use heaters, or smudge pots (opposite). The smudge pots trap heat between the ground and a thick smoke cloud that hovers over the orchard or vineyard.

well. The edible members of this clan are good sources of vitamin C. Soanaceae plants like slightly acidic soil, so you don't want to add lime where you will plant them. They do like potassium, so adding a source of potash, such as wood ash, is a good idea.

Vitaceae: The final family of importance for gardeners, farmers, and wine drinkers is the Vitaceae family, which brings us the grape. Most areas of the country can grow one or more varieties of grapes, but grapes are very geographically specific. Some grapes can't grow in high humidity areas, others crave humidity; some tolerate heat well, others are hardy enough to survive a Minnesota winter. If you are interested in trying grapes, research varieties suitable to your area before purchasing any vines.

Hardiness

You can successfully grow most annuals throughout the United States (though in cold climates you may need to start annuals indoors and transplant out if they are to reach maturity). Unfortunately, biennials and perennials won't grow everywhere; climate dictates where they will grow. In 1960, Henry T. Skinner, then director of the U.S. National Arboretum, in cooperation with the American Horticultural Society, supervised the creation of the *Plant Hardiness Zone* map. The map is broken down into hardiness regions, based primarily on average annual minimum winter temperatures. It has become a valuable tool for gardeners interested in growing perennials.

When shopping for perennials, you will see references to the zones that the plant you are looking at will grow in. Plants may survive in warmer or colder zones than those listed, but the range represents the optimum for that plant's performance.

Be aware of microclimates, localized areas where weather conditions may vary from the norm. A sheltered yard may support plants not normally adapted to the region, or a north-facing slope may be significantly cooler or windier than surrounding areas, thereby reducing the survival of plants normally adapted to the area.

METHODS OF PROPAGATION

Plants that grow from seeds are classified as either monocotyledons (also known as monocots) or dicotyledons (dicots), depending on how their first leaves grow. Monocots start life with a single, straight leaf and include many grasses and grains. Most fruits, vegetables, and legumes are dicots, sending up two leaves. The dicots have thicker, tap-type roots, and the leaves are often patterned with veins in a weblike design.

A seed coat protects most seeds from the elements until the time is right for them to grow. Some seeds only remain viable for a short period, measured in days, but others can remain dormant for many years and then spring to life when the time is right. Lotus seeds, for example, remain viable for thousands of years. Most garden seeds, however, last no more than a few years.

When it comes to many heat-loving plants, transplants give you a head start on the growing season. They are readily available in the spring at garden centers, grocery stores, and discount stores. You can also start them in the house with little effort. The biggest benefit of starting your own plants is that you have more seed varieties to choose from. Starting your own transplants is cost-effective as well. It's almost essential if you want fully organic produce because commercially available transplants are often fertilized with petroleum-based fertilizers and treated with chemicals to protect from insects and diseases.

Cutting, division, and layering are techniques that offer an alternative to starting plants from seeds when you wish to propagate perennial and biennial plants. These are asexual techniques that start new plants from a parent plant's stems or roots.

From spotting your first seedling such as the one above, to a sea of green, like the vegetable garden shown opposite, you'll discover the true meaning of "enjoying the fruits of your labor." Waiting for perfect temperature and soil conditions (among many other factors) that seeds require to sprout can be tough; consider purchasing transplants instead.

Starting with Seeds

You can start seeds directly in the garden, indoors for transplanting outside, or in containers for remaining inside. Seeds sprout when temperature, moisture, light, and other conditions are just perfect.

For some seeds with particularly hard seed coats, breaking dormancy naturally may take years, but you can opt for some intervention strategies that trick the seed into breaking dormancy when you want it to. Scarification helps break dormancy; out in nature, it is the result of years of freezing and thawing, and of living creatures (ranging from microscopic organisms to birds and animals) working over the seeds. To scarify seeds, scratch the seed coat (an emery board works well), freeze and thaw, or soak the seed in hot water (170 to 212 degrees Fahrenheit). For hot-water treatment, allow seeds to soak in the water as it cools, for twelve to twenty-four hours right before planting.

After germination occurs, seedlings require ten to sixteen hours of intense light a day. Without strong light, the seedlings become spindly or leggy and may lean toward whatever light source is available. For indoor sowing, light from a south-facing window may be sufficient, but if not, use a grow light for supplemental light. (You can make a light stand for a fluorescent fixture from PVC pipe.) Not all grow lights are created the same: A combination of cool white and warm white fluorescent bulbs placed three inches from the top of the tallest plants you are supplementing does the trick. (Just remember to move the light up frequently, or you will find a plant cooking itself right against the light.)

You can seed in the garden by hand or with a single-row seeder that you push. Different models use different approaches for delivering the seed. Fluid, belt, and vacuum seeders are expensive specialty seeders, probably only justified for very large commercial gardens.

FRUITS AND VEGETABLES

Family	Common Name	Companions	Antagonists
Liliaceae	Asparagus	Tomatoes, parsley, basil	
Leguminosae	Beans	Potatoes, marigolds, cucumbers, corn, strawberries, celery	Onions, garlic, gladiolas
Chenopodiaceae	Beet	Lettuce, cabbage, onions	Beans, mustard
Cruciferae	Broccoli	Nasturtium, aromatic herbs, potatoes, celery, dill, beets, onions	Strawberries, tomatoes, beans
Cruciferae	Brussel Sprouts	Nasturtium, oregano, potatoes, celery, dill, beets, onions	Strawberries, tomatoes, beans
Cruciferae	Cabbage	Nasturtium, oregano, potatoes, celery, dill, beets, onions	Strawberries, tomatoes, beans
Apiaceae	Carrot	Peas, lettuce, chives, onions, rosemary, sage, tomatoes	Dill
Cruciferae	Cauliflower	Nasturtium, oregano, potatoes, celery, dill, beets, onions	Strawberries, tomatoes, beans
Apiaceae	Celery	Leeks, tomatoes, beans, cauliflower, cabbage	
Cucurbitaceae	Cucumber	Beans, nasturtium, corn, peas, radishes, sunflowers	Potatoes, aromatic herbs
Poceae	Corn	Potatoes, peas, beans, cucumbers, pumpkins, squash, marigolds, sunflowers	
Solanaceae	Eggplant	Beans	
Liliaceae	Garlic	Beets, strawberries, tomatoes, lettuce, chamomile	Peas and beans

*Aromatic herbs include oregano, basil, rosemary

Sowing	Minimum Soil Temperature for Germination	Space in Beds in Inches	Culture
From roots in trenches; seeds do not yield for at least three years	50	12	Mulch in the winter; tolerates part of day shade; this is a perennial, so once established it stays productive for years; cut ferns to the ground in fall; cut shoots just below soil surface
Sow at least 2 inches deep in the garden	60	6	Moist, rich soil; benefit from trellising, string or wire frames so plants can grow up off the ground; may benefit from seed innoculation; like lime
Sow in place, in batches 3 weeks apart, but presoak seed	40	3	Sow in batches, 3 weeks apart, likes well drained soil high in humus
Indoors 4 weeks before you want to set, out or outdoors for later crops	40	15	Grows in a wide variety of soils, but doesn't tolerate heat
Indoors (4 weeks)	40	18	Likes frost, and limed soil
Indoors (4 weeks)	40	15	Good soil, high in nitrogen and lime. Growing near aromatic herbs helps repel cabbage moth
Sow in place, but not in very wet soil	40	2	Well drained rich soil with lots of phosphorous; don't wash carrots until ready to use, as washed carrots rot more quickly than those that are left unwashed
Indoors (8 weeks)	40	15	Likes frost, and limed soil high in nitrogen
Indoors (4 weeks); sowing in a coldframe is advantageous to get it going; plant in trenches	60	6	Deep, rich soil, high in humus, with constant moisture; slightly acidic soil; requires mounding of soil over the plant as it grows so that only the top leaves are exposed to sunlight; frost needed for full flavor
Indoors (8 weeks) or under a coldframe	60	12	Well drained, yet moist, rich soil, neutral pH; needs calcium for crispness; protect transplants from frost; pinching male flowers will improve the quality of the crop
Outdoors after last frost; speed things up a little by starting in a tunnel	50	15	Must be protected from frost; loves rich, well drained soil; may require hilling
Indoors (8-10 weeks) or outdoors in a coldframe	60	18	Deep, rich soil, high in humus; slightly acidic soil protect from frost
Cloves in fall for harvest the next fall	40	2	Rich, loose, and well drained soil is best, but will grow in a wide variety of soil; likes cool temperatures, and will tolerate shade

FRUITS AND VEGETABLES

Family	Common Name	Companions	Antagonists
Compositae	Lettuce	Carrots, radishes, strawberries, cucumbers	
Cucurbitaceae	Melons	Pumpkin, corn, nasturtium, radish	
Liliaceae	Onions	Broccoli, marigolds, beets, carrots, eggplant, strawberries, tomatoes, lettuce	Peas and beans
Leguminosae	Peas	Potatoes, aromatic herbs, carrots, turnips, radishes, cucumbers, corn, beans	Onions, garlic, gladiolas
Solanaceae	Pepper	Basil	
Solanaceae	Potato	Eggplant, aromatic herbs, beans, corn, cabbage, marigold	Pumpkins, squash, cucumbers, sunflowers, tomatoes, raspberries
Cucurbitaceae	Pumpkin	Corn	Potatoes
Cucurbitaceae	Radish	Peas, nasturtiums, lettuce, cucumbers, beets, spinach, mellons, tomatoes, beans	Cabbage family
Liliaceae	Shallots	Broccoli, marigolds, beets, carrots, eggplant, strawberries, tomatoes, lettuce	Peas and beans
Chenopodiaceae	Spinach	Strawberries, radishes	
Cucurbitaceae	Squash (winter)	Nasturtium, corn, radish	
Cucurbitaceae	Squash (summer)	Nasturtium, corn, radish	
Rosaceae	Strawberries	Beans, spinach, lettuce	Cabbage family
Solanaceae	Tomatoes	Chives, onions, parsley, asparagus, marigolds, nasturtium, carrots	Potatoes, and cabbage family
Cruciferae	Turnips	Peas, vetch, beans	
Cucurbitaceae	Watermelon	Potatoes	

*Aromatic herbs include oregano, basil, rosemary

Sowing	Minimum Soil Temperature for Germination	Space in Beds in Inches	Culture
Outdoors	35	12 for head; 8 for leaf	Rich, well drained soil on the acidic side; once leaves dry back, dig crop and let dry in sun for a day or two before you handle; then braid and hang in bunches in a dry room for storage
Indoors (4-8 weeks) or outdoors in long growing season regions	60	15	Light, rich soil with alkaline pH
Indoor (8 weeks) or outdoors for seeds, outdoors for sets	35	4	Seeds are more challenging than sets; like potassium and phosphorous (likes wood ash); mulch helps keep weeds in check
Outdoors at least 2 inches deep; presoak seeds	40	3	Rich, well drained soil; likes wood ash; protect seed from birds; benefit from trellising, string or wire frames so plants can grow up off the ground; may benefit from seed innoculation
Indoors (8 weeks) or outdoors in long growing season regions	60	12	Light, well drained soil; good sun; mulch plants to maintain moisture
Sets, in place after last frost, or earlier in a cold frame; plant about 5 inches deep	40	9	Rich soil; likes acidic soil, but benefits from some wood ash; tolerates partial shade; requires mounding of soil over plants as they grow
Indoors (4-8 weeks) or outdoors in long growing season regions	60	30	Likes humus; often found growing as volunteers from compost piles
Outdoors; sow successive batches about 2 weeks apart for a constant supply	40	2	Grow almost anywhere, but like moist soil, with neutral pH; tolerates some shade
Sets in place	35	2	Rich, well cultivated and -watered soil
Indoors for an early start, or outdoors about 1 inch deep	35	4	Moist, rich soil; seeds do not store well
Indoors (3 weeks) or outdoors	60	20	Well drained, rich soil
Indoors (3 weeks)	60	16	Well drained, slightly alkaline soil
Roots	50	12	Light soil; good sun; slightly acidic; mulch with pine needles; allow plants to become established for several years before harvesting much fruit
Indoors (8 weeks)	65	20	Rich, moist soil with neutral pH; requires good sun
Indoors (4 weeks) or outdoors	40	3	Cool, moist soil; likes wood ash
Indoors (8 weeks) or outdoors in long growing season regions	60	20	Light, rich soil with alkaline pH

Plate seeders, such as those made by Earthway Products of Indiana and the Lambert Corporation of Ohio, are reasonably priced and accurate in seed placement, making them an ideal choice for smaller gardens. Adding seed to a pasture to improve the diversity of grasses and legumes is easy to do with a broadcast seeder. Broadcast seeders are available as bags that fit over your shoulder or in larger units that you pull behind a tractor or ATV. Seeding field crops requires specialized planters or seed drills.

You can buy started plants at a home-and-garden store or grow your own in pots (above), then relocate the plants when they're ready. Transplanting started seedlings (opposite) gives you a jump on achieving a thriving garden.

Transplants

You can start seedlings indoors in almost any kind of container, or you can use a soil blocker, which presses out soil cubes in sizes ranging from three-quarters to four inches. I have used both, and for large-scale planting the blocks can't be beat. For starting a small batch of transplants, however, pots, yogurt cups, milk cartons, egg cartons, flats, or any container in which you can poke a hole in the bottom works fine. I keep plantings watered from beneath as much as possible, and until the first seedlings emerge I keep the container or blocks lightly covered with plastic wrap (plastic produce bags or the ones you buy for cooking turkeys work well for containers, which can be set right in the bag). Make a few slits in the plastic to allow airflow.

Some people recommend against using anything but commercial potting mixes for starting seeds, but I like to use a home brew that incorporates my ever-improving garden soil, compost and/or well-aged manure, some commercially purchased sphagnum moss or peat, and perlite. If my base soil were high in clay, I would add some purchased sand. My proportions are one part garden soil, one part compost/manure, one part moss, and a quarter part perlite (for clay, add half part coarse sand). This mixture works well in any container, and it does well in blocks if you keep stones and rocks from the garden out of it. A few grass seedlings or weeds may pop up in the transplants, but they are easy to pluck right out.

To water plants from beneath, run a piece of un-dyed wool yarn through the soil as you place it in the pot and out the bottom of the pot. This will act as a wick that brings water up from the pan placed below the pot.

Cutting, Division, and Layering

Layering is suitable for many perennials with flexible branches. It is the simplest and most reliable method to increase perennials. The idea is to produce roots on a stem while the stem is still attached to the parent plant. Once the root is established, cut the new plant from the parent plant.

Select a healthy branch that is growing close to the ground and that is flexible enough to bend down to the soil. While holding the branch close to the soil, bend the top 6 to 10 inches of the stem into a vertical position. It's helpful to scrape the bark on the underside of the branch at the bend. Bury the bent, scraped portion three to six inches deep, and anchor it with a wire loop. Insert a small stake to hold the top upright. Keep the branch moist.

You can take cuttings any time during late spring and summer from healthy, well-established plants. Those taken in fall have to over-winter in pots or temporary beds, so they take longer to fully develop. Healthy tip growth makes the best cuttings. Cut below a node to form a cutting that is 3 to 5 inches long, and root in potting soil. Keep the soil well moistened and in partial shade until the roots form. Rooting can take anywhere from two

Fragrant sage (above) is a broad-leafed herb commonly used in cooking for its powerful flavor. Herb gardens bring the hobby farmer a kick for cuisine, medicinal benefits, and just plain aromatic goodness.

weeks to two months depending on the plant; the woodier the cutting the longer it will take. Transplant once the roots take off.

Division is useful for multiplying healthy, established plants that may be two to four years old. Dig up the old plant and cut or pull it apart into sections. Replant the sections and keep them moist until the new plants are established.

GARDENS, GROVES, AND FIELDS

Mention gardening, and the first thought that comes to mind is a small vegetable patch, or some ornamentals planted near the house. We farmers, however, can grow things on different scales and in different places. A field of alfalfa, just sprouting after a spring rain, or a grove of trees, grown for fruit, nuts, shade, or other forest products, are as much a farmer's garden as the rose bushes next to the house or the potatoes by the kitchen door.

Herbs

From a botanist's point of view, a true herb is a plant that does not produce a woody stem and that dies back to the ground each winter. But in general terms, gardeners have expanded the term *herbs* to include aromatic plants grown largely for their ability to flavor foods, for medicinal

SAVING SEEDS

If you want to experiment with developing locally adapted plants, or keep heirloom plants, which can be great fun to grow, you will need to learn how to save seeds. The process can be challenging. There are a few essential rules:

- **Don't try to save seeds from "hybrids."** Don't save these unless you want to get into serious plant breeding. They won't reproduce true to the plant you had last year. Look for heirloom, or open-pollinated varieties.
- **Save seeds from the best plants in the garden.** These include plants that resisted disease or insects, had high yield, and good size fruits, vegetables or flowers, and those that produced the most flavorful fruits and vegetables.
- **Avoid cross-pollination.** Cross-pollination is the acceptance of pollen from a different plant of similar genetic makeup. Some plants, such as cucumbers, pumpkins, and squash, are very easily cross-pollinated; others, such as beans and peas, peppers, and tomatoes, are less vulnerable to cross-pollination. A few, such as carrots and radishes, not only cross-pollinate with domestic garden mates, but also easily cross-pollinate with nearby wild relatives.

You can avoid cross-pollination by providing sufficient distance (anywhere from a few garden rows to a mile, depending on how easily a crop crosses) between plantings intended for seed production, or by staggering planting times so that flowering and pollination are not happening in two varieties at the same time. Alternatively, you could use a cheesecloth plant cover to protect flowers from receiving "foreign" pollen. The cheesecloth approach requires you, the gardener, to hand-pollinate, so if you are going to go with that approach, you're making a real commitment.

The easiest crops to experiment with initially are beans, peas, peppers, and tomatoes, because they are annual crops and have low or moderate susceptibility to cross-pollination. (Biennial crops, which include most root crops as well as some herbs, take an extra commitment because they require a two-year cycle to produce seed.) For tomatoes and peppers, separate varieties by at least 200 feet or only grow one variety. Allow the "fruit" to fully ripen, but not rot, on the vine. For beans and peas, allow the pods to dry on the vine. Separate seeds from fruit or pods, and allow them to dry completely at room temperature. I find this easiest to do by spreading seeds out on a glass dish. As the pulp dries, keep moving seeds apart and allow them to continue drying. Once fully dry (which may take up to several weeks for large seeds), store the seeds in clearly marked envelopes to protect from light damage, then place the envelopes in tightly sealed glass jars. Stored like this, most seeds will last at least a couple of seasons; dry bean and pea seeds can remain viable for many years.

The Seed Savers Exchange is a great nonprofit group dedicated to preserving seldom-seen and heirloom varieties. They publish excellent information regarding seed saving and an annual list of available heirloom seed varieties—such as sun and moon melons and Cherokee purple tomatoes—that are available from their members all over the country. Visit them at www.seedsavers.org or write to them at Rural Route 3, Box 239, Decorah, Iowa 52101.

Winter
Savory

HERBS

Family	Common Name	Companions	Antagonists	Sowing
Apiaceae	Angelica	Peas, lettuce, chives, onions	Dill	Do not cover seeds, they need light to germinate; may be sown in spring or fall
Apiaceae	Anise	Coriander	Dill, carrots	May be sown in spring or fall
Lamiaceae	Basil	Tomatoes, peppers	Rue	Indoors (4 weeks) or outdoors
Lauraceae	Bay			From cuttings or nursery stock
Lamiaceae	Bee Balm	Tomatoes		Indoors (4 weeks) or outdoors
Compositae	Calendula	Tomatoes and asparagus		Indoors (4 weeks) or outdoors
Compositae	Chamomile	Cruciferae, cucurbitacea, and liliaceae families		Indoors (4 weeks) or outdoors
Umbelliferae	Chervil	Radishes		Outdoors; seeds germinate better with light
Liliaceae	Chives	Broccoli, marigolds, beets, carrots, eggplant, strawberries, tomatoes, lettuce	Peas and beans	Indoors (3 weeks) or outdoors
Umbelliferae	Coriander (or cilantro)	Anise	Fennel	Outdoors
Umbelliferae	Dill	Crudiferae, lettuce, onion	Carrots, tomatoes	Outdoors
Compositae	Echinacea			Outdoors in the fall; for spring planting stratify seeds by keeping moist in the refrigerator for 21 days prior to planting.
Umbelliferae	Fennel		Peas, beans, peppers, coriander	Outdoors
Lamiaceae	Lavender			Indoors (8 weeks)
Lamiaceae	Oregano	Corn, melons		Indoors (4 weeks), or from cuttings of existing plants or nursery stock
Umbelliferae	Parsley			Outdoors when soil temperature reaches 50
Lamiaceae	Rosemary	Beans and peas		From cuttings or nursery stock
Lamiaceae	Sage	Cruciferae, lettuce, tomato, strawberries	Onions	Indoors (4 weeks) or from divisions or nursery stoc
Lamiaceae	Thyme	Eggplants, potatoes, strawberries, tomatoes	Kohlrabi	Indoors (6 weeks) or from nursery stock or divisions/cuttings

Space in Beds in Inches	Culture	Uses
24	Hardy biennial During the second growing season, it sends up a 4–5 foot tall flower stalk with umbrella-like clusters of flowers that attract many beneficial insects to the garde; grows to 6 feet tall; likes moist, slightly acidic ground; tolerates shade	Medicinal for indigestion, congested respiratory tract; cooking
6	Will grow in poor soil; likes it acidic	Medicinal for indigestion, flatulence; cooking; used in licorice
8	Likes well drained, but rich soil with pH down around 6.0; does well in pots	Critical for French and Italian cooking, and a primary ingredient in pesto sauce
	Perennial that grows to 10 feet tall; tolerates partial shade	An evergreen tree, bay leaves are used decoratively, medicinally and culinarily
12	Tolerates partial shade; likes moist soil	Attracts butterflies and beneficial insects; medicinal as an antiseptic; culinary and in potpourris
6	Tolerates partial shade; likes well drained, slightly acidic soil	Repels insects; adds color to garden; medicinal as an antiseptic
8	Likes full sun and light, dry soil	Medicinal for aiding sleep, ornamental, and in potpourris
6	Likes partial shade, moist soil	An important culinary herb in French cooking; also medicinal as a diuretic and ornamental
4	Tolerates partial shade; mulch to control weeds; grows well in pots	Culinary and medicianal uses
18	Tolerates partial shade; likes well drained, slightly acidic soil	A staple of Mexican food, also medicinally for digestion
36	Well drained but moist soil, pH around 6.0	Medicinal and culinary (where would pickles be without dill)
12	Hardy perennial that likes full sun and well drained soil	Medicinal and ornamental; attracts butterflies and beneficial insects
36	Well drained but moist soil, pH around 6.0	Medicinal and ornamental; attracts butterflies and beneficial insects
18	Well drained, neutral to slightly alkaline soil; can be grown in pots	Used extensively in cosmetics and potpourris; medicinally as a seditive; limited culinary use
12	Perennial (hardy to zone 5); likes well drained soil in full sun	An important culinary herb in Italian cooking; medicinally for coughs and headaches
18	Biennial that likes rich, well drained soil with slightly acidic pH; tolerates partial shade	Medicinally as a diuretic, as a culinary herb it is full of vitamin C and calcium
24	Tender perennial; slightly acidic, well drained soil; full sun; does well in pots	Culinary; used extensively in cosmetics
12	Hardy perennial; likes well drained, but moderately rich and slightly acidic soil	Culinary; used extensively in cosmetics and in potpourris
8	Perennial (hardy to zone 5); likes light, well drained, acidic soil; tolerates partial shade	Medicinally for coughs and intestinal upsets, and an important culinary herb in French cooking

Versatile, easy-to-grow herbs make themselves at home almost anywhere—in a dedicated plot or nestled among other plants—but they'll do best in slightly acidic soil (above). For gardening on a grander scale, you could grow apple trees (below), which explode with color in the spring and delicious fruit in the summer or fall.

purposes, for cosmetic uses, and as ornamentals. They include woody and non-woody annuals, perennials, biennials, bulbs, and grasses in their definition. The broad classification comprises hundreds of plants that you can plant in gardens or as part of landscaping.

Most herbs are easy to grow. They can be mixed in beds with other plants or have dedicated areas, but whichever approach you opt for, remember that they generally like a sunny location. The oils, which account for an herb's flavor, are produced in the greatest quantity when plants receive six to eight hours of full sunlight each day. Herbs will grow in any good garden soil, but they don't need a lot of extra fertilization. Highly fertile soils tend to produce excessive foliage that is poor in flavor. Most herbs like soil that is slightly acidic.

Many herbs do very well as potted plants, growing on a windowsill throughout the year. For potted herbs, watering from below works well, providing adequate moisture without soaking the roots. After the outdoor growing season is over, enjoy dried herbs in fragrant potpourris and sachets, or grow them indoors in pots on sunny windowsills, and use them for culinary purposes.

TREES

One thing I really miss living at 9,200 feet above sea level is the ability to have an orchard. On our Minnesota farm, we had about a dozen kinds of apples and several kinds of plums. With such an extensive variety, we were able to pick apples and plums for several months. What we didn't use, we shared with friends and neighbors—and what they didn't use, our livestock enjoyed immensely.

Trees (and shrubs) provide shade and wind protection; they yield not only fruits, but also nuts, Christmas trees, lumber, firewood, and fence posts. They invite wildlife to share our world as well. Planting them and nurturing them is really not all that hard, and the rewards are great.

Container-grown versus bare root stock

Trees are usually sold as container-grown, balled and burlapped (B&B), or bare root stock. Container-grown trees are the easiest to plant and successfully establish in any season, including summer. With container-grown stock, the plant has been growing in a container for a period of time, so little damage is done to the roots as the plant is transferred to the soil. One disadvantage to container-grown trees is that they may be root bound if the nursery kept them in one size pot too long, and root-bound plants may suffer from problems. When you remove root-bound plants from their containers, you will notice that the roots are wrapped tightly in circles at the edge of the soil they were planted in. You can help these plants get a better start by pulling the bound roots apart and spreading them out in the planting hole.

Growers dig B&B plants from a nursery, wrap the tree in burlap, and keep it in the nursery for an additional period of time to give the roots an opportunity to regenerate. B&B plants can be quite large. It's best to transplant B&B plants in fall or early spring, while the plant is dormant; they do not do well in summer transplanting without a tremendous amount of babying.

Bare root plants are usually extremely small. Because there is no soil on the roots, you must plant them when they are dormant to avoid drying out. Seed and nursery mail-order catalogs and wholesale traders frequently offer bare root trees. Many state-operated nurseries and local conservation districts also sell bare root stock in bulk quantities for only a few cents per plant. Bare root plants usually are offered in the early spring and should be planted as soon as possible upon arrival.

Cherry blossoms announce the arrival of spring. Flowering trees are generally pruned in the dormant season, but you should contact a local horticulturist for precise instructions for the species on your farm.

Fruit and nut trees

Most fruit and nut trees have a chilling requirement, which is defined as the accumulation

TREE PLANTING STEPS

1. *Before digging,* call your local utilities to identify the location of any underground utilities.
2. Dig a hole two to three times as wide, and just about the same depth, as the root ball. Roughen the sides and bottom with a pick or shovel so that roots can penetrate the soil. For poor, compacted soils, you can give trees a boost by digging down deeper and then filling in the bottom of the hole with compost.
3. With a potted tree, gently remove it from the container, or remove the strings that hold the burlap on a B&B tree. If roots are growing in a circular pattern around the root ball, slice through the roots on a couple of sides of the root ball.
4. Root tips die quickly when exposed to light and air, so work fast once they are exposed.
5. Place the root ball in the hole. Leave the top of the root ball (where the roots end and the trunk begins) a half to one inch above the surrounding soil, making sure not to cover any more of the stem than is necessary to get the roots covered.
6. For bare root plants, make a mound of soil in the middle of the hole and spread plant roots out evenly over mound. As you add soil to fill in around the tree, lightly tamp the soil to collapse air pockets, or add water to help settle the soil.
7. When the hole is about three-fourths refilled, straighten and level the tree, tamp the soil down carefully, and water heavily. Then bring soil up to the surface and tamp.
8. For all plantings, build a temporary water basin around the base of the tree. You can accomplish this by mounding the extra soil that comes out of the hole around the tree. This encourages water penetration. Water thoroughly after planting, and once a week during dry weather.
9. Mulch around the tree. A 3-foot-diameter circle of straw mulch or wood chips works well.
10. Depending on the size of the tree and the site conditions, you may need to stake the tree. Staking supports the tree while the roots establish themselves to properly anchor the tree. Staking should allow for some movement of the tree. After a tree is established, remove all support wires. If you do not remove the stakes, they can girdle the tree, cutting into the trunk and eventually killing it.

of hours that the tree needs to spend below 45 degrees Fahrenheit and above 32 degrees Fahrenheit during the course of the year. The requirement varies by species and variety. For example, apples require between 250 and 1,700 hours, depending on the variety, and blueberries require 250 to 1,200 hours. After an unusually mild winter, or an unusually severe winter, you may notice that fruit crops are poor despite the fact that the variety normally performs well in your hardiness zone. This is simply because that particular winter did not meet the tree's chill requirements.

Some fruit and nut trees, like apples and pears, need cross pollination with another tree of the same species, though the tree must be of a different variety (in other words a Jonah apple and a Jonah apple can't cross-pollinate, but a Jonah and a red delicious can). Nursery stock for some trees that need cross-pollination may come with two varieties grafted onto the same root, thereby allowing a single tree to cross-pollinate. Other trees, such as apricots and sour cherries, are self-pollinators, so male flowers pollinate female flowers on one tree by pollen from the same tree. In a few fruit species, such as kiwifruit and persimmons, different plants produce the male and female flowers. In these species, only the female plants bear fruit, though a male plant must be nearby to produce compatible pollen.

Fruit trees for some species, such as apples and pears, come in standard size, dwarf size, or semi-dwarf size. The standard-size trees produce more fruit, for more years, but they take longer to begin producing, and they may present difficulties at harvest time to get fruit from the tops of the trees. Gardeners can train dwarf and semi-dwarf varieties along a fence or wall in an espalier; this provides fruit in small areas, such as a backyard.

Most fruit and nut trees benefit from pruning. Pruning is done to open a tree's crown, thus providing good air circulation and light to the fruit, and to keep branches from crowding one another. Pruning lightly every year or so is far better than heavy pruning every few

GRAPES AND CANE FRUITS

You can propagate grapes and cane fruits fairly easily from cuttings off existing plants or by layering. Nursery stock is also readily available. Spring is the best time for planting, and also for pruning, which you should do before the plants break dormancy. Most cane and vine fruits bear the best fruit on new or one-year-old shoots, so pruning out older shoots will help production. Grapes, blackberries, blueberries, currants, gooseberries, and raspberries all grow on canes or vines and are typically long lived. There are varieties that work in most plant hardiness zones.

If you're thinking of planting orange or apple trees such as ones on these pages, consult your local nursery to determine which types fare well in your area. Valencia oranges, for instance, grow best in the western and southwestern states.

TREES

Fruit	Distance Between Plants (Feet)	Minimum Yield*	Minimum Bearing Age (Years)	Pollination	Life Expectancy (Years)	Chill Range
Apple (standard)	25	8 bushels	6	Cross	35-45	250-1700
Apple (semi-dwarf)	18	4 bushel	4	Cross	20-25	250-1700
Apple (dwarf)	12	1 bushel	2	Cross	15-20	250-1700
Apricot	12	2 bushels	2	Self	23-30	300-1000
Almond	25	40 pounds	5	Cross	40-50	50-450
Cherry (sour)	20	60 quarts	4	Self	15-20	600-1500
Cherry (sweet)	25	75 quarts	5	Cross	20-30	500-1450
Fig	15	25 pounds	2	Self	30-40	50-300
Hazelnut (filbert)	18	800 pounds	4	Cross	50+	850-1700
Pear (standard)	25	3 bushels	5	Cross	35-45	600-1500
Pear (dwarf)	12	1/2 bushel	3	Cross	15-20	600-1500
Peach or nectarine	18	4 bushels	3	Self	15-20	375-1200
Persimmon	25	2 bushels	4	Self	30-35	50-450
Plum	18	2 bushels	4	Cross	15-20	600-1800
Walnut	35	50 pounds	8	Self	60+	400-1550

* Assuming healthy plants in normal conditions

years. After pruning, treat bare wood with shellac or tree paint to minimize decay and prevent insect attack and disease.

Forage Crops

Forage crops are often the first field crops that new farmers need to deal with, since livestock often plays a role in the life of small farmers. Like everything else in the world, forage has its own lingo:

Pasture is a field of grasses, legumes, and forbs (broad-leaf plants) that farmers grow to feed livestock. Though pasture may require some maintenance (liming, spreading manure for fertility, clipping to reduce weed and brush pressure), it is not routinely tilled.

Hayfields are cropped fields that farmers periodically till, plant (with grasses and legumes), and harvest, producing bales of dry forage. (You can put up small quantities of hay in piles—say, enough to feed a couple of sheep or some rabbits—rather than making bales.)

Straw Many nonfarmers confuse hay and straw. Hay is made from grasses and legumes before the plants have gone to seed and died back. Straw is the residual dead vegetation that a grain crop, such as wheat, rye, rice, or oats, leaves in a field after harvest. Farmers bale this dry material, much like hay, but with few nutrients remaining, straw is best used for bedding (or straw-bale construction) rather than for feed.

Haylage is an ensiled feed, prepared from cuttings off the hayfield. You can first bale forage and then bag it. Or you can chop and blow it directly into long tubular bags. You can make haylage when crop moisture is between 40 to 60 percent.

Silage is another ensiled feed, prepared from crops like corn or sorghum. Farmers ensile many grain crops. You can put silage in a silo with moisture content between 60 to 70 percent.

COMMON FORAGE PLANTS

Grains (particularly oats) can make good hay or haylage if harvested early, when the grain is just beginning to form. You can use dozens of grasses for hay, but some of the most common are bent grass, bluestem, bromegrass, fescue, orchard grass, ryegrass, timothy, and wheatgrass. Alfalfa, clovers, vetch, and birdsfoot trefoil are common legumes for hay.

At left, a tractor makes its way back and forth across a field of dried cornstalks, chopping it up for silage. On the opposite page, a field of golden wheat, nearing harvest time, sways in the breeze beneath lowering clouds.

Above, a tractor packs silage into a bunker silo. Below, round bales of hay rest in a field surrounded by trees kissed by autumn's shades of orange and red.

Making hay

Properly harvested and stored hay can last for extended periods, with the bulk of its nutrients intact, though hay that is a little damp when it's baled will mold, and hay stored outdoors may lose valuable nutrients to leaching by the weather. Hay should have less than 15 to 20 percent moisture when it is baled and stored. The quality of hay is dependent on several factors:

- the moisture content at baling and stacking
- the time in storage and storage conditions
- age when baled
- what cutting you are taking (first cutting of the season, second, and so on)
- the species present (including not only the grass or legumes present, but also the weeds present)

Cut hay when grasses are just beginning to reach the flowering stage but before the plants begin setting seed. This is the time when the nutritional value of the plants is at its peak. Hay cut with a sickle mower or by hand with a scythe is windrowed (piled and raised off the ground to dry). Windrowing is usually done with a hay rake, though it can be done by hand for a small patch. Hay cut with a haybine is dropped by the machine into a windrow.

Mother Nature plays a big role in how well the hay turns out. If she grants you a few nice, sunny, breezy days after cutting, the hay dries quickly and the windrows don't have to be turned before baling. But if she spits moisture on your hay, the process can take longer and you may need to turn the rows with a rake several times before they are ready to bale. Each time you have to turn windrows, you lose a little more nutritional value. But wet hay that molds is worse than bleached hay, because moldy hay can contain toxins or cause respiratory problems in animals that eat it.

This garden snail can munch an entire seedling in one evening. You can discourage destructive snails and slugs by sprinkling eggshells a round your greens; these pests don't like to drag their bodies over the jagged pieces.

Preparing silage and haylage

Prepare both silage and haylage by packing the harvested crop into an airtight container (a silo or large agricultural plastic bags in the field), so that bacteria ferment the feed. Although the upfront costs for an operation that allows haylage and silage making are stiff, for larger operations they offer benefits. The operations are cost-effective when handling large amounts of feed; weather and crop moisture are more forgiving for ensiling than for haymaking; and you can chop and ensile stubby, drought-stricken crops that would make poor hay.

PESTS

You won't be the only one who likes your plants: Animals, insects, and microorganisms will find your vegetables, fruits, and flowers to their liking as well.

Although commercial agriculture has come to depend on harsh chemicals to control pests, it's best to resist the temptation to use these chemicals. The chemicals reduce biodiversity, thereby killing off the good organisms that work on your behalf. In addition, they are often dangerous to use for you, your family, and your livestock. You can raise crops successfully without toxic chemicals.

A healthy garden, with plants that are well cared for, is much less susceptible to pests than an overgrown garden, so keep up with weeding, pruning, and other chores. Catch problems early by performing regular checks. You'll catch the most pests by checking at different times of the day and night, Be sure to check right around dawn and dusk, as these are the times many unwanted and unsavory characters are busy in the garden. An ounce of prevention is worth a pound of cure. Try these approaches to animal, insect, and disease control:

- Use manual methods, such as pulling and hoeing weeds or picking off and disposing of pests or infested leaves, regularly to keep the situation under control.
- Practice crop rotations, even in the garden. Many pests become a problem only when you grow the same crop in the same place for years.
- You can attract pill or sow bugs (which like very ripe fruit) to cut-up pieces of raw potatoes placed on the ground, and then drown the bugs in a bucket of soapy water.
- Fences can keep out large animals, such as rabbits or deer.
- Recognize that not all bugs are bad. Spiders, ladybugs, lacewings, and minute parasitoids ("mini-wasps") are all bugs that eat bad bugs in your garden. Create an environment that beneficial insects like, and they will control many problems for you. Plant asters, calendula, chervil, chrysanthemums, coriander, cosmos, dill, fennel, fleabane, poppies, Queen Anne's lace, rosemary, rudbeckia, sunflowers, sweet alyssum, and yarrow around the garden to attract these good insects.
- Keep slugs and snails (check several hours after dark for these guys) away by grinding up eggshells and sprinkling them in a ring around each plant. Powdered ginger sprinkled around a plant can also help keep slugs and snails at bay. Remember to reapply after rain. Make traps by placing upside-down flowerpots, dark-colored plastic sheeting, and wooden boards around the garden; then collect snails and slugs in early morning from your traps and drown them in soapy water. Wrap a strip of copper around a tree trunk, flowerpot, or the wooden sides of garden beds or fences. The unpleasant reaction between their bodies and the copper will repel snails and slugs.

A birdhouse, swinging from a tree branch over a garden, waits for the arrival of feathered guards. Birds offer a natural way to keep pests out of your vegetable patch. The bad guys don't include ladybugs (below), however, who feed on soft-bodied pesky insects and larvae that would destroy your leafy greens.

• Diatomaceous earth sprinkled around the base of plants and on leaves will reduce populations of soft-bodied insects, such as aphids.

• Hose down plants and shrubs with water to rid them of aphids, whiteflies, and spider mites, being careful not to damage flowers or buds.

• Place a tin can with its ends cut out around plants to a depth of 1 inch to keep cutworms away from plants.

• Use agricultural fabrics to create a physical barrier that keeps insects away from plants. For example, floating row covers are very effective at protecting brassicas from cabbage loopers.

• Brew your own bug sprays. Mix 100 ml of crushed hot peppers with 400 ml of water. Strain the concoction and spray it on infested plants. (Note that hot peppers can irritate eyes and skin.) Do not spray when it is windy or in strong midday sun. Or, finely chop ten to fifteen cloves of garlic and soak them in 500 ml of mineral oil for twenty-four hours. Strain the solution and spray as is, or dilute it with water before applying. (Be aware that use of these solutions may also repel beneficial insects.)

• Use commercially available nematodes, which are microscopic worms that prey on grubs and other pests, to control grubs.

• Place bat houses and birdhouses near your garden.

• Use companion planting, as many pests have a natural aversion to mint, garlic, basil, chives, dill, onions, marigolds, and other aromatic plants. These plants may be interspersed with more vulnerable plants in your garden.

• For bad infestations, try using insecticidal soap (dissolve one part dishwashing liquid in forty to eighty parts water). Spray infected plants, covering undersides of leaves, and rinse off after fifteen minutes to avoid damage to foliage. For severe infestations, repeat three times during a ten-day period to treat successive generations.

• *Bacillus thuringiensis* (Bt) is a commercially available, naturally occurring soil bacterium that infects and kills caterpillars when they eat it. It's used for many garden pests.

CHAPTER 7

Farm Animals

A FARM IS HARDLY A FARM WITHOUT SOME ANIMALS. A FEW chickens can provide eggs for the family. A cow or a goat can provide milk and meat. Sheep and goats can control weeds, and their fiber can be used in handcrafts. Farmers use horses for work and play. For some, animals are companions; for others, they provide sustenance; and for those looking at commercial production, animals provide opportunities to turn a profit.

Animals have certain basic needs: plenty of clean, fresh water; good quality feed, in appropriate amounts for their age and the work they are required to do; and shelter from the elements and predators. They deserve a life free of fear and distress and the right to exhibit natural behaviors. These come readily to animals that have physical and mental stimulation. Give them room to move about relatively freely and companionship (preferably from their own species), and you will provide an atmosphere that is perfect for happy, healthy animals. In spite of our best efforts, however, animals can become ill or injured, so you need to be prepared to meet their medical needs through preventive care and doctoring.

A SITTER FOR YOUR ANIMALS

Leaving the farm overnight can be a whole lot more difficult than leaving a home in the city. If you are a dedicated traveler, you'll need to develop a relationship with a farm-sitter. You may be able to trade sitting duties with a neighbor, bribe a relative, hire an area teenager, or hire a professional sitter. Whoever it may be, before you leave, meet with him or her and walk through all the chores. Make sure there is enough food on hand for all your pets and livestock and that the sitter knows where all food is stored.

Take time to legibly write out the following information for your sitter:

- emergency contact numbers for you, the name and number of your veterinarian, and the name and number of a neighbor, friend, or family member to contact in case the sitter can't reach you
- feeding regimens for every animal or class of animals
- individual animals' specialized needs, such as medication schedules, and behavioral or safety considerations (e.g., "the gelding can open gates if the latch isn't secured; stay out of the ram's pen because he butts")

FEEDING ANIMALS

The single most important function you serve in the lives of your animals is meeting their nutritional needs. Most farmyard animals are herbivores, so plants should be the exclusive source of their nutrients. Pigs and poultry are an exception to the rule. Like humans, they are omnivores, and at least a portion of their natural diet is composed of animal matter, including insects.

Food needs vary, changing with age, the amount of work performed, and the seasons. One ration isn't always suitable for all animals, and the true husbandman must develop an eye for the condition of his or her animals, adjusting feed regimens according to the ever-changing needs and conditions of the stock.

Maintenance rations represent the food required to support the animal when it is doing no work and producing no product (milk, meat, or fiber). A maintenance ration basically supports all minimum body functions, such as respiration and cardiovascular function. It maintains the animal's weight at a steady state: no gain, no loss. For most farm animals, up to half of their food ration represents their maintenance requirement.

Providing adequate feed for growth, reproduction, and work is really the goal of every good farmer. And *adequate* is a key concept in my mind—you want to feed enough to keep your animals healthy and strong, but you don't want to overfeed them. Overfeeding not only costs too much, it isn't good for the animal. An overly fat breeding animal has trouble breeding. If you feed young animals too much, too quickly, the animals can develop severe joint and bone problems from growing too fast (this is especially true for young horses).

Feed Components

Whether the source of feed is from a plant or an animal, there are certain basic properties all feedstuffs share. Three major components make up feed: water, organic matter, and

mineral matter or ash. Carbon, hydrogen, and oxygen make up organic matter, though other elements may be present. You can group organic matter into four parts: the carbohydrates; the fats and fatty substances; the nitrogenous compounds, or proteins; and the vitamins.

You can further break down the carbohydrate group, made up of carbon atoms attached to water molecules, into sugars, starches, and fiber. The proportion of these components varies according to the type of plant, its age, and environmental factors, such as drought. The sugars and starches are easy to digest, so they provide a relatively high feed value. Lignins primarily make up the fiber component and are completely indigestible. Cellulose, which accounts for about 50 percent of the organic carbon on earth, is also present in fiber. Cellulose requires bacterial fermentation to break it down into useable sugars and starches. Animals are able to ferment small amounts of cellulose in their intestines, but only ruminants, such as cattle and sheep, can convert the bulk of the cellulose in their diet to useable sugars and starches.

As with carbohydrates, carbon, hydrogen, and oxygen make up fats and fatty substances, though in different proportions than in sugars and starches. In spite of our current fear of fat, it is an essential nutrient, especially for young animals. Fat provides more than twice the energy that a carbohydrate does, and it helps animals maintain body condition and temperature.

Proteins are essential for the development of all cell walls and for forming muscle, internal organs, blood cells, hair, horn, and bone. In most animals, protein accounts for 15 to 20 percent of the animal's weight. Unlike sugars, which may contain as few as twenty atoms, thousands of atoms make up each molecule of protein. In nature, as in construction, it's often easier to build a complex structure by using substructures, like building blocks or prefabricated roof trusses. In the case of proteins, amino acids are the building blocks

Beef cattle eat at a well-stocked trough (above), and farm children prepare feed for animals on a dairy farm (below). Hardworking livestock, including draft horses (opposite), benefit from a consistent nutritional supply.

Animal type, age, and weight	Dry matter lb.	Crude protein %	Crude protein lb.	TDN %
Growing goats (live weight)				
50 lb.	2.0	10	0.2	57
75 lb.	2.8	9	0.25	57
100 lb.	3.5	8.5	0.28	56
125 lb.	4.0	8	0.32	56
Breeding goats				
First 2/3 of Gestation	2.5	9	0.23	55
Last 1/3 of Gestation	3.5	10	0.35	56
First 10 weeks of lactation	4.4	11.7	0.51	69
Last 14 weeks of lactation	3.5	10	0.35	56
Billies at moderate work	4.0	9	0.36	55
Growing sheep (live weight)				
50 lb.	2.2	12	0.26	55
75 lb.	3.5	11	0.39	58
100 lb.	4.0	9.5	0.38	62
125 lb.	4.6	8	0.37	62
Breeding sheep	**Per 100 lb. of body weight**		**Per 100 lb. of body weight**	
First 2/3 of gestation	2.5	8	0.20	50
Last 1/3 of gestation	3.5	8.2	0.29	52
First 10 weeks of lactation	4.2	8.4	0.35	58
Last 14 weeks of lactation	3.5	8.2	0.29	52
Rams at moderate work	3.5	7.6	0.27	55
Growing horses	**Per 100 lb. of body weight**		**Per 100 lb. of body weight**	
3 mo.	4.5	20	0.9	62
6 mo.	2.6	15	0.4	62
1 yr.	1.9	12	0.23	62
1.5 yr.	1.6	11	0.18	62
2 yr.+	1.3	10	0.13	62
Mature horses (850-1100 lb.)	**Per 100 lb. of body weight**		**Per 100 lb. of body weight**	
Not working	1.21	10	0.12	63
Light work	1.63	10	0.16	63
Medium work	2.13	10	0.21	63
Late pregnancy	1.31	11	0.14	63
Peak lactation	2.12	13	0.28	63
Growing beef cattle (live weight)				
300 lb.	8.1	14	1.1	78
400 lb.	10.3	13.5	1.4	77
500 lb.	11.9	13	1.5	76
600 lb.	13.6	12.5	1.7	75
700 lb.	15.4	12	1.9	74
800 lb.	17.1	11.5	2	73
900 lb.	18.5	11	2	73
1000 lb.	19.8	10.5	2.1	73

TDN lb.	Calcium %	Phosphorous %	Notes
1.14	0.4	0.28	
1.6	0.3	0.2	
1.96	0.28	0.21	
2.24	0.28	0.21	
1.38	0.28	0.21	
1.96	0.35	0.25	
3.04	0.42	0.27	
1.96	0.35	0.21	
2.20	0.28	0.2	
			Don't feed sheep feed formulas or mineral mixtures that are not specifically recommended for them. The amount of some trace minerals, like copper, that are in feed for other classes of livestock may be toxic to sheep.
1.21	0.23	0.21	
2.03	0.21	0.18	
2.48	0.19	0.18	
2.85	0.18	0.16	
Per 100 lb. of body weight			
1.25	0.24	0.19	
1.82	0.23	0.17	
2.436	0.28	0.21	
1.82	0.25	0.19	
1.93	0.18	0.16	
Per 100 lb. of body weight			Ponies need about 125% feed relative to their size, and draft horses only need about 90% relative to their size. In other words, ponies at rest need about 1.5 lb. of Dry Matter per 100 lb. of body weight, and draft horses at rest need about 1.1 lb./100 lb. Pony (1.21 x 1.25) and Draft Horse (1.21 x 0.9) All other figures can be adjusted the same way.
2.8	0.6	0.4	
1.6	0.8	0.5	
1.2	0.4	0.3	
1	0.4	0.3	
0.8	0.3	0.2	
Per 100 lb. of body weight			
0.76	0.32	0.25	
1.03	0.25	0.18	
1.34	0.2	0.15	
0.83	0.37	0.29	
1.34	0.47	0.38	
6.3	0.5	0.4	
7.9	0.5	0.4	
9	0.4	0.3	
10.2	0.3	0.3	
11.4	0.3	0.3	
12.5	0.2	0.2	
13.5	0.2	0.2	
14.5	0.2	0.2	

Animal type, age, and weight	Dry matter lb.	Crude protein %	Crude protein lb.	TDN %
Breeding beef cattle	**Per 100 lb. of body weight**		**Per 100 lb. of body weight**	
Dry pregnant cow - Middle 3rd of pregnancy	1.6	7	0.1	50
Dry pregnant cow - Last 3rd of pregnancy & lactating cows late lactation	2	8	0.16	57
Lactating cow first 3 mo. - Average milking ability	2.4	10	0.24	50
Lactating cow first 3 mo. - High milkers	2.7	12	0.32	67
Lactating heifer first 3 mo.	2.3	12	0.28	64
Bull - Moderate work	1.9	7	0.13	55
Growing pigs (live weight)				
1-10	0.55	27	0.15	85
10-20	1.1	20	0.22	85
20-40	2.2	18	0.4	79
40-70	3.3	16	0.53	79
70-120	4.4	14	0.62	74
120-240	6.6	13	0.86	74
Breeding swine	**Per 100 lb. of body weight**		**Per 100 lb. of body weight**	
Bred gilts & sows; Young & adult boars Summer	1.3	12	0.15	74
Bred gilts & sows; Young & adult boars Winter	1.8	12	0.21	76
Lactating Gilts & Sows Summer	3.5	13	0.47	74
Lactating Gilts & Sow Winter	4	13	0.51	76
Growing llamas (live weight)				
Bred Gilts & Sows; Young & Adult Boars Summer				
50 lb.	1	14	0.14	65
100 lb.	1.9	13	0.25	62
175 lb.	3.1	11	0.34	62
250 lb.	4.5	10	0.45	60
Breeding llamas	**Per 100 lb. of body weight**		**Per 100 lb. of body weight**	
First 2/3 of gestation	2.5	12	0.30	60
Last 1/3 of gestation	3.5	14	0.49	65
First 12 weeks of lactation	4	14	0.56	65
Last 12 weeks of lactation	3.5	12	0.42	60
Buck at moderate work	3	14	0.42	60

TDN lb.	Calcium %	Phosphorous %	Notes
Per 100 lb. of body weight			
0.8	0.18	0.18	
1.1	0.26	0.21	
1.2	0.28	0.23	
1.8	0.45	0.3	
1.5	0.35	0.25	
1.1	0.2	0.2	
0.47	0.9	0.7	
0.94	0.8	0.6	
1.74	0.65	0.55	
2.61	0.6	0.5	
3.26	0.55	0.45	
4.88	0.5	0.4	
Per 100 lb. of body weight			
1	0.75	0.6	
1.4	0.75	0.6	
2.6	0.75	0.5	
3	0.75	0.5	
0.65	0.8		
1.2	0.8		
1	0.7		
2.7	0.6		
Per 100 lb. of body weight			
1.5	0.65		
2.28	0.8		
2.6	0.9		
2.1	0.7		
1.80	0.6		

POULTRY

LAYERS

Age in weeks	2	2 to 4	4 to 6	6 to 8	8 to 10	10 to 12	12 to 14
Typical egg production (percent of hens laying each daily)	0	0	0	0	0	0	0
Feed consumption per hen in oz. (lb.) per week	1.6 (0.1)	3.2 (0.2)	6.4 (0.4)	9.2 (0.6)	11.5 (0.72)	13.6 (0.85)	15.1 (0.94)
Crude protein %	18	18	18	15	15	15	15
Crude protein per hen per week	0.29 (0.02)	0.58 (0.04)	1.15 (0.07)	1.38 (0.09)	1.73 (0.11)	2.04 (0.13)	2.27 (0.14)
Calcium %	0.8	0.8	0.8	0.7	0.7	0.7	0.7
Phosphorous %	0.4	0.4	0.4	0.35	0.35	0.35	0.35

BROILERS

Age in weeks	1	2	3	4	5	6	7	8	9
Feed consumption per cockerel in .oz (lb.) per week	4.2 (0.26)	9.2 (0.57)	13.7 (0.86)	18.8 (1.18)	26.1 (1.63)	34.5 (2.16)	38.5 (2.40)	42.6 (2.67)	46.5 (2.90)
Feed Consumption per pullet in oz. (lb.) per week	3.9 (0.24)	8.4 (0.53)	12.5 (0.78)	17.6 (1.10)	22.7 (1.41)	28.2 (1.76)	32.0 (2.00)	34.1 (2.13)	35.6 (2.22)
Crude protein %	23	23	23	20	20	20	18	18	18
Crude protein per crockerel in oz. (lb.) per week	0.97 (0.05)	2.12 (0.13)	3.15 (0.20)	3.76 (0.24)	5.22 (0.33)	0.69 (0.48)	6.93 (0.43)	7.67 (0.18)	8.37 (0.53)
Crude protein per pullet in oz. (lb.) per week	0.90 (0.06)	1.93 (0.12)	2.88 (0.18)	3.52 (0.22)	4.54 (0.28)	5.64 (0.35)	5.76 (0.36)	6.12 (0.38)	6.41 (0.40)
Calcium %	1	1	1	0.9	0.9	0.9	0.8	0.8	0.8
Phosphorous %	0.45	0.45	0.45	0.4	0.4	0.4	0.35	0.35	0.35

14 to 22	22 to 24	24 to 26	26 to 30	30 to 40	40 to 50	50 to 60	60 to 70
0	10%	38%	64%	88%	80%	74%	68%
16.2 (1.01)	18.5 (1.16)	21 (1.31)	23.4 (1.46)	27.1 (1.69)	26.9 (1.68)	26.6 (1.66)	26 (1.63)
12	14.5	14.5	14.5	14.5	14.5	14.5	14.5
1.94 (0.12)	2.68 (0.17)	3.05 (0.19)	3.39 (0.21)	3.29 (0.25)	3.90 (0.24)	3.85 (0.24)	3.77 (0.24)
0.6	3.4	3.4	3.4	3.4	3.4	3.4	3.4
0.3	0.32	0.32	0.32	0.32	0.32	0.32	0.32

Above, a mare and her colt rely on pasture for daily sustenance—as do a gathering of cattle (below) and a gilt (opposite). However, each animal group processes the grasses and grains differently, according to their complex digestive systems.

nature has developed to simplify construction. There are about twenty critical amino acids. You build words by varying the combinations of the twenty-six letters of the alphabet, and similarly, you build proteins by varying the combinations of these twenty amino acids.

Vitamins are also organic in nature. They are required in very small quantities, but deficiencies of vitamins in the diet can lead to a wide range of diseases, including rickets, anemia, and muscular dystrophy. At the same time, some vitamins, such as vitamin A, can be toxic if given in too high a quantity.

As with vitamins, most minerals aren't required in very large quantities, but deficiencies cause a wide range of health problems and toxicity can occur when there are mineral excesses in the diet. The minerals include elements such as sodium, calcium, phosphorous, and selenium. Mineral deficiencies (or excesses) usually occur where soil mineral imbalances exist. When you grow plants in a soil that is either too low or too high in any given minerals, the soil imbalance will be reflected in your animal's tissue. Your extension agent, a reputable feed dealer, or your veterinarian should be able to provide you with information on the soil mineralization in your area and recommend the mineral supplements needed for your situation.

Digestion

We classify animals according to the configuration of their digestive systems:

- monogastric—those with a single stomach (such as pigs, poultry, and humans)
- post-gastric fermenters—those with a single stomach but a well-developed cecum, a fer mentation chamber located between the small and large intestines (such as horses and rabbits)
- pre-gastric fermenters, or ruminants—those with four stomachs (such as cattle,

Preferring woody and weedy species, a goat selects a young growing points first, then browses downward (above). The goat's close digestive cousins, llamas (below), graze in a woodland pasture.

sheep, and goats), including the rumen, or first stomach, which acts as a large fermentation chamber. Pseudo-ruminants (such as llamas and alpacas), a smaller class of pre-gastric fermenters. The pseudo-ruminants have three stomachs instead of four, but their digestive process is very similar to that of true ruminants.

Animals with monogastric digestive systems have some disadvantages when it comes to digesting food. They can ferment only a very small amount of the fiber in their diets, and they can synthesize only a few of the many amino acids their bodies require. This means they get almost no feed value out of hay or straw. (Young and vegetative green grass, however, can provide them some feed value.) It also means that monogastric animals must have a wide variety of protein sources in their diets to meet their amino acid needs. Although they can't use grass to supply amino acids, these monogastric critters have teeth and stomach enzymes that allow them to break down meat.

The post-gastric fermenter's cecum performs a similar function to a cow's or sheep's rumen. Although all mammals have this organ, it is only well developed and highly effective in post-gastric fermenters. However, since the cecum comes fairly late in the digestive process, it is less efficient at both fiber digestion and amino acid synthesis than a rumen.

When it comes to fiber digestion, ruminants are the clear winners. The rumen ferments food very early in the process, so by the time the waste leaves the body, almost all the cellulose-fiber has been broken down into useable sugars and starches. Through bacterial and enzymatic action in their rumens, the ruminants are also able to synthesize all of their necessary amino acids from whatever nitrogenous compounds are present in the plants they eat.

Instead of top teeth, ruminants have a hard palate in the top of the mouth. A ruminant grabs a piece of grass or hay between its lower teeth and hard palate and tears it off. It lightly chews the food, just enough to moisten it a little and form a ball, before swallowing. The ball of food travels down the esophagus and enters the rumen.

Heavy food items, such as whole grains, (or the stray stone or piece of hardware) usually bypass the rumen altogether and enter the reticulum, or second stomach, directly. Grain that bypasses the rumen generally remains intact, which is why you'll see grain kernels in the manure if you're feeding whole grain to your ruminant livestock. Those whole kernels cost you money but don't provide all the available nutrients for your animals, so try one of these two approaches to get full feed value from the grain you grow or purchase: feed ground or cracked grain, or feed the whole grains with hay or other light fibrous feeds so the rumen captures the whole grains.

Bacteria, protozoa, yeast, and fungi populate the rumen. For each gallon of rumen capacity, there are up to two hundred *trillion* bacteria and four *billion* protozoa. The quantities of yeast and fungi are more variable but still number in the millions under normal circumstances. Now multiply these figures by the usual twenty-five to thirty gallons of rumen content in a cow—or three to five gallons in a sheep—and you get a good idea of just how large the workforce is that ferments food in the rumen. An important objective of a ruminant feeding program is maintaining an environment that is good for these micro organisms so they can do their jobs well. A key approach to keeping microbes happy is to make any dietary changes slowly—say, over the course of two weeks—so the bugs can adjust to the change.

A calf enjoys a meal of young green grass. The calf's rumen will guarantee maximum nutritional benefit—sugars, starches, and amino acids—from every mouthful.

Ruminants spend up to six hours per day eating and up to eight hours per day chewing "cud," or ruminating. Cud is simply a bolus of food that has been floating in the rumen for some time, forced back up by the esophagus into the mouth, and chewed again. Cud-chewing serves two purposes: It provides some extra mechanical breakdown of food, and it provides lots of saliva for the rumen.

One side effect of fermentation in a ruminant is that it produces a significant amount of gas. In fact, a mature cow can produce up to twenty cubic feet of gas per hour, which is enough gas to fill a balloon the size of a large chest freezer. The cow passes this gas through regular belching, or eructation.

FEED DEFINITIONS

- **Balanced ration:** A ration that provides all the nutrients, in the proper proportions (including energy, fiber, protein, vitamins, and minerals) for the animal's needs based on age and level of work.
- **Concentrate:** The grain or grains portion of the ration.
- **Dry matter:** The mass of the ration or feedstuff if the water is "baked off." For instance, a sample of mixed meadow hay might contain 85 percent dry matter, so your 60-pound bale of hay would actually weigh 51 pounds on a dry matter basis (0.85 X 60 pounds).
- **Energy:** The part of the ration that is made up of sugars, fats and fatty acids, and starches used by the body for muscle and nerve activity, growth, fattening, and milk secretion.
- **Feedstuff:** Any food intended for livestock consumption.
- **Fiber:** The part of the ration that comes from cellulose and hemi-cellulose in plant matter and is broken down in ruminants and horses to create additional sugars and fatty acids.
- **Forage or roughage:** The hay or pasture portion of the ration.
- **Protein:** The portion of the ration that contains amino acids. The body requires protein for cell formation, development, and maintenance, especially for muscle and blood cells.
- **Ration:** The combination of foods in a specific diet, for a specific animal or class of animals, at any given time. It includes everything the animal is receiving.
- **Supplements:** The vitamins, minerals, or protein added to the ration.
- **TDN:** Total digestible nutrients. These make up the portion of the ration the animal can take advantage of. Feed reports, feed tags, and feed charts give the TDN of feedstuff. If the TDN on the previous sample of hay (see dry matter definition, above) was tested as 60 percent on a dry matter basis, the bale would contain 30.6 pounds of digestible nutrients (0.6 X 51 pounds).

A gray mare (above) and dairy cows (below) feed in rich, open pastures, free from the feeding stable flies that cause Holsteins (opposite) to bunch together. Bunching damages pasture vegetation, causes heat stress to the cattle, and increases injuries, especially to calves.

Quality Pastures

Livestock are capable of turning grasses inedible for people into a high-quality protein for human consumption, making pasture a critical component of livestock operations. If they have access to high-quality pasture or hay, most animals (pre- and post-gastric fermenters) do fine with no supplemental concentrate. When hay or pasture is inferior, your animals may need a concentrate supplement. Dairy animals and those working hard (pulling a plow, riding for hours each day) also require supplemental concentrates, such as corn or oats. In addition, pregnant, lactating, and breeding animals may need supplementation if the pasture or hay isn't at its highest quality. Balance the ration first for dry matter and total digestible nutrients (which represents the food in the feed). Then use supplements as needed to balance for protein, calcium, and phosphorous.

Drive around the country, and where there is livestock, there is often lots of bare dirt and weeds in pastures. But the good news is, with a technique known as managed grazing, you can take excellent care of both your animals and your land. With just a little extra money and time spent initially to develop a subdivided pasture, you will reap benefits year-round, including:

- good grass cover, which is aesthetically pleasing and increases your property values
- reduced bills for purchased feed
- reduced weed pressure
- reduced animal-health problems, such as those related to parasites and dust
- reduced erosion (both from wind and water) and nutrient pollution. In fact, the Environmental Protection Agency (EPA) recognizes the technique of subdividing your pastures as environmentally beneficial.

In a healthy pasture, there's a complex and diverse group of animals and plants that interact with each other. One goal of managed grazing is to foster this healthy complexity. The variety of plants, animals, insects, and microscopic organisms that inhabit a healthy

pasture differ regionally. But wherever you live, if the pasture is healthy, many creatures call it home.

Ideally, a pasture should contain about 60 percent grass and 40 percent legumes. If yours doesn't have enough legumes, talk to your local county extension agent to find out what types grow well in your area. Introduce legumes simply by spreading seed in early spring on top of the ground, either with a whirlybird seeder or by throwing handfuls out as you walk around.

Growth primarily takes place near the soil surface at the plant's basal growth point. Initially, a new plant gets all its energy from the seed, and seed-dependent growth is slow. Once you see sufficient green, leafy matter exposed above the basal growth point, the power plant (photosynthesis) kicks in and growth speeds up. As a plant reaches maturity, its growth slows, and the energy it creates through photosynthesis begins flower and seed-head production.

You want to control things so that you maintain the plant's activity in the quick-growth phase. To accomplish this, you need to clip the plant just before its growth slows with flower and seed production, but leave enough green surface showing to keep the power plant operating at full steam. Typically, this requires taking off about 40 to 50 percent of the leaf. You can do this mechanically, with a mowing device, or with those animated clipping units—your animals.

After you graze (or mechanically clip) a plant, it requires a recovery period. The recovery period is the time it takes the plant to regain the energy it lost by being cut back—or the time that it takes for the plant to grow back to the length before you clipped it. If plants aren't allowed an adequate recovery period before they're bitten a second time, they weaken—and may die.

GREAT SOURCES OF FEED

Lawns, gardens, and orchards are great sources of feed. Use portable electric fencing to allow animals to graze the lawn. If you're worried about what the neighbors will think, use a bagger on your mower and toss the fresh, chopped grass clippings to your livestock. You can also toss garden waste and windfall apples over the fence. Pigs and birds, with their omnivorous diets, can eat many of the items we eat, so table scraps don't go to waste if thrown into the pig or poultry pens.

Above, sheep munch away in a mountain pasture, reducing the amount of larkspur and thus making the place safer for the next set of grazers, cattle, who have a higher sensitivity to the plant's toxicity. Below, a farmer inspects an electrical fence used for rotational grazing. On the opposite page, an agronomist conducts a different kind of inspection—collecting fescue samples for microscopic examination for fungus.

Set-stocking versus rotation

Set-stocking is the most common grazing method. Farmers put animals into a pasture and keep them there indefinitely. Like kids in a candy store, the animals first go around eating the things they like best. Then, before their feed of choice has had an adequate recovery period, they come along and bite it again. Meanwhile, a plant they don't like quite as much, or one that's got manure near it, never gets bitten, thereby reaching slow growth. The paradox: Both plants continue to lose energy, one because it is bitten too often and the other because it isn't bitten often enough.

Set-stocking results in overgrazing and over-resting of plants in the same pasture at the same time. While the over-rested plants do well in the short term, many of them are noxious weeds, so weed infestations usually increase with set-stocking.

You can manage grazing by subdividing the pasture into multiple paddocks, usually with electric fencing. Rotate the animals through before they have a chance to regraze the same plants, and keep the animals out of the paddock until the plants have had time to recharge their batteries. Generally speaking, the more paddocks available, the better. Paddocks may be either permanent or temporary. Four to eight permanent paddocks, which you can further subdivide with portable and temporary electric fencing, offer the most flexibility and allow you to time your animals' movement between paddocks.

The timing of animal movement from one paddock to the next is critical. In the spring and early summer, the grass is growing very quickly, and recovery may take only seven to ten days. Later in the summer, the plants may require a month or more.

As an example, let's say you've subdivided your five-acre pasture into five permanent paddocks. It's May, and the grass is growing quickly. When you move the animals out of a paddock, they can return in about ten days. With four paddocks left, you can move them every two to three days (ten days divided by four paddocks equals two and one-half days

per paddock). Now let's consider the same setup, but it's the dog days of July. The grass is growing much more slowly and requires about forty days to recover. If you move the animals out of a paddock, they'd have to spend about ten days in each of the next four paddocks (forty days divided by four paddocks). The problem during this period is that at ten days between moves, the animals are starting to bite the same plants twice. How do you allow an adequate recovery period but not let them regraze plants? Use temporary subdivisions to cut the permanent paddocks in half. Now the animals graze each temporary paddock for only five days, but the paddock you're leaving gets its full forty days to recover (forty days divided by eight paddocks).

Poisonous plants and feeds

It is tragic to lose an animal to food poisoning, but each year it happens to farmers around the country. Many poisoning agents have no antidotes, so prevention is truly the best medicine.

The first step to take is to learn what poisonous plants grow in your area. This is another time your county extension agent should be able to help you. He or she will know what those plants are, what they look like, if their toxicity is strictly seasonal or continuous, and to which classes of stock the plant is toxic.

Some crop plants are poisonous at certain periods in their growth. Sudan grass and sorghums, for example, can cause prussic acid poisoning if consumed while the plants are immature or immediately following a frost. Grazing of these plants at a stage where prussic acid levels are high can result in very quick death.

Animals often become ill due to spoiled feed. Unfortunately, it isn't always easy to tell that the feed is spoiled. Mold is the most common cause of spoiling. Cattle tend to be less sensitive to mold than horses, sheep, and pigs, but all species can develop health problems

BETTER GRAZING

You can improve grazing if you do the following:

- Aim for 40 percent legumes, such as alfalfa, clover, and birdsfoot trefoil, in your pasture.
- In a well-developed pasture, don't graze plants until they have reached at least six inches and do graze plants before they reach twelve inches. In a newly seeded pasture, let the plants reach at least eight inches before grazing.
- Remove 40 to 50 percent of the plant's leaf matter in each grazing period.
- During the growing season, don't graze plants lower than three inches from the soil surface. In winter, you can allow animals to graze plants to within about an inch of the soil surface.
- When the grass is growing fast during the spring and early summer, move the animals quickly; when it's growing slower, slow down the movement.
- If the grass is getting too far ahead of you (getting too long) during fast growth, mechanically clip it for hay or to leave on the paddock as green manure.

POISONOUS PLANTS

Common name	Scientific name	Animals most affected	Season	Habitat
Bitter weed	Hymenoxys odorata	sheep cattle	Spring	Flooded areas, overgrazed range
Water hemlock	Cicuta spp	All	Spring	Open moist to wet areas
Larkspur	Delphinium spp	All	Spring, Fall	Either cultivated or wild. Wild usually in open foothills and meadows among Aspen or Poplar stands
Pokeweed poke	Phytolacca americana	Pigs most affected, also cattle, sheep, horses, man	Spring	Disturbed areas with rich soil, pastures, waste areas
Cocklebur	Xanthium spp	Pigs most affected, but also all other animals	Spring, Fall	Fields, waste places, edges of ponds and rivers
False hellebore, Corn lily	Veratrum spp	Cattle, sheep, fowl	Spring	Low, moist woods and pastures, mountain valleys
Horse chestnut	Aesculus spp	All grazing animals	Spring, Summer	Woods and thickets
Oaks	Quercus spp	All grazing animals	Spring, Summer	Deciduous woods
Mesquite	Prosopis glandulosa	Cattle and goats, sheep are resistant	Summer, Fall	Dry ranges in brittle areas
Yellow star thistle, Yellow knapweed	Centaurea solstitialis	Horses	Summer, Fall	Waste areas and roadsides
White snakeroot	Eupatorium rugosum	Sheep, cattle, horses	Summer, Fall	Woods, cleared areas, waste areas, moist and rich soils
Choke cherry, Cherries, Peaches	Prunus spp	All grazing animals	All seasons	Waste areas, orchards, fence rows, dry slopes
Milkweed	Asclepias spp	All	All seasons	Waste areas, roadsides, streambeds
Jimson weed, Thorn apple	Datura stramonium	All	All seasons	Fields, barn lots, trampled pastures, and waste areas on rich bottom soils

This is by no means a complete list. In fact, it is estimated that there are about 300 plants in North America that are capable of causing poisoning in animals at some point during their growth cycle. Some are as common, and widely used in pastures, as Ryegrass. In the case of Ryegrass, the problem occurs in seed heads that become infected with bacteria or fungi.

Effects	Comments
Vomiting, green nasal discharge, anorexia	Toxin is cumulative; avoid overgrazing
Salivation, muscular twitching, dialated pupils	Generally fatal, extremely toxic
Arched back, falling constipation, bloat, vomiting	Moderately toxic, causes death in some cases. Young plants and seeds are most toxic.
Vomiting, abdominal pain, bloody diarrhea	Mildly toxic in small doses, but may result in death when consumed in large quantities.
Anorexia, depression, vomiting, weakness, muscle spasms	Extremely toxic
Vomiting, excessive salivation, cardiac arrhthmia, muscle weakness, paralysis, coma, birth defects in offspring of dams who have consumed	Moderately toxic
Depression, incoordination, twitching, paryalysis, death	Young shoots and seeds are highly toxic, otherwise moderately toxic.
Anorexia, rumen stasis, constipation followed by black diarrhea, dry muzzel	Moderately toxic; diet must consist of over 50% buds and young leaves for an extended period.
Chronic wasting, excessive salivation, facial tremors	Moderately toxic; animals must graze for extended periods. Mixed species grazing reduces losses.
Involuntary chewing movement, twitching of lips, unable to eat	Moderately toxic; horses only graze it when there is a lack of other forage. Death results from extended period of consumption.
Weakness, trembles, weight loss, constipation	Extremely toxic, often resulting in death. Toxins may be passed to man through milk from affected animals.
Excitement leading to depression, incoordination, convulsions, bright pink mucous membranes	Extremely toxic. Generally fatal in less than 30 minutes; animals that live two hours normally recover.
Staggering, bloating, dialated pupils, rapid and weak pulse	Moderately toxic, but may result in death if sufficient amount is consumed.
Weak and rapid pulse, dialated pupils, coma	Extremely toxic; generally fatal within 48 hours.

A newborn lamb sucks milk from a bottle (above), a calf suckles from her mother (below), and a herd of cows gathers by a well-maintained pond (opposite). A customized nutritional plan and a good, clean water supply are essential for young and adult livestock alike.

from mold. Though mold itself isn't generally fatal, some kinds produce fatal mycotoxins as byproducts of their life cycles (as do some fungi). Mycotoxins are common throughout the world and can be found on both stored feeds and feeds in the field. Fescue poisoning, a common problem in many southern and western states, is the result of a mycotoxin. Again, talk to your county extension agent or your veterinarian to learn whether mycotoxins could be a problem for your operation.

Feeding Babies

The best feed for baby animals comes right from their mothers. At times, though, farmers need to step in and hand-feed little ones. In commercial dairy production, almost all calves (or kids) are bottle-fed.

It is crucial that all newborns receive colostrum within the first twenty-four hours of life. Colostrum is the first milk a mammal secretes after it gives birth, and it jumpstarts the baby's immune system. If the mother's colostrum isn't available (as with an orphaned animal), there are commercial colostrum products you can purchase from your vet. If you have planned ahead, you can use the colostrum saved (and frozen) from other animals in your herd. It's best if the colostrum comes from the same species, but in a real pinch you can use cow's colostrum for other species. Most dairy farmers keep frozen colostrum, which they will usually share in an emergency.

When bottle-feeding, the rule of thumb is to provide 10 percent of the baby animal's body weight per day in whole milk, preferably from their own species. However, goat's milk or cow's milk will work for most babies. If this milk is unavailable, you can always use commercial milk. Manufacturers make commercial milk, called replacer, for most classes of livestock (and even for dogs and cats). Calf milk replacer is readily available from feed stores, but you may need to special-order replacers for other species. Look for

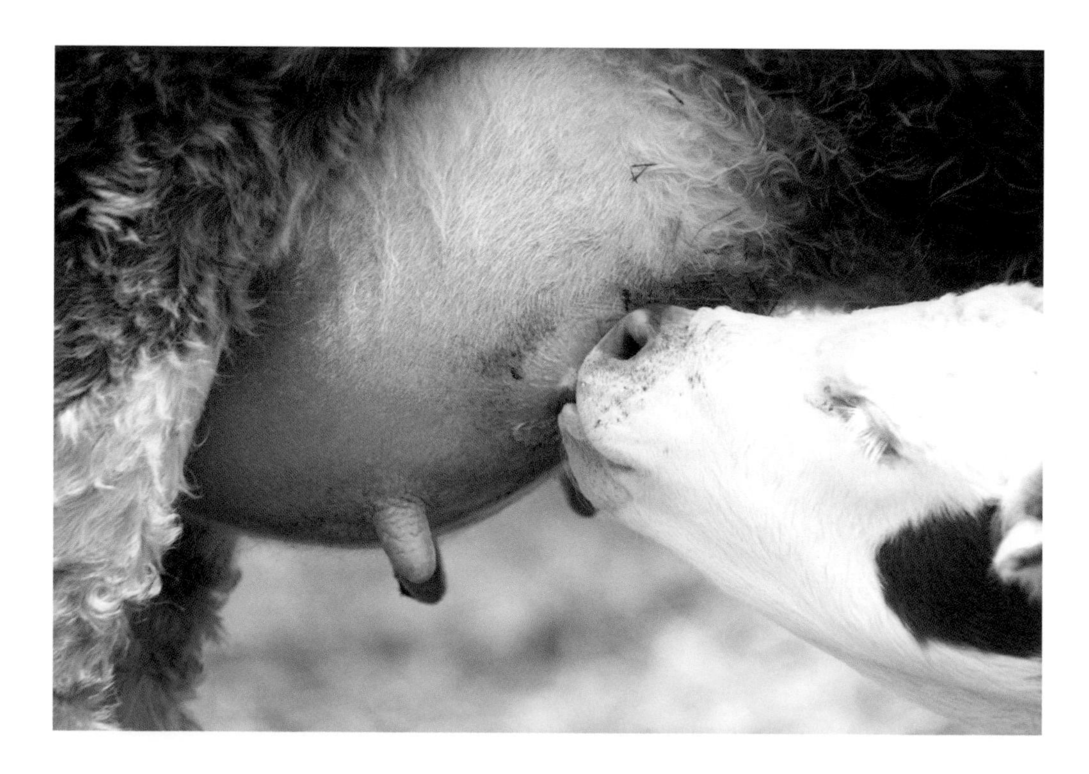

unmedicated milk replacer. As Dr. C. E. Spaulding says in *A Veterinary Guide for Animal Owners*, "There is not enough antibiotics in a pound of feed [medicated milk replacers] to prevent scours or other diseases, and the antibiotic fed daily can damage enough of the natural and necessary bacteria in the gut to cause scours." In addition, look for milk replacer that lists milk as the first ingredient on the ingredient list; cheap brands often include no milk at all.

Don't feed babies more than they are supposed to have just because they act crazy when their milk is gone. If possible, feed them smaller, more frequent milk rations throughout the day, rather than one or two big feedings. Don't feed out of a bucket, as the animals will inhale the milk too quickly. Use a nipple appropriate to the animal's size. Some nipples are designed to work on a bucket or barrel and require a suction hose. These are convenient (especially for feeding groups of babies) and offer some advantages, but you may need to order them from a catalog. You can purchase nipples designed for use with individual bottles at any farm supply store.

Start babies on dry food quickly. If they aren't on pasture, offer a small pile of hay for them to nibble at right away. Whole oats are an excellent starter food, though for the first few days, you may have to teach the young animals to eat the oats. After feeding them their milk rations, and while they're still smacking their lips together, place a small handful of oats in their mouths. They may dribble out more than they swallow in the first day or two, but then they'll quickly start to eat the oats.

Water

Water is the elixir of life. It provides structure to cells, transports and breaks down nutrients, flushes toxins from the body, and moderates the body's temperature. An animal could live without any food for a couple of weeks. But keep it from an adequate supply of

GOOD WATER STANDARDS FOR LIVESTOCK USE

- **Total solids** less than 1,000 ppm*
- **Hardness** less than 1,000 ppm
- **Sulfates** 500 ppm or less
- **Nitrates** less than 45 ppm
- **Iron** less than 5 ppm
- **Sodium** 500 ppm or less

*ppm = parts per million = mg/liter

Beneath a crystal clear sky, sheep drink from an irrigation canal on a farm in Oregon's Wallowa Valley (above). When temperatures drop, however, they will need shelter from the elements. Tawny goats peek from the window of a warm barn (below), protected from wind, rain, and snow.

water on a very hot day, and it can succumb to heat stroke after only a few hours. Even during the winter, three waterless days can result in an animal's death.

One of the biggest challenges in the water department is keeping it clean. No animal wants to drink manure- or urine-contaminated water. Yet if I had a dollar for every time we had to drain and clean a tank with manure or urine in it, I'd be a heck of a lot richer. Even if your water system is automatic, check your tank every day: Make sure the water is clean and there is plenty of it.

SHELTER

Large animals that have their babies on pasture during the spring flush (the early part of the grass-growing season) and have shelter from wind and sun can get along pretty well without buildings. They can also use portable or temporary structures. Windbreaks and shade structures are easier to build and cost far less than a barn. We have raised all kinds of animals for decades and have done so without a barn more often than not. Don't get me wrong; a nice barn can be a great asset. But you don't need one to keep most large livestock, though you definitely need windbreaks and preferably some available shade from the heat of summer. An open shed is ideal, providing relatively inexpensive wind protection, midday shade, and a dry place in inclement weather. If your critters have access to wind protection from walls or trees, you can even do without an open shed.

Small animals, such as chickens, ducks, and rabbits, will need some type of structure for nighttime protection from both the elements and predators. It won't take predators long to see your farmstead as a place for free dinner when chickens are roosting unprotected or a duck is waddling around the yard near dusk. For poultry, a small, traditional hen house will work, or you can build a "chicken-mobile," which will let you move your chickens around your pastures for maximum productivity. Raise rabbits in individual hutches or in a pasture rabbit cage similar to the chicken-mobile.

Alternatives to conventional housing include straw bale structures, hoop-house structures, small metal or plastic hutches, and even tents or teepees.

HEALTHCARE

Though sometimes an animal's illness results from chemical agents (poisoning), from improper diet, or from a sudden change in diet. Most illnesses are generally caused by a biological agent. Complex organisms, such as birds and mammals, regularly act as hosts to a rather large menagerie of microorganisms. Scientists estimate that a hundred billion microorganisms routinely share human bodies. They call these regular guests "normal flora." For the most part they are harmless, and, in some cases, actually beneficial, as with the digestive bacteria that help break down food. Under certain circumstances, however, these usually benign bugs can cause disease. When a microorganism causes disease, whether it is a member of the normal flora or a recently introduced bug that is just passing through, it is called a pathogen.

When conditions are right for them, pathogens proliferate until their numbers simply overwhelm the animal, like weeds taking over a garden. Some produce toxins as a byproduct of their bodily functions. Clostridium bacteria, for example, produce toxins that can cause tetanus, botulism, or black leg. Such toxin-producing pathogens are capable of causing illness with only a few organisms present. The biological agents include bacteria, viruses, yeast, fungi, worms, and other parasites.

You can treat bacteria with antibiotics. Not all bacteria, however, respond the same way to all antibiotics. If a bacterium responds to treatment by a particular antibiotic, it's said to be sensitive to the antibiotic; if it doesn't respond to the treatment, it's resistant. When you treat an animal for a bacterial infection, it's best to have your veterinarian perform a culture and sensitivity test (unless you're dealing with an immediately life-threatening situation).

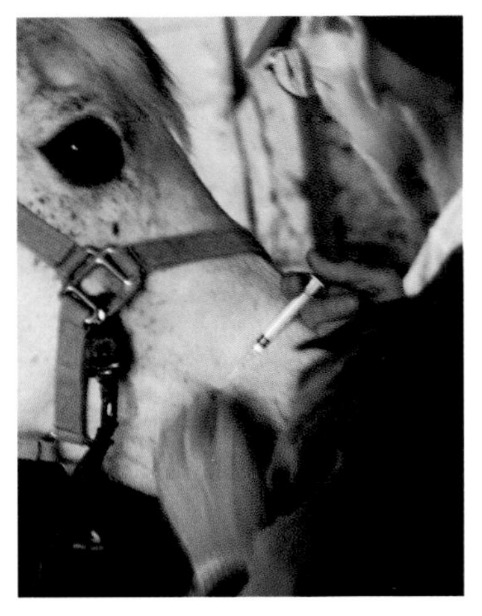

A veterinarian administers a local anesthetic before freezing a melanoma on a gray horse's muzzle (above), and a husband-and-wife team of ranch hands doctors a sick newborn calf (below). Both professional treatment and preventive care are crucial for maintaining healthy livestock.

This test will tell you which antibiotic will be most effective against the bacterium that's causing the illness.

Unfortunately, antibiotics do not affect viruses—not even a little bit . While some antiviral drugs have come on the market, for the most part, once a viral infection has begun, the animal's immune system must combat the viral organism with antibodies or the animal will die. However, though antibiotics won't cure a viral infection, they may delay secondary bacterial infections, some of which can be deadly. Bovine viral diarrhea (BVD) is a good example of a viral disease that is highly contagious and results in high mortality levels (large numbers of exposed animals will die). The virus itself isn't usually the cause of death; it's the secondary bacterial pneumonia that follows. So as soon as a veterinarian diagnoses BVD, antibiotic therapy begins. Veterinarians also administer drugs to help alleviate certain symptoms (for example, aspirin to reduce fever).

Viruses may not succumb to antibiotics, but you can prevent many common livestock viruses from causing illness through the use of vaccinations. Basically, what a vaccine does is teach the body to recognize the protein sequence of a given virus. Once the body's immune system has recognized the virus as a foreign invader, it will quickly recognize it again. This pre-programming allows the immune system to deploy antibodies when the virus first shows up, cutting down the immune system's response time to a point where the invading virus has little chance to begin reproducing.

Unlike bacteria and viruses, yeast and other fungi are multi-celled organisms. These organisms normally don't cause problems in healthy animals. But when an animal's immune system is already compromised, multi-celled organisms can cause a variety of skin problems, respiratory problems, and mastitis (an infection in the udder—or milk-secreting gland—of a female animal). Often, these infections follow antibiotic use because the balance of normal flora has been upset, providing an opportunity for the existing flora to multiply or invaders to take off.

A veterinarian prepares to inject a cow with the new vaccine for bovine leptospirosis. The disease can cause abortion, weakness in newborn calves, mastitis, and even seizures and sudden death.

The definition of a parasite is "an organism that obtains food and/or shelter from another organism." Parasites aren't a single class of organisms. Instead, they run the gamut from protozoa (single-celled members of the animal kingdom) to far more complex organisms such as worms and insects.

Some parasites are relatively benign. Others, such as biting flies, are nuisances; still others cause serious illness. Parasites are capable of attacking most parts of the body. In cows alone, there are almost one hundred known pathogenic parasites. You'll find pathogenic parasites throughout the digestive system, on the skin, in the blood, throughout the respiratory system, in the eyes—everywhere. Luckily, you won't find some of the worst parasites in the United States. In addition, strong, healthy animals rotated on clean pastures are less likely to suffer from parasitic diseases. In this country, the intestinal worms tend to be the biggest parasite problem. Though not often fatal, intestinal worms reduce weight gain and milk production, and they simply tax an animal's system. There are medications available for treating worms; however, before treating, have your vet run a stool sample from one or two animals in the herd to check for worm eggs. If worms are significant, the vet will find eggs; if he or she doesn't find any eggs, then you don't need to treat the herd.

THE POWER OF OBSERVATION

Some illnesses and injuries cause readily apparent discomfort, but many don't. The power of observation is one of the best tools available to small-scale farmers when it comes to caring for their animals. So what should you be looking for?

- **Listlessness** Healthy animals are "bright-eyed and bushy-tailed," as the old saying goes. They are active, moving around freely. They hold up their heads and respond with their ears and eyes to their environment. They have a good appetite and drink plenty of water. An animal that is lying around, not eating, and not showing interest in *its* surroundings is probably ill. There are some exceptions to this rule. On really hot days, critters may just lay around in the shade looking pretty lethargic—but as the heat of day breaks, they'll get up and eat again. Even if they're lethargic from the heat, they should still respond with their eyes and ears.

  Newborns can also be an exception to the listlessness rule. For the first week or two, a newborn eats and sleeps. Its sleep tends to be very, very deep. Sometimes, you'll see a newborn baby animal that you think has died because it's in such a deep sleep, but when you go over to it, you realize it's not. Coming into the world from the safety and warmth of the womb is hard work for a little thing.
- **Sunken eyes or gray or white gums** Sunken eyes usually indicate dehydration, which often accompanies illness. If gums and tongue are gray or white, instead of pink, chances are, the animal is probably in shock—either from dehydration accompanying an illness or from an injury.
- **Poor-quality hair or wool** The hair or wool should cover the body fairly evenly and look shiny and healthy (unless animals are shedding out their winter coats in spring and early summer). Poor-quality coats can indicate nutritional deficiencies, external or internal parasites, or other systemic diseases. In addition, if the tail-head and the backs of the legs display caked-on manure, it is a sure sign of diarrhea or "scours."
- **Discharges from nose, mouth, ears, or eyes** While a bit of watery discharge from eyes or nose isn't anything to worry about, indicators that can mean an animal is not well are a discharge that looks like pus, crusty stuff built up around the muzzle or eyes, excessive slobber or frothiness around the mouth, or any kind of discharge from the ears.
- **Coughing or wheezing** Healthy animals breathe easily through their noses, not their mouths, though sometimes they may mouth-breathe after excessive exercise or during extreme heat. Coughing is a sign the animal may have an infection or there's a physical irritant, such as dusty feed, present.
- **Hot, red, or hard udder** Though most common in dairy cows, mastitis can occur in any female animal producing milk in its udder. On rare occasions, a young female that hasn't bred can develop mastitis. A healthy udder should be warm, but not hot; pink, but not red; and soft, not hard. The milk should flow smoothly and—except for colostrum—will be very liquid, with no clots or lumps. Colostrum is almost the consistency of pudding, but it shouldn't have any lumps in it after the first few squirts.

Common illnesses

Just like us, our animals are subject to a variety of illnesses. We get the common cold; so do they. We sometimes suffer from "Montezuma's revenge"; so do they. What follows are some of the more common afflictions your animals might suffer from.

Scours (or diarrhea)

In adult animals, diarrhea, or scours, usually isn't fatal. Most often, adult diarrhea is the result of a change in diet or the consumption of very lush pasture. Mild cases of diarrhea from changing diets will clear up in two to three days and don't have many symptoms other than the diarrhea itself. Lush-pasture cases will continue for as long as the high-quality, moist feed lasts; but, like change-of-diet cases, it doesn't tend to have other symptoms associated with it. If you haven't adjusted the animal's diet and it's not on lush pasture, the next most common cause of adult scours is excessive parasite loads. Animals don't typically have a fever with parasitic scours, but the animal will appear lethargic and its coat may appear dull. Diagnosis of parasitic scours requires your vet to check a stool sample (unless you actually see worms in the stool). If an adult animal is suffering from both diarrhea and a fever, it's time to call your veterinarian. The animal is suffering from either a viral or bacterial case of scours.

Scours in baby animals is always a very serious and life-threatening situation. Normal baby-animal stools are yellowish, with a consistency similar to soft peanut butter. Sometimes the stools stick to the tail-head for the first day or two. During the fly season, wipe away stools to prevent screw flies from laying their eggs (which develop into maggots) there. With scours in very young animals, the stool becomes watery or slimy and, if left untreated, the baby will die within a few days. Scours is quite common in bottle-fed babies. The most prevalent cause of scours in bottle babies is overfeeding, especially overfeeding of milk. It's easiest to cure the scours caused by overfeeding, but without treatment, an otherwise healthy baby can die in just a few days. Other causes of scours in babies include bacteria, viruses, and parasites.

ELECTROLYTES

Chemically speaking, an electrolyte is a solution—such as salt water—that will conduct electricity. When you dissolve things such as sodium, potassium, or chloride in water, they create an electrolyte solution. (Pure water, found only in a laboratory, won't conduct electricity.) Living creatures depend on a proper balance of electrolytes in their blood stream. When illness upsets that balance, body functions (such as liver and kidney function) suffer. Most weak or sick animals benefit from the use of an electrolyte solution, though weak babies—especially those suffering from dehydration associated with fever or scours—*must* be given additional electrolytes if you hope to save them. Although sugar dissolved in pure water isn't electrolytic, people usually add it to electrolyte solutions to supply extra energy.

You can purchase electrolytes from farm supply stores or veterinarians in convenient packages to keep on hand, or you can prepare a homemade electrolyte solution. The homemade solution doesn't have the variety of ions and doesn't contain some of the added vitamins or probiotics that commercial products do. But when you need something in a hurry and the nearest farm store is an hour away, the homemade version can mean the difference between life and death. Here is a recipe: In one gallon of warm water, dissolve four tablespoons of corn syrup, two teaspoons of table salt, and two teaspoons of baking soda. (A friend of ours swears by the addition of a teabag to her homemade solution, and another friend uses a sports drink instead of the homemade solution.)

If you're treating a baby animal, dilute its normal milk ration by half with water. In between the milk feedings, feed it a comparable ration of your electrolyte solution. Don't feed the electrolyte with the milk, as the digestive process interferes with absorption of the electrolytes into the animal's system.

You should institute treatment of scours as soon as it's recognized. The first thing to do is to replace fluids and electrolytes. Babies suffering from the overeating version of scours often require no more treatment than this, but continue treatment for two to four days, or until the stool returns to normal. If you do suspect that a pathogen caused the scours, antibiotics may be in order. Check with your vet.

Bloat

Bloat is limited to ruminants. When the rumen traps excessive quantities of gas, bloat occurs. In extreme cases, bloat can be deadly within an hour or two. It is usually the result of eating lush, leguminous pasture and is aggravated by moisture from dew or rain. It is most common on alfalfa, slightly less common on clover, and doesn't happen on birdsfoot trefoil pastures. Pastures with a high percentage of grass compared to legumes are the least likely to cause bloat, but even these can do it in the early spring. The most prominent symptom of bloat is a bulge on the animal's left side, just below the spine and in front of the hipbone. This area usually appears caved-in, but in a bloating animal it sticks out. Bloating animals also quit eating and belching.

For bloating cows, we'd mix and administer the following mixture: a cup of cooking oil, a cup of water, and three tablespoons of baking soda. A squirt-water bottle (like those that bikers and hikers use) works well to administer the mixture. Dribble the contents into the animal's mouth over a few minutes. The animal won't consume the entire mixture, but it will get enough. Sheep and goats are much less likely to suffer bloat, but if they do, administer about one-quarter of the amount. After the animal drinks the mixture, hold a smooth stick in its mouth—sort of like a bit. This gets the tongue working, which helps to kick-start the belching process. As soon as the animal begins belching, you can remove the stick and watch its side go back down.

A cow grazes in a pasture of flowering birdsfoot trefoil. This perennial legume contains tannin, a natural antibloating compound.

RESTRAINT

Through all the health discussions, I talk about things to do; but if you can't control an animal, taking care of its problems is quite difficult. We work to get all breeding animals tame enough that we can move them easily into controlled areas. We can then move them into smaller pens, where restraint comes more easily. This is something to begin early. At times you can exert enough control in a confined area, such as a stall, to do what you need to do without additional restraints, but often you'll need more control. Halters, ropes, nose rings, and twitches are all good tools for controlling animals.

If you are dealing with fairly wild animals, you'll need extensive handling systems that include catch pens, chutes, and head gates. These can be expensive, but plan on spending the money if you don't have the time, the patience, or the type of animals that can be tamed.

In a life-or-death situation, cut through the animal's side into its rumen to release the gas. Vets carry a two-part tool for this purpose, called a trocar and cannula. In lieu of the trocar and cannula, a thin, sterilized knife (boil in water or soak in bleach for about five minutes) might save the animal's life. In either case, place the animal on antibiotics following the procedure, because infection is likely.

Hardware disease

Unless you purchase a piece of completely bare land that has never had any buildings on it, chances are that you will, at some time, come up with hardware disease if you have any cows. Even baby calves can suffer from it. Sometimes it can happen in other ruminants, but it's most prevalent in cattle.

When an animal eats a sharp piece of metal, such as a nail or a small hunk of wire, hardware disease occurs. The reticulum traps the piece of metal, which can puncture the wall. Symptoms include obvious pain, kicking at the side, a slight rise in temperature, and getting up and laying down repeatedly. The cure, at least, is simple: Insert a magnet (specially made for this purpose) in the cow's stomach to "catch" the hardware. Some cattlemen insert magnets as a matter of course in all their animals; we simply kept magnets on hand, in our vet supplies, and inserted them when an animal showed the signs. If the problem is indeed hardware disease, the animal recovers almost immediately when you insert the magnet.

Pneumonia and other respiratory disorders

Respiratory illnesses can occur in all species. A stressed animal's normal flora can get out of control. Stress caused by poor management (drafts or ammonia fumes in buildings, poor nutrition, and other hazards) or transportation of animals is often the underlying cause of respiratory illnesses. It is very common in young animals of all species.

In mature animals, if an animal has no fever and is still eating well, we simply keep an eye on the animal. In young animals it is, again, far more serious. Keep the animal warm, administer electrolytes, and call the vet if the condition persists for more than twenty-four hours or seems to be getting worse.

If your animals will come in contact with other animals (for example, if you plan to show them) or if you'll be bringing new animals into your herd, vaccination can prevent or greatly reduce the impact of many contagious respiratory diseases.

Reproduction

For most of us, one of the greatest joys of raising livestock comes from the miracle of reproduction. The opportunity to witness the birth of a calf, to see the first bumbling steps of a colt, or to spy a chick peaking out from under its mother's ruffled feathers is part of what draws us to animal agriculture in the first place. However, the reproductive process can also be a source of trouble.

Sexual reproduction requires a male to supply sperm and a female to supply an egg. Males produce sperm in the testicles. In mammals, the testicles hang outside the body in the scrotum, but in birds, they are internal. The scrotum helps to regulate the temperature of the testes. It drops lower to reduce temperature during warm weather and pulls in closer to the body during cold weather to maintain a higher temperature. Generally, sperm require temperatures that are four to five degrees cooler than normal body temperature to survive.

With protective gloves, a firm grip, and a well-placed knee, a veteran cattleman restrains a struggling calf (opposite). Novice hobby farmers may require the aid of restraining gear in a similar situation (see above).

Haystack

SEXUAL INFORMATION

Species	Ovulation rate	Gestation period	Estrus period	Estrus cycle
Cow	1 egg/estrus	275-285 days	13-17 hours	21 days
Horse	1 egg/estrus	330-345 days	90-170 hours	22 days
Pig	10-20 eggs/estrus	112-115 days	48-72 hours	21 days
Sheep	1-3 eggs/estrus	112-115 days	24-36 hours	17 days
Chicken	28 eggs/month	26-29 days	na	na

With each ejaculation, males send billions of sperm cells in search of an egg, though only one sperm is required to fertilize each egg. Unlike males, who regularly produce new sperm cells from puberty until a very old age, females have their full complement of eggs at puberty. Females produce eggs and then store them for life in their ovaries. All species contain two ovaries, but a quirk of nature provides poultry with only the left ovary as a developed, working unit.

When females release eggs from the ovaries, we call it the estrus cycle. This complicated process begins at puberty and extends into fairly old age. The cycle is controlled by the ebb and flow of four major hormones: the follicle stimulating hormone, estrogen, luteinizing hormone, and progesterone. The length of the cycle varies from species to species; and in most species, the female will allow the male to breed her only for a short period during the cycle, called *heat*, or estrus. Males sense the estrus period through their sense of smell.

Normally cows and mares release one egg per cycle, so twins are unusual, and triplets are a real rarity. Ewes typically drop between one and three eggs per cycle, though some breeds are capable of dropping up to six. Sows are the big producers, dropping as many as twenty eggs per cycle. Chickens can drop about twenty-eight eggs per month. Multiple births are most often the result of dropping multiple eggs. Occasionally, however, one fertilized egg splits in two at the beginning of development. This is the anomaly that causes identical twins.

The estrus cycle in some species, such as horses, sheep, and chickens, is seasonally cyclic. That is, the number of hours of daylight controls their cycles, and during part of the year, they do not come into heat at all (or their heat isn't very powerful). Cows and pigs cycle regularly, all year long.

When eggs leave the ovaries, they travel down the fallopian tubes. As the egg travels down the tube, it will be fertilized by a sperm and settle into the uterus for development. (Birds are the exception, with development taking place outside the body.) The period of development is called gestation, or, in the case of birds, incubation.

Fertilization may take place either naturally—through copulation between a male and a female—or through artificial insemination (AI). AI is now a common practice for most species of livestock. Dairy cows and turkeys are almost all bred artificially in commercial agriculture. The use of AI is also increasing dramatically in the pork industry. Farmers breed other species largely the old-fashioned way: boy meets girl. AI does have some good points. All farmers have access to high-quality sires, and they do not need to keep male breeding stock on site—and the price isn't exorbitant.

The fertilized egg is called a *zygote*, and although it starts out as two unique cells (an egg and a sperm), it is considered a single cell in its own right. It begins to split into additional cells almost immediately. The zygote implants itself in the wall of the uterus, at which point it's called an *embryo*. In a truly remarkable process, embryonic cells continue to split into more cells. Those cells differentiate into the various types of cells that are ultimately required for a fully developed organism, such as blood cells, muscle cells, and skin cells. The instructions for how to correctly split and differentiate are in the chains of genetic material that each parent provides.

At the end of gestation, the fully formed embryo is ready to enter the world. During the last few days before delivery, the mama begins to show signs that the big event is near. The udder starts to swell with milk. The area around the tail-head begins to flatten out and appears sunken. Mucus begins discharging from the vulva, and the vulva itself looks puffy.

Minutes after giving birth, a two-year-old beef cow licks down her newborn calf.

INFERTILITY PROBLEMS

Infertility problems can occur in both males and females but are more common in females. The main cause of infertility in females is an infectious process in the uterus, following the birth of last year's baby. The infection occurs when the animal has failed to pass the afterbirth. If you haven't seen the mother pass the afterbirth, keep an eye on her for any discharge over the next week or two. Clear to slightly turbid, mucous discharges with some blood are quite normal, but if the discharge is thick (like pus), have the vet come out and check the animal.

When male infertility does occur, it is a much bigger concern than female infertility, as one male is responsible for breeding many females. If a female is infertile, she won't have any lambs, but the rest of the flock will still be producing. If the prize ram for which you paid dearly is a dud, there will be no lambs next year. Ask a veterinarian to check the male for infertility problems when purchasing a breeding male.

A nanny goat offers warmth and security to her kids (above), but not all new mothers know how to care for their offspring. If mothers neglect their newborns—for instance, leaving a calf (below) lying unattended after birth—hobby farmers need to act as emergency surrogates.

Often, during these last few days, mothers act kind of oddly. They often go off by themselves, avoiding people and other members of the herd; they may talk more than normal; or they may act quite restless, laying down and getting back up frequently. Close to the time of birth, a sack of fluid may show up and break.

Labor can last just a few minutes, or it can last for hours. First-time mothers generally take longer for labor than those that have delivered babies in the past. The most common delivery position is front feet first, followed by the nose. After the shoulders pass through the cervix (the strong muscle that protects the uterus from the outside world), the baby just about shoots out, but getting to that point can take time. Rear presentations, or breech births, are far less common than frontal deliveries, but they can happen.

Troubled deliveries are really few and far between if the mother is in good health. Over the years, and among the hundreds of babies born to our animals, we had to assist only a few times. As a rule of thumb, any animal that has struggled in labor for more than an hour, or that is obviously weak and tired, needs assistance.

Call a vet the first time you run into a problem delivery. After you've worked through the procedures with an experienced guide, you'll know what to do most of the time, but that first exposure definitely benefits from guidance. Be cautious about asking other farmers for help and advice in this particular department; many old-timers we met were too quick to pull babies, used too much force and the wrong kind of force, and caused more problems than they prevented. Most vets can confirm this observation first hand.

Once the infant comes into the world, Mom will lick the mucous-covered newborn down. Sometimes a first-time mom is confused about what's going on. In this case, make sure to clean the baby's air passage (the area around its nose and mouth) so it can breathe. If the animal isn't breathing, give *it* a good strong slap on the side.

ANIMAL DEFINITIONS

- **Barrow** A castrated male pig
- **Billy or buck:** Mature, intact male goat
- **Boar** Male pig
- **Breed** A group of animals purposefully bred to demonstrate similar traits
- **Brood** 1) To sit on, or hatch, eggs 2) To protect young, as if by covering with wings
- **Bull** Immature or mature male cattle (also bison, elk)
- **Calf:** Newborn cattle (also bison, elk)
- **Calving** Cattle giving birth (also bison, elk)
- **Capon** A castrated male chicken
- **Chevon** Goat meat
- **Chick** A newborn chicken
- **Chunk** A cross between a draft horse and a saddle horse
- **Clutch** The number of eggs produced or incubated at one time
- **Cockerel** Immature male chicken
- **Colt** Immature male horse
- **Conformation** The animal's physical structure of bone, muscle, skin, and other attributes
- **Cow** Mature female cattle (also bison, elk)
- **Crossbred** Animals known to have more than one breed in their lineage. Many crossbreds perform well, due to an effect known as *hybrid vigor.*
- **Doe or nanny** Mature female goat
- **Dual-purpose breed** A breed of animals that is well suited to meeting two production functions, such as eggs and meat for chickens, or milk and meat for cows
- **Ewe** Female sheep
- **Exotic** An exotic animal that is from a species not traditionally or normally raised for commercial agricultural purposes in the United States, such as buffalo, camel, elk, red deer, potbellied pigs, and alpaca
- **Farrowing** Act of giving birth to pigs
- **Free martin** Heifer born as a twin, with the other twin being a bull. These heifers cannot breed.
- **Filly** Immature female horse
- **Foal** Newborn horse
- **Gelding** Castrated male horse (also donkey, llama)
- **Gilt** Immature female pig
- **Grade** An animal that may or may not be purebred, that shows the traits of a known breed, and that is not registered with a breed association. For example, a grade angus cow may be purebred angus, through and through, but if she comes from an unregistered, she is called a grade angus. Or, a mare may have the color characteristics of a paint horse, but if her breeding is unknown, she is called a grade paint.
- **Heifer** Immature female cattle (also bison, elk)
- **Hen** Mature female chicken
- **Hinny** A cross between a stallion and a jenny. Hinnies are sterile crosses.
- **Hybrid vigor** Constant inbreeding, which often happens with registered animals, can result in bad traits emerging. By crossing two breeds you tend to get a healthier and more vigorous animal; this is known as *hybrid vigor.*
- **Jack** Male donkey
- **Jenny or jennet** Female donkey
- **Lamb** Immature or newborn sheep
- **Kid** Immature or newborn goat
- **Mare** Mature female horse
- **Minor breeds** Minor breeds are those breeds of livestock that have fallen from favor with current commercial agricultural ventures, but which played an important role in our agricultural past. As these breeds lose popularity with the industrial agricultural sector, their numbers decrease, sometimes to the point that the breed becomes extinct.
- **Molting** The regular seasonal shedding of feathers
- **Mule** A cross between a mare and a jack. Mules are sterile crosses.
- **Papered** A registered papered animal
- **Polled** An animal that naturally doesn't have horns
- **Pullet** Immature female chicken
- **Purebred** A purebred animal has 100 percent (or more than 15/16) of its bloodlines coming from a particular breed. A purebred Boer goat has no other breed of goat mixed in.
- **Ram or buck** Mature intact male sheep.
- **Registered** Registered animals are purebred animals, or bred in accordance with the rules of a breed association, and their owner has recorded their lineage with the breed association. For example, a registered Quarter horse comes from two parents that are registered Quarter horses, or from a cross of a registered Quarter horse and a registered thoroughbred (as allowed by the American Quarter Horse Association rules). Most major breeds, and many minor breeds, have breed associations that record the registrations of animals within their breed. Registration costs money, and registered animals aren't necessarily better than unregistered animals, but there is a detailed breeding record and breeding goals going back generations.
- **Rooster** Mature male chicken
- **Shoat or piglet** Newborn pig
- **Sow** Mature female pig
- **Springer** Cow or heifer nearing calving
- **Stallion** Mature male horse
- **Steer** Castrated male cattle
- **Wether** Castrated male goat or sheep

Baby animals need to begin nursing soon after birth for two reasons: one, to get the colostrum, and two, for the energy. Watch mother and baby from a distance for about forty-five minutes. If Junior hasn't found the teat by then, it's time to get involved. First, hand strip a little milk out of each of Mom's teats to make sure they are open. Then, nudge the baby into position and hold its mouth against the teat, working the mouth like an air pump. Once or twice over the years, in the case of especially weak babies, we simply had to strip a little milk into a bottle with a nipple and feed the first serving that way. This usually gave the animals enough energy to feed themselves.

A day after birth, fuzzy yellow chicks cluster together (above), inexpensive and cuddly additions to the farm. A dairy cow (below) is also an asset, providing fresh milk in exchange for feed and care. Ideally, a variety of livestock (such as the mix shown in the quirky picture (opposite) offers hobby farmers a wide range of benefits.

THE MENAGERIE

The farmyard is a cacophonous, wild, and joyous place. You are greeted by the neigh of a horse or the bray of a donkey, the gentle lowing of a mother cow talking to her calf, a gaggle of geese hissing a warning at a visitor. A llama guards the flock of sheep, who are playing king-of-the-hill on a pile of manure. Life is abundant and entertaining. What kind of animals do you want? The possibilities are wide open.

Horses, Chickens... Llamas?

Horses are often the first animal people new to the country get—responding to the lobbying of their kids or to the yearnings of a child trapped in an adult body. Horses have worked for people for more than 8,000 years—providing power and yielding progress. Horses are expensive pets, but they can earn their keep providing recreation or working in field and forest.

Chickens are almost a must-have item. They are economical, supplying meat and eggs that taste so much better than grocery store fare, with little effort. Chicken meat and eggs from small flocks are easy to market. Other members of the bird clan include turkeys (which are smarter than most people give them credit for), guinea fowl, pigeons, peacocks,

A contented pig (above), an affectionate pair of goats (below), and a smirking llama (opposite) appear to pose for the camera. Though farm animals may be purchased with profit in mind, they often become beloved members of the family.

ducks, and geese. You can often purchase baby birds at feed stores in the spring, or you can order them from hatcheries, which ship them to you as day-old chicks (poults, ducklings) via the U.S. mail. The day they arrive, the post office personnel will call you as soon as the truck pulls in, so you can pick them up quickly. It is always a great day. You can also purchase eggs to incubate, or, from time to time, find someone willing to sell a few adults from his or her flock.

Cows are wonderful animals. Beef cattle require no housing, unless calves will be born in the winter, and dairy animals can do with minimum housing. For a homestead approach, one dual-purpose animal, such as a Jersey cow, can raise a calf and supply milk for the family—just milk her once a day.

Pigs have personality plus. They are very intelligent and entertaining, but they can also be challening. They are really curious, so they often get into things that you don't necessarily want them in (the garden, for example). And, since they are omnivores, they may eat things you don't want them to consume (such as one of your chickens).

Goats are the magicians of the farmstead—able to escape from enclosures. Contrary to popular myth, they don't eat tin cans, but they do play havoc on things. For example, given the opportunity, they will climb all over your vehicles, leaving dainty little hoof dents on the roof, the hood, or the trunk. They have good market potential, as numerous ethnic communities prefer their meat.

Sheep are sweet and vulnerable but also high-strung, making them somewhat difficult to handle. Sheep move like a school of fish, in a tight bunch, so working with them requires patience. Yet it is inexpensive to start sheep, you can raise them in a small area, and you can build an impressive-size flock pretty quickly from a few animals to start with.

Llamas and alpacas are members of the camel family. Farmers raise them primarily for their fleece, which handspinners and weavers crave, though you can also train them as pack animals. Llamas make good guardian animals for sheep.

Whether you're in the market for a chicken (above), a calf (below), or a horse (opposite), remember the Latin phrase *Caveat emptor*—or at least the English translation—"Let the buyer beware." Know what you need to watch out for before you go shopping.

Shopping for Animals

Buying your first animals is an adventure. At this stage, you probably don't know much about markets, conformation, disposition, or animal health. You will probably have the best luck by buying through a "private treaty" deal. This means directly from the animal's current owner, instead of at an auction or through a broker. Owners selling directly are more likely to be honest about the animal's disposition and health, but remember that when buying any animal from anyone, there is a certain amount of "buyer beware": you may find an owner who isn't totally scrupulous.

Some of the best advice about going to view animals is to apologize profusely, but arrive approximately five minutes to an hour earlier than you told the owner that you would. Mark Rashid, who is author of three of my favorite horse-related books, including *A Good Horse is Never a Bad Color* (Johnson Printing, 1996), makes the following observation: "By 'accidentally' arriving early when looking to buy a horse, I've seen supposedly quiet and gentle horses that kicked when you walked behind them, bit or bloated when you tried to cinch them, pulled back when you tried to tie them, and threw their heads when you tried to bridle them. In one case, I even walked in on a fellow as he was injecting the horse he wanted to sell me with a sedative."

If you have a friend or acquaintance familiar with the type of animals you are looking at, ask him or her to go with you. That person will be able to help you evaluate the animals' health, condition, and suitability for your needs. Also, if you are buying expensive animals (breeding stock, show animals), I strongly recommend having a veterinarian check out the animals before you close the deal. The money you spend on a pre-purchase exam could save you not only dollars, but also heartaches down the line.

CHAPTER 8

Preserving the Harvest: Fruits and Vegetables

AT LAST, YOUR WORK PAYS OFF WITH FOOD AND FIBER FROM from plants and animals that you have raised. The good news is, you have a harvest; the bad news is, you have a harvest. It all seems to come at once. You need to store the crops, some requiring processing before they go into storage.

In many homes today, cooking and preserving are lost arts, sadly replaced by restaurant fare and "convenience" foods from the grocery store. Those old skills are still necessities on the farm, however, when tomato plants are weighted down with luscious red globes, strawberries available in profusion, and sweet corn ready by the bushel.

During harvest time, the kitchen becomes the center of life. In an ideal world, harvesting of crops is done in the morning, after the dew has dried but before the midday sun begins heating up the crop. Crops spoil more quickly if stored hot, so when you must harvest during the heat of the day, if at all possible, cool crops with a cold water misting and then dry them before storing. Likewise, they spoil more quickly if they're moist when stored, so if you must harvest while dew is on the crop, make sure the crop is dry prior to storing.

STORAGE OPTIONS

Many vegetables and fruits store well for later use if you can control the temperature and humidity. A root cellar is often the perfect answer. (It can even do double duty as a wine cellar.) If you have a basement in your house, you may have the ideal place to construct a root cellar closet. The one absolute must for a basement to work as a root cellar is that it remain dry—if yours is subject to serious dampness it will not serve the purpose. If you don't have a suitable basement, other options include buried barrels or metal garbage cans, straw bales, or drain tiles. Temporary pits or piles also work, though they are less convenient and, once you open them, you must empty them quickly.

Several factors are crucial for root cellar success. Consistent temperatures in the appropriate range, proper humidity, and ventilation to provide clean air and remove excess gasses are all essential. An ideal situation for a basement root cellar is a northwest or northeast corner of the cellar that has a window in it. Partition off the corner with insulated walls and an insulated door. When a window is available, remove the glass and place metal screening over it to keep critters out; then install a flue board that has an air intake flue bringing cool air in and dropping it near the floor. Install an air outlet flue that allows hot air to escape. You can make flues out of wood or PVC pipe. Open and close both flues with a damper. You will quickly get the hang of controlling temperature by manipulating the flues. If you need additional humidity in a root cellar, simply add a pan of water.

The length of time produce keeps in a root cellar depends on several factors: maturation period, storage conditions, and condition of produce. Late-maturing varieties harvested in the fall store better than varieties harvested in summer. Less-than-ideal storage conditions will shorten storage life (see sidebar for best conditions). Crops you store in a root cellar must be of the highest quality.

Bruised or blemished fruits or vegetables are sure to go bad, and once they go, they tend to take others with them. Some fruits and vegetables don't mix, even though temperatures

Produce can be preserved for use throughout the year, keeping your pantry well stocked (above). A basket of succulent lettuce leaves sits on a table, ready for immediate consumption (opposite).

FOOD FOR THOUGHT

The best piece of advice I can offer about food is this: eat as close to sustainable as you can. The average beef animal travels more than 1,500 miles in its short life; industrial egg farms keep 100,000 chickens under one roof, each bird with less space than the size of the page you are now reading. A typical 5,000-hog factory produces 9,500 tons of manure per year (about the same amount generated by a small town). The manure is stored in open lagoons or cisterns that often leak, killing fish, contaminating drinking water supplies, hatching massive swarms of flies, and yielding odors that make it unbearable for people who live near a hog factory to spend time outdoors.

Vegetables and grains from industrial agriculture are grown less for taste than for consistent size and ship-ability; they are sprayed with known carcinogens. (If imported, chances are the chemicals they are sprayed with are completely banned from use in the United States due to their environmental or health impacts.) The laborers who work in the fields are practically slaves, poorly paid and poorly treated, with young children and very old people laboring in conditions you wouldn't subject a dog to.

The salad from your own garden, the eggs from your own flock, and the milk from your own goat are always better than food from other sources. Try to grow as much as you can of your own food, using sustainable practices such as managed grazing and vegetable and grain production that relies on healthy soil and crop rotation instead of chemicals.

If you can't supply all your own sustenance, purchase locally grown food from family farmers who use sustainable practices. Many farmers are now marketing directly from their farms, and most areas of the country now have a farmer's market that caters to local growers. Buy food produced by family farmer-controlled cooperatives that use sustainable practices, and when you must shop in stores, purchase "labeled" foods, such as those that are certified organic or free trade. You'll find these foods in regular grocery stores and they are readily available in natural food stores.

PEAS

and moisture requirements are similar. For instance, apples, tomatoes, peaches, pears, and plums all give off ethylene gas, which can cause potatoes to sprout. In addition, other fruits and vegetables can absorb the odor of strong-smelling vegetables such as turnips and cabbage, so store these fragrant vegetables separately from other food and where the odor cannot waft into the house.

When blanched to ensure optimum quality and nutritional value, garden-grown produce, like the tomatoes above, may be enjoyed for months to come.The peas, asparagus, green onions, radishes, artichokes, sweet corn, and other fresh fruits and vegetables shown opposite are ready for preservation.

PRESERVATION TECHNIQUES

Preserving the harvest through techniques such as drying, canning, and freezing allows us to enjoy the bounty of summer throughout the year. Each method has advantages and disadvantages. Which method you use depends on the crop.

For a wide variety of recipes and food preservation information, visit the National Center for Home Food Preservation at www.uga.edu/nchfp/index.html. The center is funded by the Cooperative State Research, Education and Extension Service, a branch of the USDA, to address food safety concerns for those who practice and teach home food preservation and processing methods. The center is operated by the University of Georgia Cooperative Extension Service.

Another web site to visit is www.homecanning.com. This site is a service of Alltrista Consumer Products, the manufacturer of home canning supplies, including Ball and Kerr jars. It has a good basic overview of canning techniques and a recipe search engine. You can order the home-canners' bible, the *Ball Blue Book of Preserving*, for a small charge to cover shipping and handling.

Choose blemish-free, fresh, firm, and ripe fruits and vegetables for preservation. Overly ripe fruits and vegetables should not be used (except when making fruit leathers).

Blanching Fruits and Vegetables

Most vegetables and some fruits require blanching prior to preservation by drying, freezing, or canning. When you blanch, you briefly heat vegetables/fruits in boiling water or steam to inactivate naturally occurring enzymes that can cause undesirable changes in the foods, including nutrient loss, vegetable toughening, and loss of flavor and color. The brief heating also reduces the number of microorganisms on food. Blanching is simple. You can either

FRUITS AND VEGETABLES FOR STORAGE

The various fruits and vegetables have different requirements for optimum storage:

- **Cold and very moist (store between 32 and 40 degrees Fahrenheit at 85 to 95 percent RH (relative humidity)** Artichokes, beets, broccoli, Brussels sprouts, cabbage, carrots, cauliflower, celeriac, celery, Chinese cabbage, endive, horseradish, kale, kohlrabi, leeks, parsnips, potatoes, radishes, rutabagas, turnips
- **Cold and moist (do not store with vegetables; store between 32 and 40 degrees Fahrenheit at 80 to 90 percent RH)** Apples, grapefruit, grapes, oranges, pears, plums
- **Cool and moist (store between 40 and 50 degrees Fahrenheit at 85 to 90 percent RH)** Cucumbers, sweet peppers, cantaloupe, muskmelons, watermelons
- **Cool and dry (store between 35 and 50 degrees Fahrenheit at 60 to 70 percent RH)** Beans (dried), peppers (dried), peas (dried, in an airtight container), popcorn (dried, in an airtight container), garlic (for long-term storage, keeps best at the low end of these temperature and humidity ranges), onions, soybeans in the pod (short duration)
- **Warm and dry (store between 45 and 55 degrees Fahrenheit at 60 to 70 percent RH)** Pumpkins, winter squash, sweet potatoes, green tomatoes

Apples seem almost infinite in the varieties available, from the crisp, juicy, firm-skinned green Granny Smith to the equally juicy, but thinner-skinned, red McIntosh, a fine choice for use in making apple butter.

dip vegetables/fruits in boiling water or steam them. (Steaming takes a little longer, but it preserves more nutrients.) Clean and cut vegetables/fruits before blanching.

To blanch in water, bring water to a boil in a large kettle. You will need about one gallon of water for each pound of vegetables or fruits. Dip the vegetables/fruits in the boiling water using a colander, wire basket, or loose cheesecloth bag. To steam-blanch, place one inch of water in an open kettle and bring to a rolling boil. Suspend a thin layer of vegetables or fruits over the water in a cheesecloth bag instead of submerging them, then cover the kettle, allowing the steam to heat them.

The blanching time varies with the type of vegetable or fruit you will be processing (see chart). As soon as the time is up, remove the vegetables/fruits and immediately put them in ice-cold water. Chill them until completely cold, then drain well (if freezing, allow them to dry completely).

Apple Butter

- 8 lb. apples (use Jonathan, winesap, golden delicious, or macintosh for good results)
- 2 cups apple cider
- 2 cups vinegar
- 2¼ cups white sugar
- 2¼ cups packed brown sugar
- 2 tbsp. ground cinnamon
- 1 tbsp. ground cloves

Wash, remove stems, quarter, and core fruit. Cook slowly in cider and vinegar until soft. Press fruit through a colander, food mill, or strainer. Cook fruit pulp with sugar and spices, stirring frequently. To test for doneness, remove a spoonful of apple butter and hold it away from steam for 2 minutes. You've finished cooking when the butter remains mounded on the spoon. Another test is to spoon a small quantity onto a plate. When a rim of liquid does not separate around the edge of the butter, you are ready to can. Fill hot into sterile half-pint or pint jars, leaving ¼-inch head space. Adjust lids and process. Yield: about 8 to 9 pints.

Applesauce

Apples*
Sugar**

Select apples that are sweet, juicy, and crisp. For a more tart flavor, add 1 to 2 pounds of tart apples to each 3 pounds of sweeter fruit. Wash, peel, and core apples. If desired, slice apples into water containing ascorbic acid to prevent browning. Place drained slices in an 8- to 10-quart pot. Add ½ cup water. Stirring occasionally to prevent burning, heat quickly until tender (5 to 20 minutes, depending on maturity and variety). Press through a sieve or food mill, or skip the pressing step if you prefer chunk-style sauce. Add sugar and reheat sauce to a rolling boil. Fill jars with hot sauce, leaving ½-inch head space. Adjust lids and process.

* You need an average of 3 pounds per quart or an average of 1½ pounds per pint. A bushel weighs 48 pounds and yields 14 to 19 quarts or 32 pints of sauce.
** You need ⅛ cup of sugar per pound of apples, or more if desired.

BLANCHING TIMES

Produce	Boiling method	Steaming method
Asparagus	2 min.	3 min.
Apples	3 min.	5 min.
Apricots	3 min.	5 min.
Beans or peas, for drying	3 min.	6 min.
Beans or peas, for freezing	2 min.	4 min.
Broccoli	3 min.	5 min.
Brussels sprouts	3 min.	5 min.
Cabbage	1 min.	2 min.
Cabbage-Chinese	1 min.	2 min.
Carrots (whole)	5 min.	8 min.
Cauliflower	2 min.	4 min.
Corn on the cob	6 min.	10 min.
Eggplant	Don't boil	2 min.
Peaches	Don't boil	2 min.
Pears	In syrup 2 min.	Don't steam
Peppers, fresh	Roast in 400° oven 4 min.	
Spinach	Don't boil	2 min.
Squash, summer	3 min.	5 min.
Tomatoes, to loosen skin	Don't boil	2 min.
Turnips	2 min.	3 min.

Drying Foods

Drying food is probably one of the oldest storage methods. The Bible mentions drying food in the sun and smoking food over a hot fire. Archaeologists have discovered samples of foods they believe people dried in Jericho 4,000 years ago. Native Americans smoked fish and meat and taught early Euro-Americans not only how to grow corn, but also how to dry it.

To successfully dry foods in the sun, you need very low humidity and long hours of very intense sunshine. A nice strong breeze, temperatures of 95 degrees Fahrenheit or higher, and humidity below 60 percent are perfect sun-drying conditions. In the eastern half of the country, this weather is rare, but those who reside in the Southwestern United States have these conditions frequently. A solar dehydrator (which may be the shelf behind the back seat of a car), a gas or electric oven, or a portable electric dehydrator offer options for drying food where nature doesn't provide ideal conditions.

Let's look at the approach to take for sun-drying if Mother Nature is cooperating with ideal weather conditions. To begin, place prepared foods (see chart) on drying trays. You can use the racks from your oven as trays, or you can construct trays using stainless steel screening or cheesecloth stretched tightly over thin wood lath frames. Don't use aluminum, galvanized, copper, fiberglass, or vinyl screening. Place trays of food, covered with tented cheesecloth, away from dusty roads and yards, elevating them on blocks at least one inch high to allow good air circulation below the food. Dry fruits (including tomatoes) in direct sunlight, and move the trays periodically to keep them in the sun. To prevent excessive color loss, move the vegetables to a shady spot. If the weather turns bad, complete the drying process using another method.

You can purchase a solar dryer commercially or construct one at home. It will increase effectiveness and reduce the time it takes to dry food, but it may still not be adequate in the eastern half of the country. During periods of cloudy days, opt for the oven or an electric dehydrator. Check the web site at www.humboldt1.com for plans to build your own solar dryer.

Oven-drying is a practical way to get started with drying food, since it doesn't depend on weather. If you plan to dry large quantities of food, though, consider investing in an electric dehydrator. They are available at most department stores. An electric dehydrator will save on energy costs and improve your success. It is also more foolproof than using your oven. It can be difficult to maintain a low drying temperature in the oven, which means that you might find your foods scorched at the end of the drying period. Oven-dried foods are also darker, more brittle, and less flavorful than foods dried by a dehydrator.

To dry foods in your oven, preheat the oven to a very low temperature (150 degrees Fahrenheit for vegetables or 170 degrees Fahrenheit for jerky). Put the prepared food on the wire oven racks, leaving room for heat to circulate between the pieces, and put the

Drying them will keep your apples, bananas, grapes, and other fruits tasty and available for nutritious snacks long after their harvest (above). Though most people buy the multicolored ears of Indian Corn merely for decorations (below), the dried kernels can be pounded into flour.

The dried apricots pictured here could be enjoyed as is or rehydrated, pureed, and formed to create a tasty treat called fruit leather.

racks in the warm oven. Rotate the drying racks carefully to ensure even dehydration. For all oven drying, leave the door propped open a bit to allow moisture to escape. To dry foods in a dehydrator, fill the trays that come with the unit and turn it on, following the manufacturer's instructions.

Drying times vary. Thicker slices take longer to dry than thin ones. Solar drying takes longer (one to four days) than oven drying (twenty-four to forty-eight hours). Dehydrator drying takes eight to twenty-four hours.

When you dry food outdoors or in an oven, you then need to pasteurize the food to kill any organisms that survived drying. Do this by preheating the oven to 200 degrees Fahrenheit, then placing the dried food on trays in the closed oven for fifteen minutes before storing.

Place dried foods in a tightly closed, large container. Stir or shake every day for a week. This will equalize the moisture (those pieces that are too dry will take some of the moisture from those that are too wet). If the dried food still seems too moist, return it to the dryer/ovens/sunshine for several more hours. Too much moisture left in a few pieces can cause the whole batch to mold. Store your dried fruits and vegetables in airtight containers in a dry and dark place, where they will last six months to a year. To keep them longer, store in the freezer in airtight bags. You can store dried tomatoes in olive oil.

You can rehydrate dried fruits and vegetables by just covering with boiling water; allow them to stand (not on a burner) until the fruits/vegetables reabsorb the moisture. Another way to use dried vegetables is to grind them to a powder and sprinkle them as you would a spice on pasta, rice, bread, or soup.

Sun-dried tomatoes, fruit leathers, fruit chips, and homemade jerky are great treats, and they make unusual—and much appreciated—Christmas gifts for citified family and friends who have almost everything. Drying herbs means you'll have them on hand throughout the year.

Fruit leathers

Many fruits (and vegetables) can be pureed and then dried to create fruit leathers. Not only does the process make a good, nutritious treat, but it also allows you to use slightly overripe (though unbruised) produce, which doesn't make a first-class product when preserved by other methods.

Pare or peel coarse-skinned fruits (such as apples), or wash thin-skinned fruits (such as berries); remove pits, seeds, and cores. Use a blender or food processor to puree the fruit, adding a small amount of water as needed to yield a very thick, yet pourable, puree. If fruit is too juicy, you can strain it to have a thicker puree. You can also use home-preserved or store-bought canned or frozen fruit to make leathers (drain the fruit and puree as above).

Add two teaspoons of lemon juice for every two cups of light-colored fruit to prevent darkening. Up to half of the puree may be made of applesauce, which acts as an extender, decreases tartness, and makes the leather more pliable.

Use a baking sheet with sides to dry the leather. Place a sheet of freezer paper on the bottom of the pan, then pour the puree onto it (a typical cookie sheet takes about two to two and a half cups of puree). Spread the puree evenly until it is no more than a one-quarter-inch thick across the bottom of the sheet. Place the cookie sheet in a dehydrator or oven set for 135 degrees Fahrenheit. Approximate drying times are six to eight hours in a dehydrator, up to eighteen hours in an oven, and one to two days in the sun. Turn the leather onto another freezer-paper-lined cookie sheet when you can pull away from the freezer paper on the first sheet (check it when about half the time specified in the previous sentence has elapsed). Allow the leather to cool on a cake rack. Once cool, sprinkle it lightly with cornstarch, then roll it up.

You don't have to buy spices from the grocery store to fill your rack (above). Create your own from the basil, oregano, thyme, and other herbs planted in your garden.

Jerky

Because of outbreaks of *E. coli* O157:H7, a sometimes deadly food-borne pathogen, the USDA now recommends that you heat homemade jerky to 325 degrees Fahrenheit before drying at a lower temperature. The following is an approach to making jerky using ground meat.

1. Thaw lean ground meat (poultry, rabbit, beef, or game) in the refrigerator.
2. Add your favorite jerky seasoning and cure in the refrigerator for six hours (try two tablespoons soy sauce, one tablespoon Worcestershire sauce, one teaspoon garlic powder, one teaspoon black pepper, one teaspoon salt, and an optional dash of liquid smoke or hot sauce; amounts are per pound of meat).
3. Shape the ground-meat jerky-type strips by hand, or with a jerky gun. Make strips no more than one-quarter-inch thick. Place on a cookie sheet with sides.
4. Preheat oven to 325 degrees Fahrenheit. Insert cookie sheet and bake for ten minutes.
5. Remove cookie sheet from the oven and pour off any liquid.
6. For continued oven-drying, lower the heat to 170 degrees Fahrenheit and place the cookie sheet back in the oven.
7. For dehydrator drying, transfer the meat to the dehydrator's trays and proceed according to the manufacturer's instructions.
8. Remove jerky before it gets too hard or brittle (six to ten hours, depending on method).
9. Let jerky cool completely, then place it in a plastic freezer-storage bag. Remove the air and seal tightly.
10. Refrigerate or freeze jerky.

Drying herbs

Depending on the herb, harvest may include one or more plant parts. In most cases you harvest the leaves, but in some cases you pick flowers, seeds, or roots. (Handle blossoms just as you would handle leaves.) Often, you harvest blossoms with the leaves and mix them together. When stored properly, dried herbs retain their quality for two to three years. Discard them if you haven't used them up in that time.

To maximize the flavor of herbs for cooking, harvest before the plants flower, in the morning right after the dew dries. Cut annual herbs close to the ground, but for perennials, never take more than a third of the plant at a cutting. After cutting, rinse them in cold running water and then pat dry with a paper towel.

Although you can dry herbs in an oven or dehydrator, it is easy to dry them by hanging them upside-down in a cool, dark place. I use an old wooden drying rack, and I hang bunches of herbs in a brown lunch bag. Each bunch hangs with the top of the plant hanging down and the stems sticking up in the air; I attach the bag to the bunch with a rubber band. I tie the bag to the rack. This type of drying takes anywhere from a few days to a month but requires no energy and retains most aromatic oils.

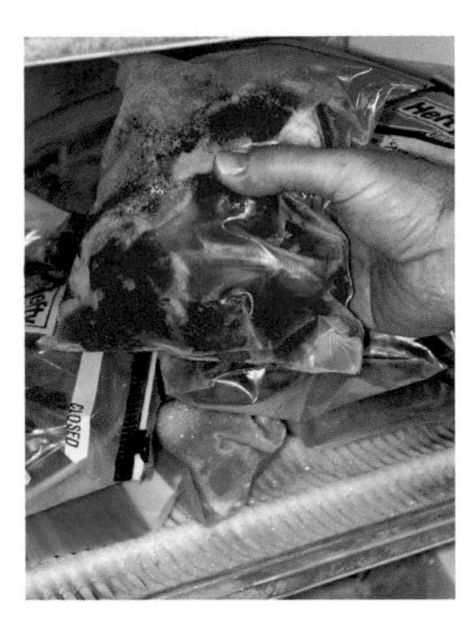

Drying herbs can be as simple as hanging bunches upside-down in a convenient place (as shown below). Your garden's bounty can also be frozen, like the produce above. Before you place food in the freezer, make sure it's clearly labeled with the contents and date.

As with other dried foods, store dried herbs in a well-sealed jar, in a cool, dark, and dry place. (Although jars of herbs look pretty on a windowsill, direct sunlight cuts down on their potency.)

Freezing Foods

The advent of the modern freezer changed our food system completely. Before its invention, food could be dried or canned for storage, but both took considerable time. Now you can quickly preserve food in a freezer. The main advantages are that freezing is simple and it keeps the texture and nutrients of food more like they were when the food was fresh than any other preservation method. But there is one disadvantage, too: to preserve any significant quantity of food requires a stand-alone freezer, which is an expensive item both to purchase and to run.

Food should be in small enough packages to freeze quickly after it is put in the freezer; slow freezing causes large ice crystals to form and contributes to freezer burn. This also means that for home freezing operations, you should limit the quantity you are putting into your freezer in any one day. Adequate packaging also helps to protect food from freezer burn. Although many people use rigid containers of plastic or glass, I mainly use plastic freezer bags because they are convenient and inexpensive. (For meat, fish, or corn on the cob, you can also use freezer paper taped up well with freezer tape to prevent air from getting to the food.) If you are freezing liquids, such as fruits packed in syrup, juices, or sauces, leave at least one inch of empty space at the top of the container. (This allows for expansion as the liquid freezes.) Label all packages with the contents and the date on which they were frozen; use a marker designated only for freezer use.

Fruits often freeze best when packed in syrup or fruit juice. To prepare syrup, dissolve two cups of sugar in four cups of water on the stove; allow the syrup to cool before pouring

over fruit. Many light-colored fruits will darken in the freezer, but you can reduce darkening by adding a tablespoon of lemon juice to your syrup.

A sparkling glass mound of canning jars waits to be filled with a variety of preserved fruits and vegetables from the farm. These are the types of containers you should use for your home canning.

Canning Foods

The art of canning has been with us for several hundred years, and although it's a lot of work, it is worth the effort. By canning foods, you can economically store them for long periods (years at a time) without refrigeration. Store canned foods in a cool, dark, and dry location for maximum shelf life.

Canning heats food to a high temperature, thereby destroying enzymes and killing microorganisms that contribute to spoilage; then as the heated jars cool, you create a vacuum so that air can't get at the food and new microorganisms can't grow. (Read about botulism in the sidebar.) Use stainless steel or enamel pots for boiling and preparing foods for canning; never, never, ever use aluminum or iron pots.

Canning times need to be increased as you go higher in altitude. Add five minutes for every 2,500 feet of altitude above 1,000 feet above sea level. For example, if a recipe calls for ten minutes, that time is appropriate for locations up to 1,000 feet above sea level. Between 1,000 feet and 3,500 feet above sea level, process for fifteen minutes, and for 3,500 to 6,000 feet above sea level, process for twenty minutes.

Use specially designed canning jars when home canning. Canning lids should vacuum-seal tightly. For safety, never use antique jars or those that are chipped around the rim; never use other types of jars (such as mayonnaise jars); and always use new sealing lids. You can reuse jars and the screw rings that hold down the sealing lids, provided that they are in good condition.

Canning jars come in narrow-mouth and wide-mouth styles. The narrow-mouth style works fine for things like jellies, jams, and relishes, but I prefer the wide-mouth jars for everything because I simply find them easier to work with and easier to clean. I use two primary canning processes at home: boiling water bath and pressure canner.

The boiling water bath uses a large kettle of boiling water. This approach is suitable for highly acidic foods, such as pickles, relishes, chutneys made with vinegar, fruits, jams, jellies,

BOTULISM

Clostridium botulinum is a naturally occurring, soil-borne bacteria that causes the potentially fatal disease known as **botulism**. Unlike most food spoilage bacteria, C. botulinum thrives in the anaerobic (or oxygen-free) environment of canned food. (Both commercially canned and home-canned foods can carry the organism.) As it reproduces in the canned food, it creates a deadly nerve toxin.

The classic symptoms of botulism include double vision, blurred vision, drooping eyelids, slurred speech, difficulty swallowing, dry mouth, and muscle weakness. These are all signs of the muscle paralysis this bacterial toxin causes. If untreated, these symptoms may progress to cause full paralysis of the arms, legs, trunk, and respiratory muscles. In food-borne cases, symptoms generally begin eighteen to thirty-six hours after eating a contaminated food, but they can occur as early as six hours or as late as ten days after exposure.

Food-borne botulism is most often associated with home-canned foods that have a low acid content, such as asparagus, green beans, beets, and corn. However, there have also been reported outbreaks of botulism from more unusual sources, such as chopped garlic in oil, chile peppers, tomatoes, or improperly handled baked potatoes wrapped in aluminum foil.

Home canners should follow strict hygienic procedures to reduce contamination and must can low-acid foods with a pressure canner instead of a water bath. (The temperature in a water bath is not high enough to guarantee killing all C. botulinum organisms.)

Lemon
Spiced Pears

WATER BATH VS. PRESSURE

High acid foods that can be canned in a boiling water bath	Low acid foods that must be canned in a pressure canner
Apples	Artichokes
Apricots	Asparagus
Berries	Beans
Cherries	Beets
Citrus fruits	Cabbage
Currants	Carrots
Figs	Catsup**
Grapes	Corn
Peaches	Fish
Pears	Meats & Stews
Pickles & Relish	Okra
Plums	Peas
Rhubarb	Peppers
Stawberries	Salsa**
Tomatoes*	Sauces (barbeque, spaghetti, etc)**

Notes: *Add 1 tablespoon lemon juice per quart; **Some recipes have sufficient acid added in the form of lemon juice, lime juice, or vinegar to be canned in a boiling water bath

fruit butters, and preserves. Place jars in the kettle with at least two inches of water over the tops of the tallest jars and two inches of space between the top of the water and the top of the pot for boiling room.

You must use a pressure canner with low-acid vegetables, meats, and fish to protect against botulism. Pressure canners are safe if you follow the directions and make sure that the petcock and pressure gage are working properly. Each year when I first use my pressure canner, I test the petcock and the gage before beginning canning. To test a pressure canner, fill the canner with water but no jars and then seal it, but leave the petcock open. As soon as the water begins to boil, steam will escape through the petcock. If steam isn't escaping, there's a plug in the petcock and you need to clean it. If steam is escaping, close the petcock and watch the gage. It should begin to climb quickly. If it isn't climbing, you need to replace it.

You can pack jars using either the hot pack or raw pack method. For the hot pack method, prepare food (as in the case of sauces and spreads) or briefly boil (in water, syrup, or juice) and pack (while still hot) into preheated jars. Then add the cooking liquid or boiling water. For the raw pack method, pack raw foods in jars and cover with boiling water,

The canning of pears is well underway in the kitchen pictured on the opposite page. The canner has decided to spice up the stored pears by adding lemon. Lemon juice can also keep the pears a bright, light color.

This succulent ear of yellow corn looks ideal for eating fresh or using in the recipe for cream-style corn below. For the fruit cocktail recipe, you'll need a delicious mix of fruits, like those on the opposite page.

syrup, or juice. The hot pack method has several advantages over raw pack. Heated fruits are easier to pack into jars because they are softer. More fruit can be put into each jar because there is less floating fruit (air is drawn out of the tissues by cooking). Fewer jars are used for the same amount of food, and the processing time is usually shorter. Hot-packing better protects the color of light-colored fruits such as apples and peaches. Do not fill jars to the very top, but leave at least a half-inch of head space.

When you finish processing the food and the jars have cooled off, clean them with a damp cloth and check to make sure that the lids have sealed properly. Manufacturers design canning lids so that the raised button in the center of the lid flattens out if you've established a proper vacuum.

Fruit Cocktail

1½ lb. slightly underripe seedless grapes
¼ cup lemon juice mixed into 4 cups water
3 lb. peaches, ripe but firm
pot of water for boiling peaches
pot of ice water for stopping cooking process
3 lb. pears
10-oz. jar maraschino cherries
3 cups sugar
4 cups water

Stem and wash grapes. Soak grapes in the lemon-juice-and-water solution. Dip peaches, a few at a time, in a separate pot of boiling water for 1 to 1½ minutes to loosen skins. Dip in cold water and slip off skins. Cut in half, remove pits, cut into ½-inch cubes, and add to solution with grapes. Peel, halve, and core pears. Cut into ½-inch cubes, and combine with grapes and peaches. Place mixed-fruit pieces in a colander to drain excess liquid. Combine sugar and water in a saucepan and bring to boil to form syrup. Add ½ cup of hot syrup to each jar. Then add a few cherries and gently fill the jar with mixed fruit and more hot syrup, leaving ½-inch head space. Adjust lids and process. Yield: About 6 pints.

Cream-Style Corn

ears of corn*
water
salt
pepper

Select ears containing slightly immature kernels, or corn of ideal quality for eating fresh. Husk corn, remove silk, and wash ears. Blanch ears for 4 minutes in boiling water. With a sharp knife, cut corn from cob at about the center of kernels. Scrape the remaining corn from cobs with a table knife or butter knife. Blend the kernels and the scrapings in a bowl. Add salt and pepper to taste. Fill the jars, leaving ½-inch of head space. Adjust lids and process.

* Amount needed depends on the quantity you want to preserve. You need an average of two ears of sweet corn per pint. A bushel of sweet corn weighs 35 pounds and yields 12 to 20 pints.

Pickling

Above, a group of canned tomatoes wait to be put away for future recipes. Opposite, a freshly opened jar of pickled cucumbers offers up its contents to the viewer.

Harvest cucumbers no more than twenty-four hours before pickling, if at all possible, or you may end up with hollow pickles. Some varieties of cucumbers are not suitable for pickling and are only good for eating fresh. Pickling varieties have a nubbier texture than eating varieties.

When pickling foods, whole, fresh herbs and fresh spices provide the best flavor. Although you can leave some herbs, such as dill or chives, in the jars when the pickles are canned, you should remove most herbs and spices when the pickles are ready to go in the jars. The easiest way to do this is to place herbs and spices in a cheesecloth bag to infuse flavor during the pickling process, then just remove the bag before canning.

Mix vinegar and water, salt and water, or a combination of vinegar, salt, and water to make a brine solution for the pickles. Temper the brine solution to taste with a sweetener. Use a good-quality, aged vinegar product and salt labeled "pickling salt." Never use brown sugar as a sweetener unless the recipe you are following specifies it, because it tends to darken the pickles to an unappealing color. You can readily interchange white granulated sugar, honey, or corn syrup for sweetening, depending on your preference.

Although we usually think in terms of cucumber pickles, all kinds of produce can be pickled or made into relishes and chutneys. Experiment, pickling your favorite fruits and veggies—from asparagus tips to watermelon rind. And don't forget—you can also pickle other foods, such as eggs, fish, and meat. For basic information on pickling or some great new recipes (pickled mushroom tapas sounds likes a winner), check out www.picklenet.com.

The water, which is often the least thought-of ingredient, is actually crucial to pickle production. When you prepare pickles with water that is high in mineral content, or with soft water from a commercial water softener, the pickles may turn out mushy and unappetizing. If your water quality is a problem, try pickling with bottled, distilled water.

Pickled Cucumbers

- 6 lb, cleaned, sliced (¼-inch thick) pickling cucumbers
- 4 cups chopped onions
- ½ cup canning salt
- 4 cups ice cubes
- 4 cups vinegar
- 4 cups sugar
- 2 tbsp. celery seed
- 2 tbsp. mustard seed
- 1 tbsp. ground turmeric

Combine cucumbers, onions, and salt in a large bowl and mix well. Cover with 2 inches of ice cubes and refrigerate for 4 hours. Combine remaining ingredients in a large kettle and boil for 10 minutes. Drain the liquid from the cucumber/onion mix, and add the vegetables to the kettle. Bring back to a boil for 2 minutes. Pack pint jars, leaving ½-inch head space. Adjust lids and process in a boiling water canner for 10 minutes. Yield: 8 pints.

Tomato sauces and salsas

The best tomatoes for sauces and salsas are paste, or Italian, types. These create a thicker sauce, or salsa that sticks to a chip. If your garden is overrun by slicing tomatoes, you can mix them with paste tomatoes (shoot for 30 percent slicing tomatoes to 70 percent paste tomatoes) for a medium-thick sauce or salsa, or add tomato paste to the recipe to thicken it.

While the garlic above would be enough to make spaghetti sauce, you'll need a lot more, and a lot bigger, tomatoes than the ones shown in a basket opposite!

For recipes that call for peeled tomatoes, dip the tomatoes in boiling water until the skins begins to split (usually less than a minute) and then immediately place the tomatoes in cold water. After this double dip, you can easily peel off the skins.

Don't have the equipment or time to deal with canning your sauce or salsa? Try freezing it. Make your recipe. Once cooled, fill appropriate freezer containers and store in the freezer. The sauce or salsa will be slightly watery when thawed, but heating for a few minutes on the stovetop will cook off the water. For salsa, allow it to cool again before serving.

Spaghetti Sauce

- 30 lb. tomatoes
- 1 cup chopped onions
- 5 cloves garlic, minced
- 1 cup chopped celery or green peppers
- 1 lb. fresh mushrooms, sliced (optional)
- 1/4 cup vegetable oil
- 2 tbsp. oregano
- 4 tbsp. minced parsley
- 2 tsp. ground black pepper
- 4 1/2 tsp. salt
- 1/4 cup brown sugar

Wash tomatoes and dip in pot of boiling water for 30 to 60 seconds or until skins split. Dip in cold water and slip off skins. Remove cores and quarter tomatoes. Simmer 20 minutes, uncovered, in large saucepan. Put through food mill or sieve. Sauté onions, garlic, celery or peppers, and mushrooms (if desired) in vegetable oil until tender.

Add sautéed vegetables to tomatoes, and mix in remainder of spices, salt, and sugar. Bring to a boil, and as soon as the mixture boils, reduce heat and simmer, uncovered, until thick enough for serving (volume should reduce by nearly half). Stir frequently to avoid burning. Fill jars, leaving 1-inch head space. Adjust lids and process. Yield: about 9 pints.

Catsup

- 24 lb. ripe tomatoes
- 3 cups chopped onions
- 1 tsp. ground red pepper (cayenne)
- 4 tbsp. pumpkin pie spice
- 3 cups cider vinegar (5 percent)
- 1 1/2 cups sugar
- 1/4 cup salt

Wash tomatoes. Dip in boiling water for 30 to 60 seconds or until skins split. Dip in cold water. Slip off skins and remove cores. Quarter tomatoes and place in a 4-gallon stockpot or large kettle. Add onions and red pepper. Bring to a boil, then reduce heat and simmer for 20 minutes, uncovered. Turn off heat and let stand for 20 minutes.

Add spices and vinegar to the tomato mixture. Turn heat on and boil mixture for about 30 minutes. Put boiled mixture through a food mill or sieve. Return to pot. Add sugar and salt, and return to a gentle boil. Cook, stirring frequently, until the volume is reduced by half or until mixture rounds up on spoon without separating. Fill pint jars, leaving 1/8-inch head space. Adjust lids and process. Yield: 6 to 7 pints.

Crushed Tomatoes (with no added liquid)
(suitable for use in soups, stews, and casseroles)

tomatoes*
water
lemon juice
salt
pepper

Wash tomatoes and dip them in boiling water for 30 to 60 seconds or until skins split. Then dip in cold water, slip off skins, and remove cores. Trim off any bruised or discolored portions, and quarter the tomatoes. Heat 1/6 of the quarters quickly in a large pot, crushing them with a wooden meat mallet or spoon as you add them to the pot. This will exude juice. Continue heating the tomatoes, stirring to prevent burning.

Once the tomatoes are boiling, gradually add remaining quartered tomatoes, stirring constantly. Do not crush the remaining tomatoes. They will soften with heating and stirring. Continue until you've added all tomatoes, then boil gently for 5 minutes. Remove pot from the stove, and add 2 tablespoons of lemon juice per quart, or 1 per pint. Add salt and pepper to taste (1 teaspoon of salt per quart is a good amount) if desired. Fill jars immediately with hot tomatoes, leaving ½-inch head space. Adjust lids and process.

*You will need an average of 3 pounds of tomatoes per quart or 1½ pounds per pint. A bushel weighs 53 pounds and yields 17 to 20 quarts of crushed tomatoes.

Red chili peppers (above) and juicy red, green, and yellow tomatoes (opposite) make the perfect combination in salsas, sauces, and spicy marinades.

Tomato Taco Sauce

- 8 quarts peeled, cored, finely chopped paste tomatoes
- 2 cloves garlic, crushed
- 5 cups chopped onions
- 4 jalapeño peppers, seeded and chopped
- 4 long green chile peppers, seeded and chopped
- 2½ cups vinegar
- 2 tbsp. salt
- 1½ tbsp. black pepper
- 1 tbsp. sugar
- 2 tbsp. oregano leaves
- 1 tsp. ground cumin

Combine ingredients in a large saucepan. Bring to a boil, reduce heat, and simmer, stirring frequently until thick (about 1 hour). Ladle hot mixture into pint jars, leaving ½-inch head space. Adjust lids and process in a boiling water canner for 15 minutes.

Green and red bell peppers, cherry tomatoes, onions, mushrooms, and other freshly washed vegetables offer possibilities for all kinds of variations on the basic recipes at right.

Tomato/Green Chili Salsa (medium)

3 cups peeled, cored, chopped tomatoes 3 cups seeded, chopped long green chile peppers 3/4 cup chopped onions 1 jalapeño pepper, seeded, finely chopped 6 cloves garlic, finely chopped 1 1/2 cups vinegar 1/2 tsp. ground cumin 2 tsp. oregano leaves 1 1/2 tsp. salt	Combine all ingredients in a large saucepan and heat, stirring frequently, until boiling. Reduce heat and simmer for 20 minutes, stirring occasionally. Ladle the hot mixture into pint jars, leaving 1/2-inch head space. Adjust lids and process in a boiling water canner for fifteen minutes. Yield: 3 pints.

Tomato Salsa (mild)

4 cups peeled, cored, chopped tomatoes 2 cups seeded, chopped long green mild chile peppers 1 cup chopped onions 4 cloves garlic, finely chopped 2 cups vinegar 2 tsp. ground cumin 2 tbsp. fresh cilantro (or 2 tsp. dried cilantro) 1 1/2 tsp. salt	Combine all ingredients in a large saucepan and bring to a boil, stirring frequently. Reduce heat and simmer for 20 minutes, stirring occasionally. Ladle hot salsa into pint jars, leaving 1/2-inch head space. Adjust lids and process in a boiling water canner for 15 minutes. Yield: 4 pints.

Tomato Sauce

tomatoes* water salt	Wash tomatoes and dip them in boiling water for 30 to 60 seconds or until skins split. Then dip in cold water, slip off skins, and remove cores. Trim off any bruised or discolored portions, and quarter the tomatoes. Puree in a blender or food processor, then simmer in a large-diameter saucepan until sauce reaches desired consistency (reduce volume by about one-third for thin sauce or one-half for thick sauce). Add 1 teaspoon of salt per quart, if desired. Fill jars, leaving 1/4-inch head space. Adjust lids and process. *For thin sauce, you need an average of 5 pounds per quart or 2 pounds per pint. For thick sauce, you need an average of 6 1/2 pounds per quart or 3 pounds per pint.

Baked Beans

dried beans*
water
molasses sauce (recipe follows)
pork or bacon

Select mature, dry beans. Sort out and discard discolored beans, then wash and dry the remaining beans. Add 3 cups of water for each cup of dried beans. Bring to a boil for 2 full minutes, then remove from heat and soak for 1 hour.

Drain the beans (saving liquid for use in making sauce), and rinse under clean water. Heat to boiling again in fresh water. Reduce heat to medium and cook until beans are soft (3 to 6 hours depending on type of bean, heat, and atmospheric conditions). Prepare molasses sauce.

Place seven 3/4-inch pieces of pork or bacon in an earthenware crock or large casserole. Add beans and enough molasses sauce to just cover beans. Cover and bake for 4 to 5 hours at 350 degrees Fahrenheit. Add water as needed, about every hour. Fill jars, leaving 1-inch head space. Adjust lids and process 15 minutes.

* You will need an average of 3/4 pound of dried beans per quart of baked beans you want to yield. I like to cook up about 3 pounds of beans and process them in pint jars. Done this way, the recipe yields 6 pints.

Hot from the pot, a bowl of savory-sweet baked beans and pork is ready to eat.

Molasses Sauce

- 4 cups water or cooking liquid from beans
- 3 tbsp. dark molasses
- 3 tbsp. brown sugar, firmly packed
- 1 tbsp. vinegar
- 2 tsp. salt
- 3/4 tsp. powered dry mustard

Heat to boiling, then reduce heat to medium. Simmer for about 15 minutes, stirring frequently.

Jellies, jams, and other sweet things

When fruit is abundant, use it to create sweet spreads such as jelly, jam, and fruit butter. These sweets are preserved with added sugar (white sugar, corn syrup, or honey may be used), and many require the addition of pectin, which is a jelling agent, or acid.

Pectin is a naturally occurring jelling agent found in all fruits. Depending on the type of fruit and its ripeness, it may not be available in sufficient quantity to produce good spreads.

Preparing pectin is easy if you have access to plenty of sour apples (underripe eating apples, or crab apples). Wash and quarter ten pounds of sour apples; remove the stems but not the skins, cores, or seeds. In a large kettle, cover the apples with cold water and bring slowly to a boil over medium heat. Simmer at a low boil for 30 to 45 minutes, until the fruit is quite soft. Drain the fruit as you would for making juice (see the recipe on page 215), though you can also squeeze the pulp to get all the juice out for pectin production. Store the pectin in the refrigerator if you plan to use it within a few days; otherwise, store it in the freezer.

Quick recipes using commercially available pectin allow you to make spreads more quickly than the old method of cooking down the fruit in an open kettle. These recipes require far more sugar, however. Most fruits are acidic, but they may not have sufficient acid for proper jelling to occur. This is why many recipes call for the addition of lemon juice or vinegar.

I know some cooks who have been making fruit spreads since before I was born, who don't need to use a candy thermometer. But for those of us who were not indoctrinated in these skills as youngsters, a candy thermometer is an inexpensive, but very important, investment for producing spreads with the right consistency. The mixture of sugar and fruit or juice is usually cooked sufficiently when it reaches 220 degrees Fahrenheit for spreads other than butters (subtract two degrees for every 1,000 feet above sea level), or 300 degrees Fahrenheit for fruit butters.

Making jams, jellies, marmalades, and other spreads (above and opposite) are great ways to preserve any abundant crop of fruit. If combined with chocolate or nuts instead (below), the possibilities for fuity sweet treats are endless.

A delicious jam that bursts with the flavors of autumn (above) can be made from apples and pears fresh from the orchard (opposite).

Fruits can easily scorch when you are making spreads, so you must stay by the pot. Stir frequently and watch your candy thermometer. You can use oven-cooking techniques to reduce the likelihood of scorching, but cooking in the oven increases the time—and the energy—needed to prepare the spread.

Pear-Apple Jam

- 1 cup peeled, cored, and finely chopped apples
- 2 cups peeled, cored, and finely chopped pears (about 2 lb.)
- 1/4 tsp. ground cinnamon
- 6 1/2 cups sugar
- 1/4 cup bottled lemon juice
- 1/2 cup pectin

Crush apples and pears in a large saucepan and stir in cinnamon. Thoroughly mix sugar and lemon juice with fruits. Bring to a boil over high heat, stirring constantly. Immediately stir in pectin. Bring to a full rolling boil, and boil hard for 1 minute, stirring constantly. Remove from heat, quickly skim off foam, and fill sterile jars, leaving 1/4-inch head space. Adjust lids and process. Yield: about 7 to 8 half-pints.

Berry Syrup

You can easily use juices from fresh or frozen blueberries, cherries, grapes, raspberries (black or red), and strawberries to make toppings for ice cream and pastries.

Select 6 1/2 cups of fresh or frozen fruit of your choice. Wash, cap, and stem fresh fruit, and crush in a saucepan. Heat to boiling and simmer until soft (5 to 10 minutes). Strain through a colander, draining the liquid into a clean bowl. Let stand until liquid is cool enough to handle. Strain the collected juice again, this time through a double layer of cheesecloth or jelly bag. Discard the dry pulp. The yield of the pressed juice should be about 4 1/2 to 5 cups. Combine the juice with 6 3/4 cups sugar in a large saucepan; bring to a boil and simmer for 1 minute. (To make syrup with whole fruit pieces, save 1 to 2 cups of the fresh or frozen fruit, combine these with the sugar, and simmer as in making regular syrup.) Remove from heat, skim off foam, and fill into clean half-pint or pint jars, leaving 1/2-inch head space. Adjust lids and process. Yield: about 9 half-pints.

SWEET TREATS DEFINITIONS

- **Jelly** Made from clear, strained fruit juice with no pieces of fruit. You can prepare jelly from commercial fruit juice or from fruit juice you have extracted yourself.
- **Jam** Made from mashed fruit. Jam is the easiest spread to prepare. It is economical because it uses all the fruit pulp and requires only one cooking step.
- **Fruit butter** Made from mashed fruit with no added juice. You make fruit butter by cooking down mashed fruit until it naturally thickens.
- **Marmalade** Made from mashed fruit, chopped fruit, and citrus fruits or citrus rind in fruit juice.
- **Preserves** Made from whole berries or large chunks of fruit in juice.
- **Conserves** Made from whole berries or large chunks of fruit in a small amount of fruit juice. May include several different fruits .

GELLING PROPERTIES OF FRUIT

Fruits that normally have sufficient pectin and acid to gel	Fruits that benefit from additional pectin or acid	Fruits that will require additional pectin or acid
Apples (green or crab)	Apples (ripe)	Apricots
Blackberries (sour)	Blackberries (ripe)	Cherries (sweet)
Cranberries	Blueberries	Grapes (Western)
Grapes (Eastern)	Cherries (sour)	Pears
Lemons or limes	Grape juice	Peaches
Plums	Oranges 	Raspberries
Quinces		Strawberries

Note: To test fruit to find out if it needs added pectin, mix 1 tablespoon of cooked fruit or fruit juice with 1 tablespoon of rubbing alcohol. When the fruit has sufficeint pectin, this mixture will coagulate into a clump. (Throw test samples away, as alcohol is poisonous.) If it doesn't clump into a single blob, you should add pectin and acid.

Fruit juice

You can prepare fruit juice for drinking or for cooking (including its use as the critical ingredient in jellies and other spreads). To prepare fruit juice, wash the fruit and drain it well. For large, round fruits such as apples or pears, quarter them, core them, and remove the stems; for berries and grapes, remove stems. Crush fruit that will lie on the bottom of the kettle, and if the fruit doesn't have a good deal of natural juice, add about half-up of water to keep the fruit from sticking to the pan. Begin cooking over low heat and stir frequently. As you draw natural moisture from the fruit, increase the heat to medium. Some dry fruits (such as apples) may require more water, but add it in small amounts (a quarter-cup at a time) so you don't overdilute. Continue to cook fruit until it loses its color.

After you've cooked down the fruit, collect the liquid in a pot. Do this by pouring the mash and juice into a wet jelly bag or into a colander or strainer lined with wet cheesecloth (or unbleached and undyed muslin kitchen towels kept for this purpose). To get the clearest juice, do not squeeze the bag, but let it drain naturally (overnight works well).

A colorful display of homemade fruit juices, in bottles of all shapes and sizes, decorates a table (above). Grapes such as pinot noir (opposite) make excellent juices (not just wines).

GRAPE JUICE

grapes*
water
sugar

Select sweet, well-colored, firm, mature fruit of ideal quality for eating fresh. Wash and stem the grapes and place them in a saucepan; add boiling water to cover grapes. Heat and simmer slowly until skins are soft. Strain through a damp jelly bag or double layers of cheesecloth. Refrigerate juice for 24 to 48 hours without mixing, carefully pour off clear liquid and save; discard sediment. If desired, strain through a paper coffee filter for a clearer juice. Add juice to a saucepan and sweeten to taste. Heat and stir until sugar dissolves. Continue heating, stirring occasionally, until juice begins to boil. Fill jars immediately, leaving 1/4-inch head space. Adjust lids and process for 15 minutes.

* You need an average of 24 1/2 pounds per canner load of 7 quarts, or an average of 16 pounds per canner load of 9 pints. A lug weighs 26 pounds and yields 7 to 9 quarts of juice—an average of three and a half pounds per quart.

CHAPTER 9

Preserving the Harvest: Dairy and Meat

DAIRY PRODUCTS AND MEAT FROM YOUR OWN ANIMALS that have had access to plenty of sunshine and fresh air, good pasture and clean water can't be beat. They provide not only great flavor but also more micronutrients, such as omega-3 fatty acids, conjugated linoleic acid, and vitamin E, than their feed-lot or factory-farm counterparts.

DAIRY PRODUCTS

Milk is a mother's food for its young, but with a dairy cow or dairy goats, you can also have your own fresh milk and produce your own butter, cheese, ice cream, and yogurt. A larger herd of dairy animals may also provide an enterprise. Even if you don't own dairy animals, you can make homemade dairy products with purchased milk or cream.

Milking is typically done twice a day, as close to 12-hour intervals as possible. Commercial-scale operations will require a milking machine, but for a cow or a couple of goats, you can get by hand milking. Hand milking isn't

Hard and soft cheeses, cream, sour cream, yogurt, cottage cheese, and butter (above and below) are among the multitude of products you can make with milk from your dairy cows or goats. Or just enjoy a delicious glass of milk at breakfast (opposite).

hard, but it takes some time to get the hang of it. Put the animal in a stanchion (a head-holding device) or restrain her with a rope halter. Clean the animal's udder and teats with warm soapy water. After they are clean, wash your hands, and then dip each teat in an iodine-based teat dip solution, which is available from farm supply stores or by catalog (see Resources).

Now that Bessie is ready, sit down beside her on a milking stool, and lightly grasp one teat in one hand, as though you were making a fist around the teat. Squeeze your hand together and apply a slight downward pressure as you do so. Release the pressure, and reapply it in a smooth motion. Discard the first several squirts of milk and collect the rest in a bucket. Milk each teat until you fully strip it of milk. This sounds easy, but at first it is really challenging, and your hands will probably begin cramping before you have fully drained the animal's udder. However, once you (and your animal) get in the groove, you can do it rather quickly, and you can milk two teats at once. Once you have stripped out all four teats (two in the case of goats), re-dip each teat in iodine solution and apply a thin coat of udder balm to keep the teats from becoming dry and cracked.

Cleanliness is critical from start to finish in dairying. Keeping your hands and the animal's teats clean during the actual milking process is crucial to preventing mastitis. I recommend purchasing a California Mastitis Test (CMT) kit if you plan to milk your animals. The kit is very inexpensive. It comes with a paddle-like device and a bottle of reagent. Test at least once a week by stripping the first few squirts of milk out of each teat; then squirt a little milk into each cup on the paddle. Add a few drops of reagent, then gently swirl the paddle with a back-and-forth rocking motion of your wrist. If the animal has mastitis starting, the milk/reagent solution will begin gelling. In advanced cases it will instantly clump together. There are a number of treatments for mastitis, so contact a veterinarian if an animal shows positive on the test.

A farmer in Poland strains raw milk into a milk can (above); a German farmer milks one of his cows out in the pasture (below). Though the equipment may differ, the basics elements of milk production are similar the world over.

Milk

Many people who come from nonfarm backgrounds worry about drinking unpasteurized milk. We drank our own raw milk all the time, as did all the dairy farmers we knew. If you use a CMT, you will know that the milk coming from the animal is safe. But, milk is excellent food not only for animals, but also for bacteria, so cleanliness must extend from milking time right through the time when you consume your milk or dairy products. Keep all utensils squeaky clean. You can purchase a home pasteurizer from many farm supply stores if you are uncomfortable using raw milk.

Milk from the store is not only pasteurized, it is also homogenized. Homogenization is a process of breaking up the fat globules in cream to such a small size that they remain suspended evenly in the milk, rather than separating out and floating to the surface.

Since you haven't homogenized your milk when it comes from the animal, the cream will separate and float to the top. You can leave the cream with the milk or skim it off the top for use in coffee or in making butter.

Many dairy products require cooking within specific temperature ranges. A thermometer with a range of 32 to 225 degrees Fahrenheit is an indispensable tool.

Butter

You can prepare butter as sweet-cream and sour-cream types. Sweet-cream butter has a much milder flavor than sour-cream butter, but it takes longer for the fat particles to coagulate than if you allow the cream to "sour" at room temperature for a day. One quart of cream will yield about one pound of butter and half-quart of buttermilk. Cream that has aged for several days in the fridge before using makes better butter than cream that just came from the critter.

You have probably seen butter churns in antique stores. They are still available from farm suppliers, though they are kind of expensive if you won't be preparing a lot of butter

regularly. For small amounts of your own butter for home use, the method I use is easy and quick: Use a wide-mouth, pint-size canning jar (you can reuse clean canning lids for this application). Fill the jar about halfway so there is plenty of room for agitation. Add a dash of salt (up to a teaspoon depending on taste) and then begin shaking the jar to agitate the cream.

Agitating incorporates air into the cream and causes it to increase in volume, so that the butter granules gather together. It is best done when the cream's temperature is between 54 and 58 degrees Fahrenheit in summer, or 58 and 64 degrees Fahrenheit in winter. At first, the cream begins to take up the entire volume, but quite suddenly butter granules begin to form and buttermilk separates out. When the granules form, continue shaking, but don't shake too vigorously or you will whip the butter, making it more difficult to handle. When the butter granules have become gruel-like, pour off the buttermilk (pigs, chickens, dogs, or cats will enjoy this treat), and then wash the butter granules with cold water, working them together with a wooden spoon. Wash and work with the spoon several more times until the liquid you pour off is fairly clear. Now your butter can be hand-formed into a block or packed into a mold to give a more pleasing shape. This approach yields about ¼-pound of butter in less than a half hour.

On the porch of her family's farm, a little girl churns butter (above). A ripe strawberry swims in a bowl of creamy yogurt (below). Enjoying fresh, homemade dairy products is one of the sweetest rewards of country life.

Yogurt

Yogurt is a fermented milk product that originated in the Middle East. You ferment yogurt through the addition of *Lactobacillus* bacteria (either *L bulgaricus or L acidophilus*) and *Streptococcus thermophilus*. These bacteria produce lactic acid during fermentation, which lowers the pH and causes the milk protein to thicken. The partial digestion of the milk makes yogurt easily digestible.

The acidity of yogurt inhibits the growth of bad bacteria, so if the lids are on properly, a container of yogurt will keep at least a month or two in the refrigerator. Baked goods rise

Yogurt Dip

Ingredients	Directions
1 pint of plain yogurt 2 tbsp. mayonnaise 1 package dry ranch-style salad dressing mix, or dry French onion soup and dip mix 1 tsp. Worcestershire sauce	Blend ingredients well. Chill at least 3 hours before serving.

well when you use yogurt, again due to its acidity. When you use yogurt as part or all of the liquid in cakes, waffles, pancakes, and muffins, cut down on the amount of baking powder.

Factors that are crucial for successful yogurt making include using good sterile technique (proper cleansing of tools and containers and keeping out unwanted bacteria), controlling incubation temperature between 100 and 122 degrees Fahrenheit (the temperature range that inhibits the growth of pathogenic bacteria, yet is ideal for the good bacteria that do the fermenting), and protection of the starter from contamination. Starter is just plain yogurt (store bought or from a previous batch). The degree of tartness of your finished yogurt depends on the time you ferment it. You ferment mild yogurt less than tart yogurt. At 100 degrees mild yogurt takes about 6 to 8 hours (at 122 degrees it takes about 3 to 4 hours).

To prepare yogurt, warm 4 cups of milk in a pot over medium heat (in a heavy pot or double boiler) until it just starts to boil, stirring continually. As soon as it begins to boil, remove the pot from the burner and set it in the sink in cold water. Ladle about 1/2 cup from the heated milk to a bowl or your measuring cup and place in the fridge for about 10 minutes. Add 1/2 cup of starter to the cooled milk from the fridge, and mix thoroughly. Once the milk that has been cooling in the pot reaches 122 degrees, return the starter/milk mix to the pot, and stir until you've distributed the starter well. For richer yogurt, substitute 1/4 cup of heavy cream for 1/4 cup of milk.

Pour the mix into sterilized canning jars (you can add chopped, canned fruit and a little syrup—or other flavors—to the bottom of the jar before adding the yogurt), and cover with new canning lids. Although making yogurt is a most-of-the-day job (it is a great project for rainy or snowy days), once it is in the jars it isn't too distracting. Keep the mix at a temperature between 100 and 122 degrees Fahrenheit until it has fermented. After fermentation, clean the jars and store them in the fridge. The way I do this is by setting the yogurt jars in my canning kettle after the water in the kettle has reached about 122 degrees. (In the winter, I place the pot on the wood stove; in the summer on the eye on the cook stove, set at a medium setting.) I take the kettle off the heat source until the temperature gets down to about 100 degrees and then reheat it to 122 degrees, repeating this step until the mix turns to yogurt. It usually takes only a short time to bring the kettle up to 122 degrees, and it takes a couple of hours to get it down to about 100 degrees. For a typical batch I might have to reheat the kettle three times during the day.

If your only experience with yogurt is the kind you buy in the store, the first thing that you'll notice that's different about your homemade yogurt is the whey (or yellow liquid) that forms on top. This is just the water-fraction of the milk, and it should be there. You can purchase a strainer (see Lehman's catalog listed in the Resources for this, and other handy equipment) if you want to get rid of all the whey, but I usually just pour it off (a favorite of my dogs) before I eat the yogurt.

I generally make plain yogurt and add fruit, nuts, or flavors as I use it. Plain is great for baking (substitute yogurt for up to ½ the liquid in your favorite recipes), or in dips and sauces that call for sour cream. The recipe yields two 1-pint jars of plain yogurt.

Cheese

You'll find cheese throughout the world, with almost every culture preparing some form. You can make it not only from cow's or goat's milk, but also from the milk of sheep, horses, buffaloes, or yaks. All cheeses fall into one of three categories: hard, soft, or cottage cheese. Hard cheeses (such as cheddar) require aging, and are more complicated to make, though they can be stored for long periods. You make soft cheeses the same way as hard cheese, but they are aged for a shorter time. Cottage cheese is a soft cheese that you do not allow to age. You can easily make soft and cottage cheeses at home without any specialized equipment. They have a refrigerator life of five to ten days.

The basic ingredients of cheese are:

- **Milk:** You can make cheese from whole milk, 2 percent milk, or skimmed milk, though the cheese's richness correlates with the amount of milk fat.
- **Rennet:** An enzyme—rennin—converts the protein, or casein, in milk from a soluble form to an insoluble form, causing the milk to clump. Rennet is commonly available in supermarkets in the pudding section, or you can purchase liquid rennet from a cheese-maker's supply house.
- **Starter:** You must add bacteria to acidify the milk so that the rennet will work and to aid in the curing. Cultured buttermilk or yogurt can serve as starter, or you can purchase pure cultures from a cheese-maker's supply house.

Sharp cheddar, creamy Swiss, and savory brie are just a few of the countless varieties of cheese made around the world.

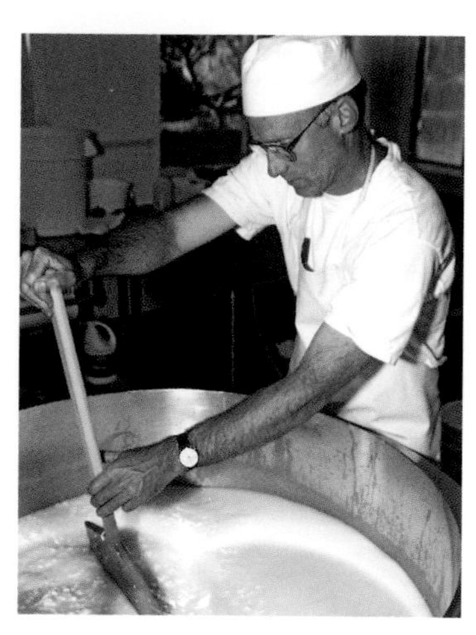

In Oregon, a farm owner stirs a vat of curds in the process of making goat cheese.

Neufchâtel

This is a soft cheese that is easy to make at home.

- 1 gal. of whole milk
- 1/4 cup cultured buttermilk or 1/2 cup plain yogurt
- 1 tablet rennet dissolved in 1 cup water (or five drops if you are using liquid rennet)
- 3 tsps. salt

1. Place the milk in the upper part of a double boiler, adding enough water in the bottom to prevent milk from scorching. Stir in buttermilk or yogurt starter and warm slowly to a temperature between 92 and 94 degrees Fahrenheit. Try to maintain this temperature through the next two steps.
2. Add the rennet and whisk into the milk/starter mixture for 2 to 3 minutes. Allow the mixture to set undisturbed for about 30 minutes or until a firm gel forms. To test for curd formation, cut a slit in the curd with a metal spatula, then slip it under the curd. As you lift with the spatula, if the cut in the curd breaks cleanly from the spatula, move onto the next step; if it is like gelatin sticking to the spatula, allow to rest longer.
3. Cut the curd into 1-inch cubes, and stir gently and continuously for 20 to 30 minutes to help firm curds.
4. Pour off whey. Allow the curds to settle and dip out the remaining whey.
5. Add 1 teaspoon salt and mix gently. Wait 5 minutes and mix in the second teaspoon of salt. Wait 5 more minutes and mix in the last teaspoon of salt. You can also add other flavors to your Neufchâtel by stirring in spices, diced dry fruits or vegetables, liquid smoke, or pepper sauce at this time.
6. Next, apply pressure using a cheese press, or create your own cheese press by poking several holes (from the inside out) in two 1-pound coffee cans. Line the cans with clean cheesecloth or muslin. Place half of the cheese curd inside each lined can. Fold the cloth over the top. Cut the plastic lids of the coffee cans so that they just fit inside the cans, and drop the lids onto the tops of the folded cloths. Apply pressure by placing a can of food on each plastic top, and allow it to press down on the cheese so the whey is forced out. Do this in the sink to allow the whey to drain out of cans. Keep the pressure on for 3 to 4 hours.
7. Remove the formed cheese and the cloth. Wrap the cheese tightly in plastic or in waxed paper and store in refrigerator. It will keep for seven to ten days in the refrigerator. You can freeze cheese for four to six months. However, freezing lowers the quality.

MEAT

Butchering involves the actual slaughtering and cutting of animals for meat. Processing is taking raw meat and making some other type of product through the addition of other ingredients (such as beans, tomatoes, onions, peppers, and spices for chili), or through specialized handling, such as smoking. With the exception of poultry (which you can generally butcher on the farm for direct marketing), I'm not going to go into the actual processes involved in butchering and processing. If you want to learn the techniques to butcher your own large animals, get a copy of Dr. John Mettler's book, *Basic Butchering of Livestock and Game* (see Resources) or check with your extension agent for a booklet on butchering.

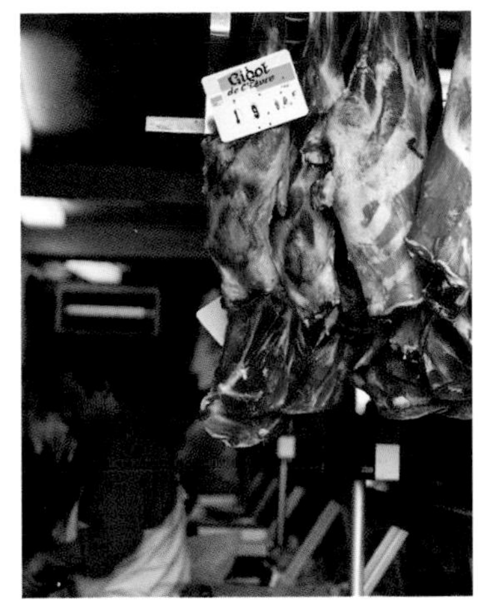

Beef hanging in a butcher's window (above) and skillfully cut short ribs (below) are familiar sights. Many hobby farmers find that raising their own livestock for meat is more challenging, but ultimately more rewarding, than purchasing meat at the local market.

Butchering Large Animals

What I do want to go over are some things you'll need to know about butchering and processing if you plan to raise animals for meat. For instance, how much meat will a 1,000-pound steer actually yield? How do you respond when the butcher asks if you want the short ribs? Or, what do you say to a first-time customer who is considering purchasing a lamb, but wants to know how much meat they'll receive, and how much freezer space it will take up?

When a butcher uses the term yield, he or she is generally referring to the "hanging" weight. The term comes from the fact that butchers hang a carcass on a rail attached to the ceiling of the cutting room to make their work easier. Typical hanging yields are:

- Lamb—50 to 55 percent of live weight
- Beef—60 to 65 percent of live weight
- Pork—70 to 75 percent of live weight

Depending on the type of animal and the age of the animal, you can either cut it up immediately, or hang it in a cooler for up to two weeks to age the meat. Aging helps cure meat, improving flavor, texture, and tenderness.

A variety of fresh, uncooked meats covers the surface of this table. Though you may not see such a spread in your own home, you should learn as much as possible about the butchering and processing of any animal you raise for meat.

The meat yield depends on how closely you trim the fat, and on how many "bone-in" cuts you prepare. Typical meat yields are:

- Lamb—40 to 45 percent of live weight
- Beef—45 to 50 percent of live weight
- Pork—55 to 60 percent of live weight

So, a 250-pound hog will hang on the rail at about 185 pounds, and when you pick up the packages of meat, you will receive about 140 pounds of meat. A 1,000-pound, grass-finished steer will hang around 650 pounds and yield 500 pounds of meat.

On average, cut and wrapped meat requires one cubic foot of freezer space for each thirty-five pounds of meat. The meat from a whole steer will almost fill a fifteen-cubic-foot chest freezer. The pig will require four cubic feet, which is about the size of the freezer space in a large combination refrigerator/freezer, but it is too much for a smaller combo unit. The lamb will fit into the freezer compartment of a small refrigerator/freezer.

When you drop off an animal at the butcher's shop, the butcher wants to know your "cutting orders." The cutting orders are simply the directions that tell him or her how you want the animal cut and wrapped. The first thing to tell your butcher is how you want the animal trimmed. Trimming is simply cutting away external fat. We go for well-trimmed meat, and our ground beef is 95 percent lean. At the same time, some processed meat products do benefit from the addition of some extra fat from the trimmings. We had all-beef wieners prepared one time, with no additional fat added, and they were too dry. Luckily, Karen, the woman who took cutting orders at the time, warned us that all-beef wieners might be too dry, so we only had a few pounds made up to try them.

The butcher also needs to know how many steaks, chops, and such you want in each package, and how thick to cut them. We have found—particularly if you plan to direct market meat—that packages with two steaks or chops are a good size. We have also found that that three-quarter-inch-thick cuts seem to be ideal for most steaks and chops. Most of the meat from the round (the butt) and the chuck (the shoulder) is best ground.

The first time we took a steer in to have it butchered, Karen asked if we wanted the short ribs. I stared kind of dumbly, and said, "Well, I don't know. Why?" She went on to explain that most people didn't take the short ribs because they're really tough and stringy and there isn't much meat on them. I didn't take them that first time, but the next time we took in a steer, I decided to keep them. By this point I was thinking they'd at least be dog food if nothing else. I also told her we wanted all of the organ meat—even the tongue—as well as packages of soup bones and boxes of bones for our dogs. Our policy became, "get everything back, because something will eat it."

Short ribs are, true to their reputation, stringy and tough when prepared by most conventional cooking methods. But we discovered they're actually pretty darn good if cooked in a pressure cooker. The technique: put about one inch of water in the bottom of the pressure cooker, load in the short ribs, pour some barbecue sauce over the top and pressure cook them for about forty-five minutes. After this treatment, they fall off the bone, and taste great, though they are messy.

Lamb, bison, deer, and elk all have similar cutting orders to beef, but pork is different. The butcher will want to know if you want hams or fresh roasts. Hams are cured (smoked) roasts. Like the hams, bacon is cured "side pork," and we have found that side pork is quite delicious. You can make the front shoulder of a hog into a picnic ham or slice it for pork-shoulder bacon. Pork-shoulder bacon is nice lean meat, much like Canadian bacon. There is lots of "trim" on a hog (and it isn't all fat) so plan on getting lots of sausage made.

HASTY HASH

1 lb. ground meat (beef, lamb, or game) 1 tbsp. oil 1 small onion, diced ½ tsp. salt ½ tsp. garlic powder ½ tsp. black pepper 4 tbsp. soy sauce 2 cups shredded raw potato (or defrosted, packaged hash browns)	Sauté the meat with oil until it is no longer pink; add onions and sauté until they are transparent. Stir in spices and soy sauce, and mix well with meat and onions. Layer potatoes on top of meat, cover pan, and cook on medium heat for 20 minutes, stirring gently from time to time. Uncover and turn the heat up a little; stir and cook until potatoes start to brown.

Butchering Poultry

Butchering poultry isn't fun, but farmers usually do it at home if raising chickens for meat. If you're planning to butcher many birds, you need to develop an assembly-line approach to butchering (or find a poultry packer). When starting out with a small number of birds for home use—or to begin assessing your production and marketing strategies for a commercial enterprise—the following directions work.

1. It is best if the birds you plan to butcher have been "starved" for 24 hours before you butcher them. This helps pass the contents of the digestive tract out—so you have less to deal with. They should still have access to water.
2. There are many ways to actually dispatch the bird. Though killing any animal isn't a pleasant task, each of these methods, when done correctly, is quick and humane: ringing the neck, chopping off the head, or slitting the throat.(See sidebar on page 228.)
3. After you kill the bird, allow it to bleed out for a couple of minutes. By "bleeding" the animal, the meat remains cleaner, and less likely to spoil.
4. Scalding loosens the feathers, making plucking easier. Submerge the bird in the scald bucket for about 40 seconds by holding it by the feet, and dunking it headfirst (130-degree water works for a small bird, and 140-degree for a large bird). If your scald water gets a little too cool, you'll need to leave the bird in longer; if it gets too hot, the bird will be over scalded, which results in "cooked" meat. Swishing the bird around a little in the bucket helps to move the heat around all the feathers. When doing multiple birds, try to keep the scald water fairly clean, as scald water can be a source of contamination. If the birds are dirty, hose them off prior to scalding.
5. Pick feathers immediately after scalding. When picking by hand, it's easiest if you hang the bird back up, so you're working at a comfortable height. Pull the feathers down and away from the body. If the scalding temperature was right, most of the feathers will come off fairly easy. If you plan on butchering lots of birds, a rubber-fingered "plucker" makes the job easier.
6. After picking most of the feathers, rinse the bird with cool water to reveal any remaining feathers and the pinfeathers. This rinse isn't in your cold-water bucket. Rinse with a garden hose or under a faucet.

7. Scrape off pinfeathers with a short, dull knife, or pick them out with tweezers. Singe any hairs with a propane torch (older birds have more hairs than young ones do). A method that is commonly used with waterfowl (they have lots of down and pinfeathers) is to dip the bird in hot wax (150 degrees Fahrenheit), then dip it in cold water to set the wax, and finally peel the wax away. The bird may require a second dip.

From this point forward, you may find it easier to work on a cutting table than with the bird hanging. Try both approaches.

8. Remove the head by cutting just below the first vertebra in the neck and then twisting off.
9. To remove the neck, first insert the thin knife in the skin above the neck, at the shoulders, and cut forward to open the skin. Then pull the skin away from the neck. Next, pull the crop, the trachea (or windpipe), and the gullet away from the neck skin, and cut off where they enter the body. Finally, cut the neck off where it enters the shoulders by cutting the muscle around the bone and then twisting off. Wash the neck, then set aside in your bucket of ice water.
10. About 1 inch in front of the oil "nipple" on the tail, make a clean cut all the way down to the vertebra in the tail. Then cut out the oil gland, by cutting from front to back, and scooping out the gland.

BUTCHERING TOOLS AND METHODS

Tools you need for butchering poultry

- Two sharp knives, one paring style, about three to four inches long, and one thin boning knife, about four to five inches long. If you don't know how to correctly sharpen knives, learn. (The best instructions I know of are in *Joy of Cooking*, the cookbook.)
- One short, dull knife, or tweezers.
- Three, five gallon buckets; one to catch blood and guts, one for the hot water, and one for the cold water.
- Hot water for scalding--ideal temperature is between 130 and 140 degrees Fahrenheit.
- Cold water for rinsing and cooling the bird--the colder the better. Add some ice cubes to keep it very cold.
- A trash can for feathers and offal. You can bury these in a compost pile after you're done, but place them deep in the pile so they don't attract vermin and so they heat up sufficiently to kill off bacteria.
- A small propane torch to singe hairs.
- A system to continuously heat the water for scalding.
- For those considering larger-scale production, consider adding an automated plucker--available from NASCO (see Resources).

Methods for killing a chicken

- Wringing a bird's neck is an old and somewhat lost skill. Pick up the bird by its head and swing it completely around in a 360-degree circle. If you use this method, hang up the bird after it is dead and cut its throat, as described below.
- Chopping off the head with an ax on a block is also an old method, though somewhat messy.
- The most common method in use today: Hang the bird upside down with its feet tied, or in a killing cone. Using a sharp knife, slit the bird's throat by making a cut directly behind the lower jaw, but try to avoid cutting through the esophagus and windpipe. When you cut the bird's throat, you cut the jugular vein; a bucket underneath the bird will catch the blood and make cleanup easier.

Evisceration methods

- *For smaller birds* Starting just below the point of the breastbone, insert the thin knife just enough to penetrate the skin and muscle. Cut down toward the vent (anus) and then cut all the way around it. When cutting around the vent, keep the knife pressed as close as possible to the back and tail. Pull the vent and a small section of the large intestine out of the way.
- *For larger birds* Make a half moon cut around the vent, pressing closely to tail and backbone. Insert your index finger into the cut and up and over the intestines. Pulling the intestines down, and out of the way, continue to cut around the vent until you have completed the circle. Pull the vent and a short section of the intestines out of the way. Next, pull the skin back toward the breastbone, then make a side-to-side cut about 3 inches wide and 2 inches below the breastbone. Finally, pull the bar of skin that remains backward and over the piece of vent and intestines.

11. Remove the shank (the lower part of the leg and foot) by cutting through the hock joint from the inside surface.
12. The next step is evisceration (removal of the animal's internal organs). This process takes practice to become adept at, so take your time when learning to do it. If you accidentally cut through the intestines, and release their contents onto the meat, you have contaminated it. There are two methods: one that is appropriate for small birds that you won't truss for roasting, and another that is appropriate for large roasting birds such turkeys. (See sidebar.)
13. Insert your hand into the abdominal opening and begin gently working your way up and around, loosening organs from the body cavity as you go. When all attachments are broken, scoop the insides out.
14. You should remove the gizzards, liver, and heart from the rest of the entrails. Cut the gizzard away from the stomach and intestines. Peel away the fat, split it open, and rinse well; add to ice water. Trim off the heart sac and heavy vessels from around heart, rinse, and add to ice water. Pinch the gall bladder off of the liver, rinse the liver, and add to ice water. (Discard gall bladder.) Retrieve the gizzard from the ice water and peel away the lining by inserting a fingernail under the lining at the cut edge and pulling away. Now, retrieve the gizzard from the ice water, and peel the lining away by inserting a fingernail under the lining at the cut edge and pull away. Return the gizzard to ice water.
15. Use your hands to check along the backbone for any remaining organs (the lungs and sexual organs are often still in the bird). Remove any you find. Rinse the bird well under running water, both inside the body cavity and on the outside of the carcass. When the carcass is clean, add to your ice-water bucket to chill. Chilling time varies depending on the size of the bird and the temperature of the water, but it may take several hours. The goal is to get the carcass temperature down to about 40 degrees Fahrenheit as quickly as possible. Once the carcass is adequately chilled, hang to drain for about ten minutes. While the carcass is draining, wrap the heart, liver, and gizzard in plastic wrap. Insert the neck and the wrapped organs into the carcass.
16. Finally, bag the bird, and label.

Chicken or Turkey Stock

Place carcass bones, with some meat still affixed, in a large kettle and cover with water. Bring to a boil, but reduce heat as soon as the water begins to boil. Simmer, uncovered, for 45 minutes, frequently spooning off the scum that forms during the cooking process. Add 1 cup chopped celery and 1 cup chopped onion. Simmer for an additional hour, continuing to spoon off scum. Strain mixture. Return to a boil, and then ladle into jars immediately, leaving 1/4-inch head space. Adjust lids and process.

EGGS
1.50
MAY 13 H
6
LARGE
U.S.

CHAPTER 10

Agripreneurship

FIRST, THE DISCLAIMER FOR THIS CHAPTER: I THINK MOST new and aspiring farmers harbor a hope that they can make some money off their operation. Maybe they just hope to sell a few foals from their brood mares to help pay for the feed and vet bills, or maybe they dream of a fully functioning value-added farming operation that will support their family in some level of comfort and security without an outside job.

You probably remember the Kevin Costner film *Field of Dreams*. In it Costner plays a baseball-loving farmer, who creates a baseball diamond in his cornfield. Needless to say, everyone thinks he is crazy—and perhaps he is, but his "build it and they will come" attitude somehow carries the story through to a fulfilling ending. It's a nice story, but it is a just a story.

Unfortunately, a lot of people who go into business for themselves (be it farming or some other type of small business) start down the business road with a *Field of Dreams* frame of mind: Build your business, and they will come.

Above, boxed apples are ready for market. Opposite, the owner of Juniper Grove Farm in Oregon, cradling two farm residents, proudly displays a variety of goat cheeses he has produced.

But business isn't a story, and to get customers to come to your business takes a great deal of planning and hard work to create a marketable product, followed by promotion, promotion, promotion—and more promotion. Even then, it is a hard row to hoe. If you think you will raise those few foals and make a profit suitable to keep the family comfortable on a single job, or if you think that the one-acre market garden or CSA will, in and of itself, result in an Eddie Bauer lifestyle of comfort and security while providing the world with wonderful veggies, think again. Unless you are *savvy*, and *lucky*, and *inexhaustible*, and *fueled by a good bit of capital*, it will be a challenge to break even; you certainly won't yield the equivalent of a real-world salary.

Now in spite of the disclaimer: Those who are willing to do the work of developing value-added, or alternative-enterprise approaches, have the potential to make a small farm into a successful, and sometimes, very profitable business. There are plenty of examples out there of people doing unusual things in and around agriculture, and doing them quite well. They are making good and comfortable incomes doing something they love.

The success stories (read some later in this chapter) all highlight people who have figured out how to deliver what consumers want. Consumers are:

• looking for local, fresh, organically or naturally grown products and are often willing to pay extra for them

• becoming interested in how and where their food is raised and produced and in how that production affects their health, the environment and society

• looking for opportunities that small farms can provide, such as educational activities, outdoor recreational activities, and agritourism.

FARM MARKETS

Traditional farmers raise commodity products, such as corn, soybeans, beef, and pork, and sell them through the commodity distribution system. For example, they sell their livestock at a local sale barn or their grain to the local elevator. If they are producing on a large enough scale, they may get into the futures market to try to increase profits, but this only works for the big guys. In the commodities game, external forces set prices, and you can't do much to differentiate yourself or your product. Commodity producers continually struggle to sell enough product to make ends meet.

HARD TIMES

In 1988, Stephanie Caughlin, a San Diego CSA operator, started a farm on ten acres. She started out selling her produce at local farmer's markets. But as the years passed, the markets proliferated, so government regulatory bodies got involved, creating arduous rules. At the same time, "the payment of a percentage of our gross to the managers became too great to keep up with." So in 1997, Stephanie got out of the markets and began operating a CSA subscription farm that delivered fresh food to area residents. Her clients received a wide variety of vegetables, fruit, herbs, flowers, and fresh eggs.

Today, sprawling growth has hemmed in her farm, yet business is down. She tells me, "This farmette is a priceless jewel in a sea of freeways and housing developments. I have had visitors from all over the world; everyone raves. Yet, it's like people think, someone else is buying our products so they don't have to. And we are not the only ones—talk to any of the growers at the local farmers markets and they too are barely hanging on. Most of us are fifty-five and older and I know of no young growers starting up. Looks like McDonald's slogan of 'One taste worldwide' will be true soon."

Stephanie is savvy and hard-working, yet she says, "Honestly, right now business is so bad and the stress so great that there is no satisfaction, only sorrow at facing selling my land after twenty-six years developing it."

A display of newly picked flowers and vegetables (above); an array of golden syrups from small enterprises on a stand (below); and woven baskets of fresh-from-the-garden beets, radishes, and peppers (opposite) are all familiar sights at a farmer's market. The direct market appeal is one aspect that sets such products apart from those found in big grocery stores.

Selling value-added products, or running an alternative enterprise, offers the opportunity to increase income by gaining a bigger share of the consumer's dollar. We define value-added products as those that:

• are changed in the physical state or form of the product, such as turning berries into jam or creating sweaters and hats from wool;

• are produced in a manner that enhances value, such as products that meet organic or humane standards; or

• result in the enhancement of the value of a commodity or product (for example, creating branded products such as Laura's Lean Beef or Organic Valley produce and dairy products).

Alternative enterprises include direct marketing to consumers, raising crops that don't relate to traditional commodity crops (Christmas trees, medicinal herbs, or yaks, for example), producing renewable energy from wind or sun, and providing activities that bring people to your farm (educational events, pumpkin patches, hunting/fishing, bed-and-breakfast operations).

Farmers engaging in value-added and alternative enterprises often build relationships with customers; they aren't faceless masses who live a thousand miles away, but individuals who count on you to provide them with a high-quality, unique product. Going into an alternative marketing system will usually require you to follow additional laws, and will always require extra planning, record keeping, and time. Advertising, or getting the word out to your potential customers, becomes a major concern for farmers pursuing alternative markets. Educating your customers about your product, why it is special, and why they should buy from you becomes an important part of your job. But the payoff can make the extra effort worthwhile.

Niche marketing requires you to differentiate your product from the tons of products that consumers look at when they wander the aisles of the local super store. No matter what

Above, crates of green apples and other fresh produce draw shoppers into a California fruit stand. Organically grown vegetables, such as the newly uprooted carrots shown below, are part of the fastest growing segment of the U.S. food economy.

product you're selling from your farm, if you're going to direct market it, you will need to think about how it will best fit in a niche. Some niches include:

- **Natural** The USDA allows the word natural to appear on the label of a minimally processed food product and one that contains no artificial colors, flavors, preservatives, or other additives.
- **Organic** The organic market is the fastest-growing segment of the U. S. food economy. Products used on, in, or around the farm must come from an approved list of substances. For example, the organic market strictly prohibits chemical pesticides, but it allows diatomaceous earth as an insect control and wormer.
- **Green and humane** Green and humane marketing attracts consumers who want to know that they are buying products raised in a manner that conserves the environment and that the animals they're eating lived in a "healthy and happy" environment.

LEGAL ISSUES

When you go into business, you will fall under a bevy of rules and regulations promulgated by federal, statc, and local government entities to protect the public. For each business idea you consider, you must explore what kind of legal concerns may come up: Do you need a license to establish the business? With what kind of regulations will you need to comply? Wandering through a maze of red tape and bureaucracies can be, at the very least, intimidating and frustrating, and at worst, a true nightmare. But don't give up; you can do it, and the payoff is worth the trouble.

Understanding your rights and responsibilities is crucial to successful alternative marketing. To find out what laws you might collide with, start with a search of the local library. Librarians can point you in the direction of the reference shelves, housing books of statutes and ordinances. Librarians are also generally happy to help you figure out how to weed out

the information you need if it's your first time reading these onerous documents. Reference materials must usually stay in the library, so bring change for the copy machine. Also, get on your computer, as all federal laws and some state laws are available via the Internet, and more and more local governments have their laws online also. Find links to federal and state laws and regulations on the Internet at a site run by the United States government: http://www.firstgov.gov/Topics/Reference_Shelf.shtml#laws.

Laws can be nestled, one within another. This means that local entities may adopt laws of other levels of government, or general codes, by reference in their ordinances, and the referenced codes can have additional references within them. The Uniform Building Code, Uniform Fire Code, Uniform Electrical Code, and Uniform Plumbing Code are all typical examples of items that are often adopted by reference. For example, say you need a fire inspection for the type of operation you plan to run: The fire inspector will most likely judge your property based on the Uniform Fire Code, which adopts, by citation, the Uniform Electrical Code.

If you plan to employ nonfamily workers, you must meet significantly more requirements, such as acquiring an employer tax identification from the Internal Revenue Service, filing payroll taxes, signing up for both unemployment insurance, and worker's compensation insurance. You must file payroll taxes on a monthly or quarterly basis, depending on the size of your payroll. Let's look at three scenarios to give you an idea of how laws work in practice.

Scenario #1 You want to start an on-farm bed and breakfast. In this case, there are probably no federal laws to worry about. You aren't carrying on interstate commerce—since your product can't possibly cross state lines—so federal business types of laws don't apply. And you probably aren't engaging in any practices that could violate other federal laws. For example, you aren't processing foods or drugs, and you aren't spewing out air pollutants or water pollutants.

A South Carolina farmer talks about crop insurance programs with a member of the Federation of Southern Cooperatives Land Assistance Fund (above). Consult officials, nonprofit organizations, and other professionals knowledgeable about the issues—and do your own research (below).

Vibrant flowers crown the entrance to a quaint bed and breakfast in a northern California town (above). Comfortable lawn chairs invite guests to lounge outdoors in sunny weather (below), and a cozy patio provides cover from showers (opposite).

So in this scenario, the only laws you need to worry about are those adopted by local governments or your state. How do you find out about them? Start with the local municipal code for your town or county. Look in the table of contents or the index for headings such as "business, licensing, lodging, and guest houses," Go to each reference you find, and read it carefully. If it sounds as though it may even remotely apply to your proposed operation, take notes or make a copy of it. If there are no local laws that apply to what you want to do, then check the state's statutes.

It is common for this type of business to need some kind of license from a local government. To obtain the license, you'll need to file an application (along with a fee) with the clerk of the entity. The application form may require a signoff from certain officials, like those employed by the local fire department or the local health department. So, make sure you check on what's required by all local government entities that have any jurisdiction over your site, including fire districts, water and sewer districts, and town or county governments. Your property tax statement should indicate who, out there in "government land," has some say over what takes place on your piece of land.

The other alternative to doing the preliminary research at the library is to call each government entity and ask the staff what you have to do to start your bed and breakfast. But, as they tell you what hoops you have to jump through, nicely ask them to show you in writing the law they are basing the requirement on and ask for copies of the pertinent parts.

Scenario 2 You want to direct market beef (or lamb, pork, or goat). Once you begin looking at direct marketing meat, you fall under the United States Code (a compendium of all federal laws). The part of the U. S. Code that deals with meat is Title 21—Food and Drugs. Chapter 12 of Title 21—Meat Inspection—requires a federal inspector to examine all carcasses intended for use as meat or meat products. The examination's intent is to "prevent

ZVCC HERO
MACBETH
WOOD & GARDEN
G. JEKYLL
LONGMANS

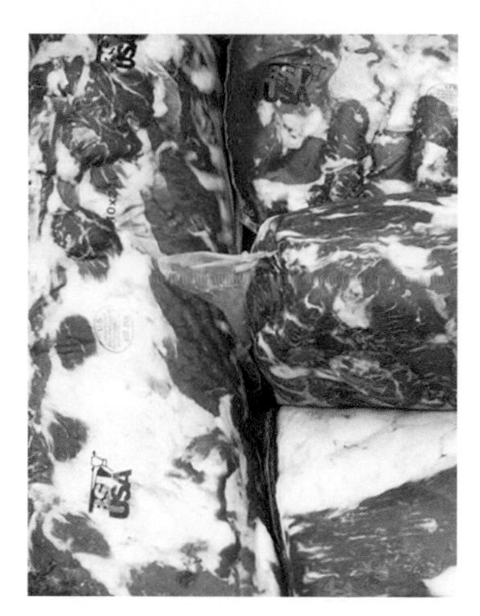

Beef is packaged for sale and stamped with approval (above), having passed inspection by a USDA official (below). If hobby farmers choose to market beef, they must follow strict federal and local regulations.

the use in commerce of meat and meat food products which are unwholesome, adulterated, mislabeled." Interestingly enough, if you're direct marketing bison, deer, or elk, they don't fall under this law because they weren't mentioned when the law was written; however, other federal laws apply to marketing these animals.

You can sell beef for meat in one of two ways: on the hoof, or packaged. Selling meat on the hoof requires less red tape than selling packaged meat, because there is a specific exemption (Title 21, United States Code, Section 623) that allows the owner of an animal to have it butchered for personal use without having it inspected. This means that you can have your animal butchered at a "custom slaughter plant" as opposed to a federally inspected plant. A federal or state inspector must occasionally check custom plants for cleanliness, but unlike federally inspected plants, there are no inspectors checking the carcasses of each butchered animal. Generally, many smaller packing plants fall into the custom category; with their small scale, they can't afford to pay for a regular federal inspector to be on site.

Selling on the hoof means you are selling the live animal to the customer, and he or she is responsible for having it butchered to his or her specifications. You may split an on the hoof animal between multiple customers—for example, two families could each be buying one half of a hog from you—but you must charge them based on the live weight of the animal. And they must pick the meat up from the butcher themselves. When you meet these criteria (selling based on live weight, butchering per customer specifications, and customer picking up meat) the exemption from carcass inspection kicks in.

If you decide to sell packaged meat (cut and frozen, or processed into meat products such as jerky and sausage), you must slaughter each animal at a plant that has a federal inspector available to view the carcass. You must label packages. Labels must say what the product is and who distributes it, and the USDA symbol must be on the label. If the pack-

age contains a product that has any added ingredients (even just a pinch of salt) the label must show all the ingredients, and the USDA must approve the label in an office in Washington, D.C. To receive approval, you must send in a copy of the recipe, along with a copy of the proposed label; you must list ingredients in order based on the quantity used in the recipe—largest-quantity ingredient listed first and smallest-quantity ingredient listed last. Labels may not include any misleading words, and you must be able to support all claims. Federal law also requires that you label meat packages with a "Safe Food Handling" label.

After you have cut, processed, frozen, and labeled your meat, you must follow laws that apply to how it is stored and transported. Although there is a federal law about storage and transport, the USDA has delegated the authority to implement and enforce this law to most of the states, so you need to check what your state requires by Department of Agriculture. Check the index of your state's statutes for key words such as *meat*, *food storage*, *food*, or *grocery*, or call your state's Department of Agriculture. You may have to apply for a "Retail Food Handler's License," or something similar.

Finally, check to see if any local laws apply to what you're trying to do. For example, if you want to open a retail meat store on your farm, you may have to go through the planning, zoning, or building department for approval.

Scenario #3 You want to sell chickens or eggs. Chickens and eggs, like the beef in Scenario #2, fall under Title 21, but there are generous exemptions for small-scale producers who wish to direct market. The exemption for poultry allows a complete exemption from any inspection for any producer who raises and slaughters fewer than 1,000 birds per year. Producers who slaughter between 1,000 and 20,000 birds per year are exempted if they market the birds within their local jurisdictions. This exemption only applies to poultry you have raised and slaughtered on your own farm, but it also extends to birds that you

A federal inspector examines poultry (above), and workers sort and package chicken eggs at a processing facility (below). Before launching such an operation of their own, prospective egg or poultry producers should investigate all applicable legal issues.

Above, a professional consultant advises a business owner of current market trends; such advice and careful research are essential to a new business's success. Below, children enjoy gathering pumpkins in a pick-your-own patch like the one owned by two agripreneurs in Gretna, Nebraska (see sidebar opposite).

sell to commercial outlets—such as restaurants and hotels—as well as those birds you sell directly to consumers.

Federal law requires you to candle and grade eggs, but again, this exempts small producers. In the case of egg production, the exemption extends to producers with fewer than 3,000 laying hens.

Even though federal law generally exempts small-scale producers from inspection of poultry and eggs, you are still required to label your products. The label must clearly state your name and address. In the case of eggs, it's a good idea to date the carton.

Though most states generally accept the federal standards, not all do. There are states and local government entities that have adopted more stringent requirements than the federal requirements for meat, chicken, and eggs, and it is your responsibility to know that. An old adage in the legal world goes: "Ignorance of the law is no excuse of the law." So, play it safe and check your state and local laws—such as county health department laws—to be sure you are in compliance with these.

Overcoming Obstacles

As you work your way through the system, you are almost bound to come up against a government employee who says, "You can't do that," or "You have to do this," but what they're saying doesn't seem correct or reasonable. What are your options? Luckily, you have options. There is always an appeal process that can go all the way to the high courts, if you choose to take your grievance that far.

First, always ask that the person show you, in writing, the laws or regulations on which he or she is basing his or her statement. If you get the line "It's our interpretation," remind the government employee that his or her job isn't to interpret, but to implement and enforce. The legislative body or the courts need to interpret the gray areas—not the staff.

Second, ask what the formal appeals process is. At the local level, the appeal generally goes quickly to the elected board. At state and federal levels, appeals work through the chain of command, from lower employees to higher employees. The final step in the appeals process is the courts, but it's often expensive to go there.

If there is a dispute, document everything. Start as soon as someone says, "You can't," or "You must." Immediately write down the date, time, name of the employee, and context of the conversation.

Review the law. During your review, read the "legislative intent." In federal laws, the legislative intent is called the "Congressional Statement of Findings." It defines why the elected officials adopted the law. For example, the Congressional Statement of Findings regarding meat inspection says, "Meat and meat products are an important source of the Nation's total supply of food. They are consumed throughout the Nation and the major portion thereof moves in interstate commerce. It is essential in the public interest that the health and welfare of consumers be protected by assuring that meat and meat food products distributed to them are wholesome, not adulterated, and properly marked, labeled, and packaged."

Ask yourself whether the requirement the employee is making is reasonable, within the law itself, and within the legislative intent of the law. If you are still confident in your

VALA'S PUMPKIN PATCH

Agritainment: A marriage of agriculture and entertainment into a fun experience for the whole family.

Jan and Tim Vala of Vala's Pumkin Patch in Gretna, Nebraska, are pioneers of agritainment. Back in the early 1980s, at a time when farmers did little direct marketing, pick-your-own operators were exploring new territory. Tim, burning with a desire to have a profitable farming operation, thought this new approach to agriculture held promise for his family's future. He went around the country to visit with farmers who were experimenting with pick-your-own operations. Then Tim went in search of a farm suitable for a pick-your-own strawberry operation. He found one less than thirty miles from Omaha, Nebraska, and just a little further from Lincoln.

The strawberry operation was, as Jan explains it, a real challenge. "The strawberries we grew were delicious, but it was a lot of work and they were never ripe the same time every year, so we couldn't advertise when they'd be ready—and when they were ready they had to be picked right away. And about the time the berries were ready to pick, it always seemed it would rain."

With twenty acres of strawberries, the Valas were barely breaking even. Then, one year, Tim planted a field of pumpkins, too, as a way to diversify his operation. He sold the pumpkins out of the back of his pickup truck, down by the highway. People seemed to like that, so the next year he planted more pumpkins. But now he had too many to sell by the road, so he used the pick-your-own approach and had buyers come to the farm. He would take them on a hayrack to the field, and the weather was usually pretty nice. By 1983 he was digging up the strawberries to expand the pumpkin business.

As Tim researched pumpkin patch operations around the country, he found that some innovative operators were adding entertainment as a way to attract, and keep, customers. They would add a haunted house or bring in local musicians to entertain visitors. Tim and Jan thought this was a great idea, and they started incorporating entertainment into their operation.

Today, the Valas' thirty-five-day pick-your-own pumpkin season attracts as many as 12,000 visitors on a Saturday afternoon. With a small staff of year-round helpers, and over 300 seasonal employees who run a dozen food booths, act the parts of spooks and goblins, and help with pumpkin sales, they have created a very successful business model. They charge admission by the day or by the season, and sell fifty-five acres worth of pumpkins to visitors from far and wide.

Jan tells me that marketing has been crucial to their success: "There is a lot of advertising you have to do, though once you have a good reputation it's a lot easier. In the early years, we would do newspaper ads, radio and cable television spots, and billboards. We still have a brochure that we print every year, and I have a company that distributes them to hotels, restaurants, gas stations, and along the interstates. Those are geared to getting new people to come to the farm."

The Valas have also worked to develop corporate and business supporters, who buy passes to give away to their customers or employees. Jan provides an example of an Omaha car dealership that purchases passes in bulk, then gives them away to potential buyers who test-drive a car. She emphasizes that these business connections provide stability and early season cash flow that helps keep their business strong.

A sales schedule and daily task sheet, such as those seen above, help keep small business owners organized and on target. Below, a homemade sign introduces visitors to a farm's horses and gives a friendly warning against feeding the animals.

stand, then ask to speak to the next higher employee, working up the line. At each point, continue documenting what is said and done. Or, if you're really confident, use the "take-us-to-court" tack.

If you have gone through all the employees, go to the elected officials. Attend a town or county board meeting, or contact your senator's and representative's offices. This step is where your previous documentation will help. Write out an outline to provide to your elected officials, detailing what has happened so far, and why you think the requirement isn't clear under the law or regulation, or why it should be waived or changed. This step, particularly at a local level, often results in a change of the law or regulation, but these changes take time.

Elected officials respond to voters, particularly when there is some volume to the voice they're hearing. By volume, I mean the number of constituents they are hearing from. Lots of potential voters (or organizations that represent voters) calling up and discussing an issue gets a much quicker response than one lone voice in the woods; so when opting to go to your elected officials, try to build support for your stand with other individuals or organizations. If the elected officials can't, or won't, do anything, your last stop for an appeal is the courts.

Liability

Unfortunately, we live in a time when there are lots of lawyers, and lawyers need lawsuits, so liability is a serious issue. Liability generally arises when one fails to meet his or her responsibilities. The best way to avoid personal liability is to pay attention to details. Make safety a top priority on your operation, studying each area of your farm, and everything you do for possible hazards. Follow all laws; they may seem like a nuisance but they offer you a degree of protection. If you have employees, develop written personnel and safety policies.

Safety policies can also extend to customers: "No shoes, no service" is an excellent policy on any farm. Place signs for your customers to see. Areas that are off limits to customers should be clearly marked: "Do not enter the barn—employees only beyond this point." Also, don't be afraid to tell customers, or their children, to stop doing something that may be dangerous: "Please stop chasing the chickens." If a customer is annoyed and leaves in a huff, count your blessings—you don't need people on your farm who aren't safety conscious, and who don't respect your rules.

Even if you are very safety conscious, accidents still occur. And, even if something isn't your fault, a customer may still sue you. Your property insurance company should be able to offer you extended personal liability coverage that will cover you for both employees and customers, but don't assume that because you have general comprehensive farm liability insurance now you're safe. These policies generally don't cover on-farm marketing operations, so check with your agent about liability and loss insurance specifically designed for direct-market farmers.

BUSINESS PLANS

Business planning is a process that will help you define your market, how you will best sell to that market, and how you will manage your operation. The process is valuable for anyone in business, as it helps you think through an approach to your enterprise, and then it helps you track, monitor, and evaluate your progress. It is absolutely critical if you plan to seek outside financing to get your business off the ground or to keep it growing. Having a plan shows

IDEAS FOR AGRIPRENEURS

By no means exhaustive, the following list is intended to spur your imagination on ways your farm can be profitable:

1. Marketing to consumers through

a. Farmer's markets
b. Pick-your-own operations
c. Farm stands
d. Community Supported Agriculture (CSA) subscription services
e. Mail order or Internet sales

2. Marketing to restaurants, specialty stores (natural food, ethnic markets, and other venues), or schools, through:

a. Farmer's markets
b. Direct delivery
c. Small-scale, specialty cooperatives

3. Developing and marketing specialty products from commodity or alternative crops/livestock

a. Clothing
b. Cosmetics
c. Food products
d. Household items
e. Crafts and decorative items

4. Non-agricultural income streams

a. Alternative energy production from wind, sun, or water
b. Special events such as music festivals and dances
c. Kennels
d. Writing, art, photography, or other creative enterprises tied to farm life
e. Creating and/or marketing products to help other farmers—for example, becoming a distributor of fencing products or building small animal cages

5. Agritourism

a. Bed and breakfast
b. Pumpkin patch/corn maze
c. Hunting and/or fishing
d. Petting zoo
e. Paintball game center
f. Bird watching
g. Demonstrations and workshops (such as weaving, preparing maple sugar, and canning)
h. Farm schools and tours
i. Horse boarding, riding, training, or instruction
j. Hiking, rock climbing, stargazing

Beautiful natural surroundings provide an inspirational setting for a businessman to draft a mission statement; a mobile phone allows him to confer with his absent partner (above). Elsewhere, a farmer opts for a hands-on approach, evaluating the year's heather crop with a NRCS representative (below).

investors that you have a well-thought-out enterprise upon which they can earn a return on their investment. Your business plan may also help you deal with things like the county zoning board or suppliers. A business plan typically includes a standard set of four parts: a mission statement, a business description, a marketing plan, and a financial plan.

Begin developing your business plan by writing a mission or goal statement. This statement should tell others—in a few sentences—what is special about you and your business and what you are seeking to accomplish. Consider a few examples:

> The mission of Smith Farms is to provide wholesome, natural foods that are pro duced in an environmentally responsible manner for consumers in the Greater Cleveland area. We plan to market our produce through area farmer's markets and at a farmstead stand that will be open from May through September.

> Our mission at Whitehorse Farm Bed and Breakfast is to provide an experience for consumers who desire a chance to get *back to the country*. We provide great personal service to visitors who have the opportunity to stay in one of several historic cabins, or in the 1920 farmhouse. We've meticulously renovated all these buildings, which are located on our working farm. During their visit, our guests have the chance to pet a cow, ride a horse, or shear a sheep. They can also fish in our stocked pond, hike on a series of trails along a river and through a native grassland that thrives with wildlife and wild flowers, and feast on farm fresh food of the highest quality.

> Kelly's Farm has long been known for an abundance of high-quality fresh produce. Today, our mission is not only to supply these exceptional fruits and vegetables for our clientele, but also to offer customers a variety of prepared foods that will excite their

taste buds, including Kelly's *Red-hot Salsa* and Kelly's *Cool Catsup*. All of our products are market driven, by the demands of discerning consumers who want the best, freshest ingredients in a locally grown and prepared product.

After you have written your mission statement, go into a more detailed description of the business. The business description can go on for a page or two and should provide as much detail as possible. It should tell who the owners are and describe their experience and/or education that is relevant to the endeavor. It should describe the type of business structure (sole proprietorship, partnership, corporation), and the history of the business if you have been operating for a while. It should also provide all other pertinent information about the business. Let's look at a hypothetical business description for Whitehorse Farm Bed and Breakfast to see an example:

In 1898 William Garry homesteaded Whitehorse Farm. Today, Gill and Jenny Garry and their family continue the tradition, operating Whitehorse Farm as an S-Corporation.

The farm is 800 acres and is located in XYZ County, about an hour from St. Louis. We raise and train American Quarter horses that are well known in horse circles for riders who participate in cutting and reining events. We maintain a purebred Angus beef herd and a commercial cow/calf herd of mixed-breed animals. We also maintain a small sheep flock for meat and for fleece, which we sell to hand-spinners and weavers.

The Bed and Breakfast (B&B) will be operated by Jenny and by Tom and Karen Smith (the Garrys' daughter and son-in-law). Tom has a degree in business administration from the University of Nebraska, and Karen has worked for seven years in hotel management for a Holiday Inn located in St. Louis. Jenny, whose cooking skills regularly win not only praise from family and friends, but awards at the Wayne County Fair as well, will provide meals to visitors.

Above, a young cowboy rides his pint-size horse. Below, a tally of figures reveals a month's total income. Being an agripreneur offers both the benefits of life in the country and the financial challenges faced by all small business owners.

Customers linger outside a country store. A break from the fast pace of urban life—and a good dose of old-fashioned charm—draws many city dwellers to rural businesses.

Visitors to the B&B will choose between three cabins and the historic farmhouse (three bedrooms), which also has a large room suitable for group events and workshops such as weddings, meetings, and parties. Cabins have small refrigerators and microwaves; the farmhouse has a full kitchen. We will supply all visitors with a breakfast of sweet rolls, buns, and fresh fruit, and will offer catering for special events such as corporate retreats.

Our objectives are to:

- incorporate this complementary operation into our overall business;
- have at least 30 percent occupancy our first year in operation, and 50 percent occupancy our second year; and
- increase exposure and market using Internet technology and direct advertising in the St. Louis area.

The marketing plan expands on the information in the business description, but before you complete it you will need to do market research, which identifies customer needs and wants; determines whether the product or service you are considering meets those needs and wants; identifies specific target markets (for example, senior citizens in Milwaukee or Arab Americans); and determines the best advertising technique for each customer group. Your marketing plan should also delve into who your competition is and how you are set apart from them, and it should provide information on how you will actually reach your target markets (for instance, through advertising, word of mouth, or promotion with corporation).

Market research looks at industry-related issues (for example, "the organics industry is the fastest-growing segment of the American food system") and at specific issues for you and your product ("we are located within one hour of the fastest-growing city in the state"). It can take place in several ways, depending on the product and the scale. You can investigate appropriate data, such as data from the census bureau on growth or data from demographic services on changing consumer interests (check out *American Demographics* magazine, usually available at larger libraries). Talking to current consumers is another good way to learn about the market. For example, Kelly's Farm, which is already growing and selling produce and wants to expand into bottled products, might provide samples of proposed products to customers and then follow up with a survey. Often you can find help with market research from area colleges that offer business degrees or from local and state government economic development offices.

The financial plan, like the name says, talks dollars and cents. It provides a proposed budget and looks at key indicators, such as your company's debt-to-equity ratio, or the relation between dollars you've borrowed and dollars you've invested in your business. The more money you have invested in the business, the easier it is to attract financing. Another key indicator is the break-even analysis, which calculates the volume of business necessary to break even—something your creditors will want to know, but which is even more important for you to know. For most aspiring business people, working with a professional is the best way to develop a financial plan. Some states have farm business advisors through their Cooperative Extension Service that can help you prepare this; if yours does not, you may need to hire an accountant.

BUSINESS STRUCTURES

Sole proprietorship is a common form of business, in part because it is the easiest to set up and to terminate. One person (or a couple) owns and controls it with funds for the business coming from the owner's personal funds such as savings and/or investments, loans from lending agencies, and sometimes loans or monetary gifts from friends or family members. Personal assets such as land, homes, vehicles, bank accounts, and investments may be encumbered to pay damages resulting from lawsuits filed against the business, or to pay claims by creditors for satisfaction of business taxes, loans, and contracts.

A *partnership* is a voluntary association of two or more people for the purpose of operating a business, with each person contributing money, property, labor, or skills to the business and each sharing in the business profits, losses, and liabilities. To protect others from using the partnership name, the partners must register the business name as a "doing business as" name with the secretary of state in any state where the partnership operates. You can form partnerships with an oral or written agreement, but a written agreement is the better option.

There are three basic types of partnerships:

- **General partnership** In this form of partnership, two or more people contribute assets to the partnership, and these general partners share the management, profits, and losses. The general partners manage the business and are personally liable for all partnership debts and liabilities and acts of any of the partners.
- **Limited liability partnership** In this form of partnership, one or more partners limit their personal liability through written agreements between the partners. All partners may be general partners, with involvement in management decisions, but the liability of an individual partner is based on his or her personal areas of responsibility or the responsibility of someone under his or her direct supervision.

In Washington State, the owner of Jones Farm proudly displays his harvested tomatoes (above). Whether seeking to start a business partnership (below), a sole proprietorship, or a corporation, hobby farmers should investigate legal and financial issues thoroughly.

• **Limited partnership** This is a way for the general partner(s) to acquire additional capital without giving up management control. In a limited partnership, there is at least one general partner and one or more limited partners. Limited partners take no active role in the management of the business, and their liability is limited to the extent of the money they contribute to the business.

Corporations have a legal and tax identity, separate from the owners, or shareholders, and they are chartered by state governments. They must file articles of incorporation with the secretary of state where they receive their charter. Once formed, corporations have to file periodic reports with the secretary of state. While the corporation is fully liable for all its business obligations, individual shareholders are liable only to the extent of their investment. In practice, however, owners of small, closely held corporations (family members, for example) are often required to personally guarantee the debts of their corporation.

For income tax purposes, business owners must choose whether the corporation is a C or an S corporation. C corporations pay taxes on income, so their shareholders do not report any portion of corporate income or losses on their individual returns, but when income is passed on to the shareholders as salary or dividends, it is taxable income for them. A corporation with 75 or fewer employees may make a special election to be taxed as an S corporation. Though an S corporation must file a federal income tax return, it allocates income to the shareholders and taxes income at their personal state and federal rates. It

COVERED BRIDGE PRODUCE

Joseph Griffin runs Covered Bridge Produce in Oley, Pennsylvania, a CSA that is a six-figure success story with 400 clients and almost a dozen employees during the growing season. With seven acres under intensive cultivation on a twenty-six-acre farm, Joseph oversees the growing, harvesting, packaging, and delivery of more than 130 varieties of vegetables, ranging from arugula to zucchini. He buys fruit, flowers, and sweet corn from other local growers, freeing him and his staff to concentrate on what they do best.

Joseph was a professor and college administrator who "sank to the level of a fundraiser" when he got tired of it all and dropped out of the system, buying his farm in 1996. He played around at first—gardening and selling a little produce at farmers markets. But in 2000, as he watched his retirement funds draining away, he decided that he either needed to have the farm make some real money, or he needed to find something else that would.

He began looking for a clientele that would support his business, and he set upon a modified CSA model as the best way to market to them. "We looked for a kind of a 'fuzzy' clientele that is really concerned about its health and that has awesome amounts of disposable income. These are people that like to cook, and that are really interested in local, organic food."

Joseph's math background, as well as his fortuitous hiring of a "down-on-his-luck computer programmer" during the dot.com bust, has helped grow this business at a phenomenal rate. Joseph and the programmer have worked to develop computerized management systems and an online form that allows CSA members to order items they would like to receive in their box. "I always felt the one thing that was wrong with the typical CSA model was that consumers didn't have choice; it smacks of socialism—you don't go to a clothing store and have them hand you a pair of jeans and a sweater because it is what they have—you get to choose what you want."

Joseph's clients go to the web site each week, and they get to choose up to ten items from a list that may include upwards of seventy-five products. The web site records their choices in a database, and then prints out sheets for harvesters and packagers, making for accurate and speedy work and saving Joseph about 40 percent over the cost of harvesting and packaging before the system was in place. The system also allows Joseph to plan better for the next season, based on buying decisions his clients made the previous year.

"I guess I should be ready to retire, and I'm not. I squandered my pension on this farm—building it up—but I've never had so much fun in my life. For years, my only output was talk and memos, but now when a truck lumbers out of here headed for the city, I think, 'That food wouldn't be there if not for my efforts'. It is tremendously fulfilling."

must file an S election with the IRS on or before the fifteenth day of the third month of the first year that the corporation is chartered.

Limited liability companies (LLCs) provide the benefits of limited liability protection, operational flexibility, and pass-through taxation without the restrictions applied to S corporations and limited liability partnerships. The owners of an LLC are called members and have both economic and management rights (including voting rights) and may constitute the management of an LLC. As with corporations, most states that recognize LLCs require management to submit periodic reports to the secretary of state. Because limited liability company laws differ from state to state, take extreme care in drafting legal documents that meet the requirements of the state where you plan to do business.

Above, signs advertising fresh produce beckon drivers to stop and visit a roadside fruit stand. Below, family members invite the public to their pick-your-own apple orchard in Oregon.

SELLING YOURSELF

Developing your clientele is one of the toughest undertakings you'll make as an agripreneur, yet a loyal customer base—folks that come back again and again—are crucial to your business's success. These customers not only come back, but are also your best advertisers. "Word of mouth" advertising grows a business better, and cheaper, than any other form of advertising.

There are two different terms that professional marketers use: *advertising* and *promotions*. Advertising is simply putting your business in the public's eye, primarily through the use of some media. Everything from business cards to paid ads in commercial media (newspapers, yellow pages, radio, television, or the Internet) falls under advertising. T-shirts or baseball caps with your farm name on them are also a form of advertising, as is providing free samples.

Promotions are a specialized form of advertising, where your business supports some community event or group. Sponsor a Little League team, and you are engaging in a promo-

Hot apple pies, delicious preserves, and a warm welcome greet visitors to this midwestern agripreneur's pie stand.

tion. Provide free or at-cost, ground beef to the local Rotary for their annual community picnic, and you are doing a promotion.

One of the most successful, not to mention cheapest, advertising tools we have found for getting our business in front of new customers has been a computer-generated sign with our busines name and phone number on "tear-offs" at the bottom. We placed these on bulletin boards in Laundromats, convenience stores, at the library, and on other readily accessible, public bulletin boards. Inevitably, each one of these signs garnered us at least one new customer.

Newspaper classifieds didn't net us many meat sales, though we did sell some breeding stock and calves using classifieds. However, some farmers have had success with marketing meat through newspaper advertising. Stephen and Kay Castner, of Kay's Home Farm Lean Meats (Cedarburg, WI), run a regular display ad in their local weekly paper. The Castners have also developed a web site on the Internet (www.kaysfarm.com). They've had it for a number of years, and although they don't feel it has had much impact on meat sales, it has helped to market breeding stock. They raise purebred Galloway cattle and Targhee sheep on their farm, and contacts made through their web site have netted breeding stock sales as far away as Kansas.

Most successful marketers encourage their clients to visit the farm, even if sales don't occur there. Some host an annual barbecue, to which they invite all their regular customers. Others just extend a fairly open invitation. No matter what approach is used, the goal is always the same: Create a proprietary interest in your operation among your customers. Melvin and Carol Moon, of Moon Berry Farm & Puyallup Jam Factory in Puyallup, Washington, began offering a farm Harvest Tour at the urging of their extension agent. Now the annual event is something they wouldn't consider forgoing: "At first, we didn't want to do it, because harvest season is so busy, and we thought it would be too big of a responsibility to have crowds here. But one of the first people to come that first year said, 'We always wanted to visit here, and when we saw your tour advertised, it was like a personal invitation.'

TIPS FROM THE EXPERTS

- **Jan Vala** says, "One of the best things we ever did was getting involved with the North American Farmers' Direct Marketing Association (NAFDMA)." Since 1986 NAFDMA has provided members with information and support to pursue direct marketing. An annual networking conference is the highlight of the year for members. The association also provides newsletters and other information, and they have published an informative book, Marketing on the Edge: A Marketing Guide for Progressive Farmers. You can contact them at 888-884-9270, or via their web site, www.nafdma.com.

- **Joseph Griffin** says, "The main thing is to realize the difficulty of the economic task. It isn't difficult to ride around on a tractor, or to plant seeds—almost anybody can learn that—but to arrange the whole process to spend less than you take in—that is the hard part. I think people think that farming is easy; the easy part is what they see.

  If you want to plant five acres, consider planting half an acre first. Keep it small initially. Remember, you can go bust a lot faster by going big."

- **Susan Robbins** says, "First of all, thoroughly investigate your own local marketing conditions. In other words try not to grow something that ten other people are doing well. Second, know what you are doing in terms of your own setting—that is to say can you know you can grow your crop successfully, or you know what you have to do or alter in your conditions to do it successfully. Third, make sure you are capitalized enough so you are not always simply trying to make it through each month. Fourth, and most importantly, see if you can develop a value-added product that makes you less reliant on the growing season."

"Once people have come on the tour, they feel more welcome—they almost take a sort of ownership interest in the farm—and they come back at other times to purchase from us, or they seek our products out in local stores."

When your farm is a welcoming place for buyers, you will find that they bring friends. And some of those visitors became long-distance customers. Again, Carol Moon tells me that they do a strong mail-order business with people who have been to the farm. She gives an example, "One man owned rental condos in Palm Desert. After a visit, he would buy little five-ounce bottles of our jam to leave on the counter for his customers. One day he called and apologized, saying he was just going to buy jam at the store because, with shipping, our product was too expensive. But not long after, he called and said that the jams he bought at the store tasted like paste, so he came back to buying from us."

Another strategy for developing a client base is doing promotions for civic groups. Offer to attend a meeting of the Rotary, a homemakers' club, or an environmental group. Prepare a slide show (or Power Point show) and presentation, describing your farm operation and the environmental benefits it brings. Have some sample products to give out after the presentation: meatballs in a crock pot, or hard-boiled eggs, or anything else you grow and market. If your goal is to offer on-farm hunting or fishing, attend a sportsmen's club meeting.

Free coverage is often available from local media; reporters (both television and print media) are always looking for stories. Prepare a media packet that will help them understand your operation, then invite one to come to the farm and do a story. Sue Robbins, of Pelindaba Farms, has done just that, and her efforts have garnered both local and national coverage. She's even done a spot on the *Today Show* and had coverage in *In-Style* and *Better Homes and Gardens* magazines. Sue offers some caution about going after media: "I have to tell you, most people have no clue how to deal with the press so they do more harm than good. Your press releases and press packets need to be professional-looking." She suggests that if you don't have experience in working with the media, you hire a consultant or join a local business association, which can help you get exposure with these specialists.

Once you've identified clients, keeping them becomes the next challenge. Find some way to keep in touch with regular customers. Hand out fliers and newsletters during presentations, or mail them to your customer list. Tell people what's happening on your place, tell stories about your animals, or let them know about food issues and policies that affect them and you—for instance, a factory farm trying to come into the area.

Becky Weed, of Thirteen Mile Lamb and Wool in Montana, works hard on keeping in touch with customers, posting regular updates on her web site. The updates are brief and written in a light and friendly fashion; they also include a few good quality pictures of animals, scenery, or events from around the farm (including wildlife spottings).

All correspondence with your customers should include information on ordering, product availability, new products, and any price changes. Computers are useful for preparing newsletters, maintaining mailing lists, and preparing flyers and labels, but they aren't absolutely necessary. Hand-prepared materials work, but they must be neat and legible.

DEVELOPMENT SOURCE

A great resource of online materials for agricultural business development is the Agricultural Marketing Resource Center, at www.agmrc.org. They have sample business plans and a spreadsheet called the Feasibility Template that can help you develop your plan.

RESOURCES

BOOKS

Ken and I have shelves and shelves of farming books that we have collected with zeal over the years. Our oldest dates to the 1860s; our newest just came out. Some of my favorites are:

Bubel, Nancy. *The New Seed-Starters Handbook.* Emmaus, Pa.: Rodale Press, 1988.

Coleman, Elliot. *Four Season Harvest.* White River Junction, Vt.: Chelsea Green, 1999.

———. *The New Organic Grower.* White River Junction, Vt.: Chelsea Green, 1995.

Damerow, Gail. *Fences for Pasture and Garden.* North Adams, Mass.: Storey Books, 1992.

———. *Storey's Guide to Raising Chickens.* North Adams, Mass.: Storey Books, 2000.

Ekarius, Carol. *Small-Scale Livestock Farming: A Grass-based Approach to Health, Sustainability, and Profit.* North Adams, Mass.: Storey Books, 1999.

———. See Simmons, below.

Kowalchik, Claire and William H. Hylton, eds. *Rodale's Illustrated Encyclopedia of Herbs.* Emmaus, Pa.: Rodale Press, 1998.

Logsdon, Gene. *The Contrary Farmer.* White River Junction, Vt.: Chelsea Green, 1995.

Gene inspired us and helped us learn how to do many of the things that we've done. (For example, his *Organic Orcharding* book is a must-read for those interested in seriously pursuing an orchard, and his *Small-scale Grain Raising* is great for anyone who wants to grow grain crops, such as wheat or corn.) Read any and all books by Gene Logsdon that you can get your hands on (many are now out of print, but you can often purchase them used or find them in libraries).

Mettler, Dr. John J. *Basic Butchering of Livestock and Game.* North Adams, Mass.: A Garden Way Publication, Storey Books, 1986.

Poisson, Leandra, and Gretchen Vogel. *Solar Gardening: Growing Vegetables the American Intensive Way.* White River Junction, Vt.: Chelsea Green, 1994.

Salatin, Joel. *Family Friendly Farming.* White River Junction, Vt.: Chelsea Green, 2001.

———. *Pastured Poultry Profits.* White River Junction, Vt.: Chelsea Green, 1996.

———. *Salad Bar Beef.* White River Junction, Vt.: Chelsea Green, 1996.

———. *You Can Farm.* White River Junction, Vt.: Chelsea Green, 1998.

Schwenke, Karl. *Successful Small-Scale Farming.* North Adams, Mass.: Storey Books,1991.

Simmons, Paula, and Carol Ekarius. *Storey's Guide to Raising Sheep.* North Adams, Mass.: Storey Books, 2000.

Spaulding, C. E. *Veterinary Guide for Animal Owners.* North Adams, Mass.: Storey Books, 1996.

PERIODICALS

Countryside
Withee, Wis.
(800) 551-5691
www.countrysidemag.com.

Hobby Farms
Lexington, Ky.
888-738-2665
www.hobbyfarmsmagazine.com

Small-Farm Today
Clark, Mo.
(800) 633-2535
www.smallfarmtoday.com

The Stockman Grassfarmer
Jackson, Miss.
(800) 748-9808
www.stockmangrassfarmer.com

ORGANIZATIONS AND GOVERNMENT RESOURCES

Alternative Technology Transfer for Rural America (ATTRA)
ATTRA is funded by the U.S. Department of Agriculture and is managed by the National Center for Appropriate Technology. It provides information and other technical assistance to farmers, ranchers, extension agents, educators, and others involved in sustainable agriculture in the United States. It is one of the best resources I know of, with outstanding information available online or mailed to you free of charge.
(800) 346-9140
www.attra.org

American Livestock Breeds Conservancy (ALBC)
ALBC is dedicated to preserving heritage breeds of livestock.
(919) 542-5704
www.albc-usa.org

National Renewable Energy Laboratory (NREL)
NREL is the nation's leading laboratory for renewable energy research and development. They offer an excellent ten-page guide, *A Consumer's Guide to Buying a Solar Electric System.*
(800) 363-3732
www.nrel.gov/ncpv/pdfs/26591.pdf

Natural Resources Conservation Service (NRCS)
NRCS is a branch of the U.S. Department of Agriculture. They have many resources available, including a really great handbook, *Ponds—Planning, Design, Construction* (Agriculture Handbook 590). This handbook will walk you through the design process one step at a time, from choosing the right site to sizing spillways and dams. It also discusses construction techniques and considerations. Look in your phone book under "United States Government—Agriculture Department—NRCS" or "Soil Conservation Service" for your local office. Information is also available at their web site.
www.nrcs.usda.gov

Organic Crop Improvement Association (OCIA)
OCIA provides research, education and certification services to thousands of organic growers, processors, and handlers.
(402) 477-2323
www.ocia.org

Sustainable Agriculture Research and Education (SARE)

SARE is an initiative funded by the U.S. Department of Agriculture. It sponsors competitive grants for sustainable agriculture research and education. Check out the CSA directory on the SARE Web site.
www.sare.org

COMMERCIAL PROVIDERS

There are hundreds of excellent commercial providers for tools, equipment, seeds, and other farming resources. Here is a selection of my favorites:

Johnny's Selected Seeds

Johnny's is a great resource for seed—for both gardeners and field crop producers. The company carries vegetable and flower seeds; culinary, medicinal, and aromatic herb seeds; gardening tools; garden supplies; and home garden accessories. Johnny's thoroughly tests all its seeds and accessories at the company's certified organic farm in Albion, Maine, and backs up its products with a 100-percent-satisfaction guarantee.
(800) 879-2258
www.johnnyseeds.com.

Lehman's

Lehman's—a company that caters to the Amish community—is the source for old-fashioned, hard-to-find items such as pickle kegs, grain mills, wooden barrels, hand water pumps, wood cook stoves, heating stoves, canning supplies, and much, much more.
(888) 438-5346
www.lehmans.com

NASCO

NASCO's catalog is like the Sears catalog for farming.
(800) 558-9595
www.nascofa.com

Premier Fencing

Premier makes high-quality fencing materials that are great for all applications.
(800) 282-6631
www.premier1supplies.com

Seeds of Change

This is an excellent source for garden and farm seeds, as well as tools, equipment, and other goods.
(888) 762-7333
www.seedsofchange.com

PHOTO CREDITS

The sources for the photographs that appear in this volume are listed below. Sources are listed by chapter in order of appearance.

COVER

Bonnie Sue
JupiterImages and its Licensors
PhotoDisc, Inc.

FRONT MATTER

Getty Images, Inc. 2
Brand X Pictures 5, 8
Corbis Corp. 6

CHAPTER 1: BACK TO THE FARM

Getty Images, Inc. 10, 14, 16 (top), 18 (top), 21 (top), 22 (bottom), 24 (bottom), 25 (bottom), 27
Monticello/Thomas Jefferson Foundation, Inc. 12 (top and bottom)
Michael A. Jensen/Mira.com 13, 21 (bottom) Greg Vaughn 15 (top)
Corbis Corp. 15 (bottom)
JupiterImages and its Licensors 16 (bottom), 17, 18 (bottom), 26
Brand X Pictures 19, 20, 23, 24 (top)
Dwight Kuhn 22 (top)
United States Department of Agriculture *Ken Hammond* 25 (top)

CHAPTER 2: ARE YOU READY FOR THE COUNTRY?

Getty Images, Inc. 28, 30 (top), 32 (top), 33 (bottom), 34, 35, 36 (top), 38 (bottom), 45, 48, 49 (top), 50, 51 (top), 52, 53 (top and bottom), 54 (top), 55
JupiterImages and its Licensors 30 (bottom), 37 (top and bottom)
Brand X Pictures 31, 33 (top), 39
James Nedresky 32 (bottom)
Ken Woodard Photography 36 (bottom), 49 (bottom), 54 (bottom)
Ron Salmon 38 (top), 41 (top)
Bonnie Sue 40, 44
Dusty Perin 41 (bottom)
David Jensen 42
Oscar Williams 43, 47
William F. McAllen/Mira.com 46
Karen Keb Acevedo 51 (bottom)

CHAPTER 3: JUMPING IN

Bonnie Sue 56
Getty Images, Inc. 58 (top and bottom), 59 (bottom), 60 (top), 61, 62 (top and bottom), 63 (bottom), 67 (top), 70, 71 (top and bottom), 72, 73 (top), 74
Brand X Pictures 59 (top), 60 (bottom)
United States Department of Agriculture *Ken Hammond* 63 (top), 75 (top); *Ron Nichols* 64
JupiterImages and its Licensors 64 (bottom), 66, 69 (top)
Ken Woodard Photography 65, 67 (bottom), 68 (top)
AgStockUSA *Ed Young* 68 (bottom); *Dave Reede* 69 (bottom)
Karen Keb Acevedo 73 (bottom)

CHAPTER 4: NATURE'S TROUBLEMAKERS AND FARM SAFETY

AgStockUSA *Dave Reede* 75; *Russ Munn* 87 (bottom); *Richard Hamilton Smith* 88 (bottom); *Ed Wargin* 90 (bottom)
Brand X Pictures 78, 79 (top and bottom), 90
JupiterImages and its Licensors 80 (top and bottom), 82, 83 (top), 87 (top), 89
Getty Images, Inc. 83 (bottom), 86, 88 (top), 89 (top), 90 (top)

CHAPTER 5: GARDENING: THE LAND

Brand X Pictures 92, 94, 95 (top and bottom), 96, 100, 104, 106 (top)
Getty Images, Inc. 97, 98, 109
United States Department of Agriculture

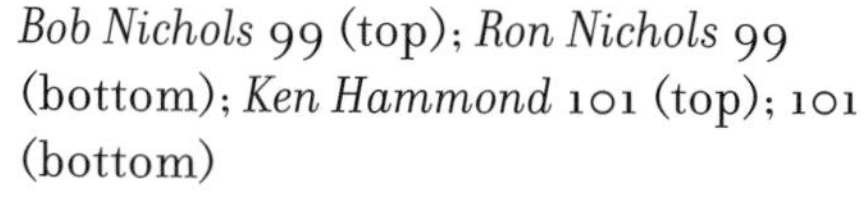

Bob Nichols 99 (top); *Ron Nichols* 99 (bottom); *Ken Hammond* 101 (top); 101 (bottom)

Agricultural Research Service, United States Department of Agriculture *Scott Bauer* 103 (top)

JupiterImages and its Licensors 103 (bottom), 106 (bottom), 108

AgStockUSA *Chester Peterson, Jr.* 107

CHAPTER 6: GARDENING: THE PLANTING

Brand X Pictures 110, 112, 113 (top), 114 (top), 120, 126, 128, 129, 132 (top), 142 (top), 143

JupiterImages and its Licensors 113 (bottom), 117 (bottom), 121, 127, 132 (bottom), 141, 142 (bottom)

Getty Images, Inc. 114 (bottom), 115, 116, 117 (top), 118 (top and bottom),119, 133, 134, 135, 137, 138, 139, 140 (bottom)

PhotoDisc, Inc. 122, 124, 130, 136

AgStockUSA *Eric Poggenpohl* 140 (top)

CHAPTER 7: FARM ANIMALS

Getty Images, Inc. 145, 146, 154 (top and bottom), 155, 158 (bottom), 164 (bottom), 165, 173, 176 (bottom), 183 (top)

Agricultural Research Service, United States Department of Agriculture *Brian Brechtel* 147 (top); *Scott Bauer* 156 (top), 161, 175; *Peggy Greb* 159; 160 (top), 171, 174 (top); *Keith Weller* 168, 174 (bottom), 179 (top and bottom)

AgStockUSA *Holly Kuper* 147 (bottom); *Mitch Kezar* 160 (bottom); *Thomas Schneider* 164 (top); *Chuck Haney* 167 (bottom)

PhotoDisc, Inc. 149, 15

Maureen Blaney Flietner 153, 157, 158 (top), 167 (top)

Corbis Corp. 156 (bottom), 166 (bottom), 182

David Jensen 166 (top)

JupiterImages and its Licensors 176 (top), 180 (top and bottom), 181, 183 (bottom)

Bonnie Sue 178

CHAPTER 8: PRESERVING THE HARVEST: FRUITS AND VEGETABLES

AgStockUSA *Keith Seaman* 184; *Maximilian Stock, Ltd.* 215 (top)

Brand X Pictures 186, 205, 213 (bottom)

PhotodDisc, Inc.187, 188, 190 (bottom), 192, 198, 199, 200 (bottom), 201, 203 (bottom), 204 (top and bottom), 207 (top left and bottom), 208 (top right and bottom), 209 (top left), 213 (top), 215 (bottom)

Maureen Blaney Flietner 189, 196 (top), 203 (top)

Getty Images, Inc. 190 (top), 191, 193 (top), 200 (top), 206, 207 (top right), 214

Charles E. Pefley/Mira.com 193 (bottom)

JupiterImages and its Licensors 194, 195, 197, 208 (top left), 209 (top right), 211 (top and bottom), 212

Sue Weaver 196 (bottom)

Karen Keb Acevedo 202, 210

CHAPTER 9: PRESERVING THE HARVEST: DAIRY AND MEAT

AgStockUSA *Alvis Upitis* 216; *Maximilian Stock, Ltd.* 218 (bottom); *Dana Downie* 220 (top); *Bryan Peterson* 220 (bottom)

PhotoDisc, Inc. 218 (top), 219, 227

Michael A. Jensen/Mira.com 221 (top)

JupiterImages and its Licensors 221 (bottom), 223, 225 (top and bottom)

Craig Lovell 224

Wesley R. Hitt/Mira.com 226

CHAPTER 10: AGRIPRENEURSHIP

Getty Images, Inc. 230, 232, 236 (top)
Craig Lovell 233, 236 (bottom)
JupiterImages and its Licensors 234 (top), 237 (bottom), 238 (top), 242 (top and bottom), 244 (top), 246 (top), 247 (top and bottom), 248, 249 (bottom), 251 (top)
Karen Keb Acevedo 234 (bottom)
Brand X Pictures 235, 238 (bottom),239
United States Department of Agriculture *Ken Hammond* 237 (top); 240 (bottom), 241 (top); *Bob Nichol*s 246 (bottom)
AgStockUSA *Scott Sinklier* 240 (top); *Mitch Kezar* 241 (bottom); *Richard Hamilton Smith* 252
Ken Woodard Photography 244 (bottom)
Greg Vaughn 249 (top), 251 (bottom)

BACK MATTER

PhotoDisc, Inc. 254-259

INDEX